AUTHORITARIAN CENTURY

'Brilliantly spins the globe to tell us not only how we got here, but why, explaining the need for a truly international, forceful response. A masterful overview of our leaders today, and a must-read!'
— Ravi Agrawal, Editor in Chief, *Foreign Policy*

'This thoughtful and articulate book could not be more timely. Liberal democracy needs its champions to speak out, and Ibrahim is doing just that.'
— The Rt Hon. Sir Malcolm Rifkind KGMC KC, former UK Foreign Secretary (1995–7)

'A very important book—in an age of new competition, Ibrahim explains what is at stake and what democracies might do about it.'
— Baroness Helena Kennedy KC FRSA HonFRSE, founding co-chair, Inter-Parliamentary Alliance on China, and author of *Eve Was Framed*

'An essential book for understanding why democracies are in difficulty— and how to address the challenge posed by rising authoritarianism.'
— Emma Sky OBE, founding director, International Leadership Center, Yale University, and author of *The Unravelling*

'We have taken the benefits of liberal democracy for granted. Ibrahim's uncomfortable and uncompromising book shows why it is in danger, and how we need to understand the authoritarian challenge so that we are better placed to resist it.'
— Sir Lawrence Freedman KCMG CBE PC FBA, Emeritus Professor of War Studies, King's College London

'Ibrahim has translated his deep research and familiarity with democratic politics into a study of the authoritarian challenge. Readable, impressive and worrying.'
— General Robert S. Spalding, former Senior Director for Strategic Planning, US National Security Council (2017–18)

'Ibrahim is one of the world's most prominent commentators. Here he tackles some of the biggest problems facing the globe and, with his usual clarity, tells us some home truths.'
— The Rt Hon. Baron Robertson of Port Ellen, 10th Secretary General of NATO and former UK Defence Secretary

AZEEM IBRAHIM

Authoritarian Century

Omens of a Post-Liberal Future

HURST & COMPANY, LONDON

First published in the United Kingdom in 2022 by
C. Hurst & Co. (Publishers) Ltd.,
New Wing, Somerset House, Strand, London, WC2R 1LA
© Azeem Ibrahim, 2022
All rights reserved.

Distributed in the United States, Canada and Latin America by
Oxford University Press, 198 Madison Avenue, New York, NY 10016,
United States of America.

A Cataloguing-in-Publication data record for this book
is available from the British Library.

ISBN: 9781787388000

www.hurstpublishers.com

Printed in Great Britain by Bell and Bain Ltd, Glasgow

CONTENTS

FOREWORD

Michael Chertoff, Chair of Freedom House
Former US Secretary of State for Homeland Security (2005–9)

Twenty-five years ago, as the world stood on the cusp of a new millennium, Western nations basked in a heady optimism about the state of the world and the future of democracy and human rights. During the 1990s, the Cold War and the real threat of a nuclear conflict seemed to dissipate, with the fall of the Berlin Wall, the dissolution of the Soviet Union, and what appeared to be an admittedly hesitant Russian movement toward democracy and capitalism.

Although economic privatisation became a fountainhead of corruption, Russia faded as a global military and economic rival of the United States and Europe. At the same time, former Soviet satellites eagerly embraced Western capitalist values. Many applied to join the European Union, thereby manifesting a commitment to honour the rule of law, democracy and free-market economics. In South Africa, apartheid was ended, and human rights activist Nelson Mandela was elected President, thereby bringing that country into the community of democracies.

Looking toward Asia, China—the other communist behemoth—had emerged from the cruelty and oppressiveness of Mao Zedong's rule into an evolving hybrid economics system and (notwithstanding the 1989 Tiananmen Square massacre) some loosening of central government control. Many observers believed that, as China engaged more with the global economic system, it would inevitably gravitate toward becoming a more democratic and human rights–respecting regime. Western businesses envisioned China as an appealing market within an increasingly globalised economy.

So, facing a new millennium, and notwithstanding conflicts still raging in places like Kosovo, it did seem that—as Dr Martin Luther King Jr famously said—"the arc of the moral universe is long, but it bends toward justice."

At the same time, the global economy, and international economic integration, also seemed to hold great promise. The G20 intergovernmental forum of the EU and nineteen other nations was formed in 1999, and the World Trade Organization was established in 1995. The vision was to enable international trade that is free, smooth and predictable, and governed by clear rules. Not coincidentally, during this period, the US economy was prospering, as were the economies of other liberal democracies. The free market seemed to have no serious ideological competitors on the world stage.

Looking back, a quarter-century later, it seems that expectations about the progress of liberal democracy and the prevalence of the global free-market systems were naively optimistic. Autocracy is on the rise in every corner of the globe. In the United States, unfounded criticism of the 2020 election results and claims of untrustworthy voting procedures persist among a significant minority of citizens, despite multiple courts ruling that there was no evidence of material fraud. This utterly baseless attack on the electoral process climaxed almost tragically when Donald Trump supporters invaded the Capitol in January 2021, in an effort to reverse the election result through use of force. And this effort has not disappeared. A number of political candidates for state or local public office in the States have made clear their unwillingness to accept election results with which they disagree.

Proto-autocrats occupy leadership positions in places such as Brazil, Turkey and Belarus. Even in the European Union, popular support is rising for parties that overtly or subtly admire neo-Nazi or neo-fascist ideologies. For example, Hungary has re-elected a President who has curtailed press freedom, eroded judicial independence, and expressed strong hostility to immigrants. Indeed, he himself characterises Hungary as an illiberal democracy.

What is notable about these developments is that, in most places, the movement to autocracy and away from freedom and the rule of law has not generally been the result of a coup or conquest. At least initially, the electorate themselves have endorsed candidates who have expressed plans to consolidate power and crack down on opponents and the press. To all too many voters, these sentiments are—to use tech speak—a feature, not a bug. The critical question is why so many citizens, in nations around the globe, do not value liberal democracy, but prefer a strongman who disdains restraints and gravitates toward exertion of raw power.

As Azeem Ibrahim masterfully illustrates in *Authoritarian Century*, the rise of this authoritarian appetite among many voters is the product of a number of experiences since the nineties. First, the glow of optimism that suffused the turn of the century dissipated almost immediately, as events undercut confidence in the competence of democratic governments and public faith in relatively unfettered globalisation. The terrible terrorist attacks of 9/11 raised hesitation about the risks and benefits of global free movement. These were reinforced when wars in Iraq and Syria led to mass migration to Europe, which to some EU residents seemed overwhelming. The EU's initial response was pallid: some ambitious politicians saw these dramatic developments as an opportunity to amplify prejudices and fears about foreigners, thereby arguing in favour of restricting refugees and cracking down on perceived or imaginary threats. The weaponisation of the refugee crisis persists in the 2020s, in the platforms of a number of European political parties.

A second blow to liberal democratic values was the crippling global financial crisis of 2008–9. For many—and especially for those in jobs that had suffered from the exporting of manufacturing during preceding decades—global institutions seemed to fail at responding to and mitigating the crisis. And this underscored a silent but growing perception among many "left-behinds" that the model of an unrestricted global free market was of benefit to upper-middle-class, well-networked elites, but not to those who lacked such advantages. More generally, the fundamental flaw in the philosophy of business leaders at the turn of the century was to treat their goal as ensuring benefit exclusively to shareholders, rather than to the broader category of stakeholders.

The culmination of this disenchantment in the United States was the 2016 election of Donald Trump, whose campaign was to channel the ensuing anger, grievance and mistrust into a political tool. Trump disdained norms of behaviour such as ethics, reciprocity and truthfulness. He exploited resentment of foreigners. And, by emphasising personal loyalty and obedience from government officials, castigating the press and applauding racism, Trump began down the road to autocracy. Happily, the electorate and the country's legal institutions have (so far) halted his progress since his defeat in 2020.

But, as noted above, the United States is not the only nation potentially gliding into authoritarianism. States around the world are doing so, and their would-be autocrats are assisting each other. It's no coincidence that Viktor Orbán has both hosted and spoken to an ultra-conservative, Trump-supporting US political organisation. And Russian disinformation efforts around the globe have sought to advance the positions of right-wing political groups, including in the US and Europe.

As Ibrahim wisely observes in these pages, if the authoritarian temptation is being fostered on an international basis, based on transnational grievances and loss of trust in democratic institutions, then the strategy to respond must equally be international. This volume is a call to action.

Michael Chertoff
November 2022

INTRODUCTION

We could scarcely imagine when the Cold War ended that in just three decades we would be where we are today. The collapse of the USSR in 1991 did not bring about 'the end of history'. Instead, it bred complacency among the leaders of the Western democracies, complacency which has sowed the seeds for the current reckoning. Across much of the world, the ideas of a democratic liberal political order, of multilateral international collaboration and of liberal free-market capitalism are now in retreat. Challenged not by a return of socialism as an alternative global, and universalist vision, but by an atavistic retreat to nativist, nationalist and populist politics. This is affecting both mature democracies and those states that made tentative steps towards a liberal political order in the aftermath of the Cold War.

This means we are now witnessing both a rise of authoritarian regimes, often through the degeneration of what were previously more functional democracies, and the decline of multinational coordination among countries now more likely to stress the primacy of the nation state as the focus for the formulation of practical policies. We are seeing how India under Narendra Modi is busily reworking its citizenship and electoral systems to exclude its huge number of Muslim citizens. Brazil under Jair Bolsonaro sees constant attacks upon the rule of law in the country, as well as callous and politically motivated attacks on the general health and security of ordinary people. The roll call of democracies that have lapsed into 'managed democracies' under populist leaders is large and increasing. The most notable examples which come to mind include Turkey, Hungary and Poland, but we are seeing worrying portents also emerging in quite a number of other European and Latin American countries.

The triumphalist hubris of the 1990s started to unravel from the 2008 Financial Crisis. The belief that there was no coherent alternative to the US model of capitalism, that societies were now on an inevitable (if sometimes bumpy) road to liberalism, and that the best way to manage economies was to allow capital the unfettered freedom to choose the location for production combined with a minimal state with a sketchy social security system, the so called 'Washington Consensus' around economic development, came to produce economic and social outcomes that have now lost broad democratic consent, perhaps even among the majority of people in the US itself and more generally across the Western democracies.

One could argue that this had initially been a problem of mismanagement in response to the 2008 crisis. Many countries elected governments committed to austerity in the 2009–12 period, blaming the financial crisis on overspending not on poor regulation of the financial sector. This austerity slowed the recovery by years, and further hollowed out the capacity of the state to meet the needs of its populace. In Greece and other poorer Western countries, the effect of the orthodoxy of austerity was essentially the destruction of both the economy and the social system.

Regardless, it should not surprise anyone that people who were pushed to the margins by austerity became increasingly distrustful of the conventional liberal politics that had failed them so badly, and are now readily attracted by those who promise easy solutions to these problems. Nor can you really blame people for being attracted to the type of politician who assures them that these problems are not of their making but a product of 'elites', 'immigrants' and globalisation—because if we are honest, in most cases, these problems really were not of the making of the ordinary people who suffered them.

As the number one representative of the global liberal order, the United States is the principal bellwether for the fate of international liberalism. Here too, the Trump presidency exemplified the retreat from all forms of liberalism, supported by factors that are all-too-familiar from other degenerating democracies: the increased venality and corruption among the economic, media and political elites who nominally represent the incumbent liberal order, the utter loss of faith by the public in their institutions as evidenced by the widespread acceptance of conspiracy theories and misinformation, and a general lack of political direction especially among the liberal political 'middle ground', with a concomitant rise in polarisation both at the top of politics, and on the street among regular citizens. A similar mindset sat behind the vote in the UK to leave the European Union in 2016.

What is at stake

A cynic might note that this is a problem most immediately for the 'old world' of American and European liberals with their particular set of domestic and international interests. But once we peer beyond this crudely 'Realist'[1] picture and look at the particular ethical and political values that are being challenged, and at the particular domestic and international institutions that are being undermined, a much more serious picture emerges. This is not one of those periods where political ascendency shifts from the centre-left to the centre-right (or vice versa); it is a much more profound rejection of an entire model for the organisation of society.

The ideological core of liberalism is that all human beings have equal inherent moral worth, and that therefore they must all have their dignity equally recognised and be given freedom to pursue their own well-being and interests, at least in so far as it does not interfere with anyone else's ability to do the same. The challenge to liberalism we are seeing today is an increasingly explicit attack precisely on this core moral axiom.

The retort to the current real and perceived failures of our nominally liberal political order is increasingly taking the form of reactionary, nativistic, 'in-group' supremacism that is the preserve of both religious fundamentalists and of ethnic nationalists. In the last century, that was the moral basis of the Holocaust, the Armenian genocide, the Rwandan genocide, the ethnic cleansing in various Balkan regions in the 1980s, and innumerable other human rights disasters. In this century, it has been the moral basis of the Rohingya genocide in Myanmar, the escalating genocide against the Uyghurs in Xinjiang, China, and of organised state violence against minorities from India to Hungary, and from Russia to the Central African Republic. Challenging liberalism, especially on this foundational tenet, and on the moral basis of humanism more generally, poses an imminent threat to the dignity and freedoms of individuals all around the world. Initially, those targeted will be visible and convenient minorities. But we should know from history that repression and conflict never stop there.

This turn in the political tides will not affect just ordinary individuals. It will also have profound geopolitical consequences.

INTRODUCTION

The next victims of this turn away from liberalism will be the traditional core of liberal democratic nations such as the US, UK, and other Western countries. The traditional foundational values of the politics of these countries, and their ability to function as cohesive societies, are predicated on a shared appreciation of liberal values, and the manifestation of these values by the incumbent institutions of the state.

What would a country like the United States become in terms of its moral foundational core if the tenets of liberalism inscribed in the Declaration of Independence and the Constitution are rejected? The US simply does not have another viable ideological organising principle. Only 60% of Americans are 'white', and a significant number of those are staunch liberals. The ethnic nationalism increasingly advocated by the far right is simply not a viable moral basis for a state where at most 40% of the population could even conceivably identify with or agree with that principle of political organisation. Despite the claims of the newly emboldened far right, multi-ethnic states are the norm and function very effectively. But they need a core organising principle and the liberal ideals of universal human rights are far superior to an authoritarian state constructed on the basis of allegiance to a ruling family, a particular religion or narrowly defined ideology.

If the United States does lose faith in its liberal moral foundations then it is going to be like Russia without faith in its former Soviet communist values in the 1990s—a scene of utter chaos and despair, haunted by the memory of past glories and achievements, yet unable to see anything bright into the future. Not a place anyone would much enjoy living in, even before the violence, the corruption, the hunger.

Other Western countries such as the UK could disband into smaller pieces with Northern Ireland seeking reunification with the Irish Republic and Scotland full independence if there are no broad liberal values underpinning the state. Even if this fragmentation was completely democratic, and the new entities full members of NATO and the EU, this has to alter the dynamics of Western foreign policy and how institutions such as NATO manage a more disparate range of members.

Between the domestic fractures within the US and the political hollowing out of other western states, abandoning liberal values would cost the countries of the West their entire global standing, influence, power and even economic prospects. It would also engender political and economic instability in the global system, with negative feedback loops further compounding the situation for ordinary people both here and in most places abroad: think more failed states, migration crises, resource wars, and all the attendant calamities that usually emerge from that.

This, at a time when the challenges of climate change, of environmental degradation, of increased global populations and of resource depletion already demand more international cooperation, not less. And that is without the challenge of how to deal with Vladimir Putin's weak but assertive Russia. But with the retreat of the liberal values of equal human dignity and worth as the *lingua franca* of international diplomacy, the long-term prospects of large-scale multilateral cooperation are under severe threat. How many bilateral, transactional deals can you make between 195 countries, and how do you make all these deals orient humanity as a whole away from all these disasters?

Climate change evidently and quite simply demands a global response, in part as the states contributing to it are spread across the globe, in part as the states most likely to be immediately affected are poorly placed to deal with the problems on their own. As discussed below, even the United States, the bastion of multilateralism since the Second World War is too often tempted to retreat to coalitions of like-minded states that can agree on specific issues. But for climate change, the response self-evidently has to be universal, and we need to find a framework to achieve that. If we allow international relations to be framed as essentially antagonistic and competitive, it is extremely difficult to see how this will allow us to avoid the kind of catastrophic climate change scenarios that would make our global complex civilisation impossible.

So we have a problem that reflects a profound threat to our entire current social structure, that needs a shared global response. On the other hand, states such as Russia and the Gulf monarchies rely on oil and gas production to balance their domestic budgets. As argued across this book, the challenges involve both domestic and international politics. The backlash against liberalism in the United States and the wider western world raises genuine existential threats not just for ideologies, identities, institutions and states, but, in the worst-case scenarios, for virtually all individual human beings on the planet, as well as their children. Humanity would most likely survive in some form. But our 'way of life' would most certainly not.

What do we mean by liberalism?

The sense of liberalism that we must rescue is that of political or civic liberalism: the notion that all human beings should have equal fundamental rights and protections, that all should be equal before the law, that all citizens should have the same rights and privileges, and that within those constraints, everyone should have the maximal level of freedom and autonomy in the social, civic and political sphere.

It is critical to distinguish and disassociate this civic and political notion of liberalism from the economic notion of liberalism, for a number of reasons.

Firstly, both the so called 'neoliberal' economic programme launched by the US and the UK in the 1980s, as well as the 'classical liberalism' of the US 'Gilded Age' and Britain's Victorian empire have proven in practice to be fundamentally about protecting predominantly the most powerful economic actors from state constraints, and not so much from the abuses of other economic actors, for example, in the forms of monopolies and cartels. And economic liberalism unfortunately favours that kind of protection from the power of the state even when concentrated economic power actually restricts the civic and political freedoms of ordinary people.

Moreover, whatever opinion one may have on the relative merits of free-market capitalism, it should be uncontroversial that this economic model is not under threat in the same way as civic liberalism is; and the consequences for its curtailment would be vastly different in any case. All around the world, economic 'liberalisation' is still going strong, and the powers of states to intervene and control economies and international trade continue to be eroded—the only notable state to challenge this with any success is China. Yet this tide of economic liberalisation has not produced a commensurate political liberalisation in most places in the world. Quite the opposite: even in the old liberal world of the US and the West, economic liberalisation has enabled concentrations of economic power which then seeped into forms of political power that have distorted the democratic character and political culture of these countries, for the interests of increasingly reactionary economic elites.

Thus the second reason to disassociate the two is that civic liberalism aims to support all people to maximise their potential, while the neoliberal economic experiment has been unable to do the same for most people in most parts of the world: it has further impoverished the working classes and decimated the middle classes in relative terms, even in some of the richest countries in the world—not least in the US. Since the 1980s wages have stagnated, levels of domestic debt increased, health care has become harder to access and at the same time rewards for those with assets have soared. The increasing casualisation of work has produced a generation with little job security and has also reduced the commitment of employers towards training their workforce. In the US, the concept of the middle class has had connotations of relative income security, asset ownership (and cross-generational transfer) and an implicit promise that the next generation will be better off. Moving to that status has been a central tenet of the expectations of US citizens for the last century. This simply does not happen any more for most American families who regard themselves as middle class.

As an example, internationalisation of the US economy in the name of economic liberalisation in part meant the export of labour-intensive work to other countries and the import of goods in return. There are strong economic arguments for this economic logic, but there needs to be a balance. And from 1990, that balance was progressively lost. Rapid de-industrialisation hit many of the older manufacturing regions of the US and this time there was little compensation elsewhere. Wages became stagnant and industrial investment fell as finance capital looked for better rewards outside the US, or in the property market and other financialised asset classes. Under the Clinton presidency, the idea of opening up access to debt as a compensation for low wages became a key economic policy. The European Union has seen the highly successful creation of a single market in goods and services within its borders, but this has also amplified existing economic differences between, say, Germany and Italy. Nor has the EU managed to protect the standard of living of its population—in effect, the focus on economic liberalism has not seen a matching commitment to citizen welfare. That, it was all too easy to assume, would axiomatically improve as a result of economic liberalisation. The failure of this policy assumption is one reason why many populist movements can gain electoral support by suggesting a return to protectionism and to economic nationalism.

And yet the middle class are the essential bedrock upon which American liberal democracy was built. The hollowing out of the American middle class produced by the neoliberal economic model undermines the liberal politics of the country and thus invites disaster. People cannot be expected to retain blind faith in an economic system that does not serve them. But to the extent to which we associate this failing economic model with the broader label of 'liberalism', we also bring into disrepute the political and civic project of liberalism. That is one of the main ways in which populists like Donald Trump have captured the imagination of so many people: disaffection with the failures of the economic model is used to foment resentment and rejection of our foundational political and civic values. This must not be allowed to go uncontested. Another positive aspect of the political liberalism that we should rescue is that, because of its fundamental moral values, it is driving towards consensus by mutual, voluntary agreement, and is therefore inherently cooperative and *democratic*, both domestically and internationally—even if, conversely, democracy can be illiberal or 'majoritarian' when a majority elects to impose arbitrary restrictions on the rights of a minority of individuals.

Liberal democracy, therefore, comes with built-in legal protections for all individuals that guarantee their rights to be 'who they are' and protects their most intimate convictions and values, so long as they do not interfere on others' freedoms to do the same. We therefore get freedom of religion, freedom of conscience and speech, the principles and legal protections of racial, ethnic, sexual and gender equality, and all the other civil freedoms. Liberal democracy protects these civil rights of the individual from the abuses of anyone, including from a potentially tyrannical democratic majority. By contrast, economic liberalism has a proven track record of concentrating power with disregard for those marginalised, and only state intervention has emerged as a bulwark against that relentless march towards the centralisation of power. Economic liberalism is therefore inherently oligarchic, in contrast to the democratic affinity of political liberalism.

For that same reason, political liberalism also naturally has an internationalist outlook which serves as a more solid foundation for international cooperation for the benefit of ordinary people, as opposed to the transactional approaches to interstate interactions observed by 'Realist' approaches to geopolitics—which at most benefit the elites of the respective countries, and often come at the direct expense of the ordinary people when these transactions come down to conflict and warfare. That kind of cooperation has served the West, the so called 'Free World', extremely well since the Second World War, and its fruits can be most immediately seen in the peace and prosperity enjoyed by many in Europe and East Asia. The European Union is perhaps the prime example of what can be achieved through liberal institutions underpinned by liberal values, even from the sorry wreckage of the War, and even among countries which have spent the last millennium fighting each other. That peace that all of us in the West have enjoyed under the umbrella of the *Pax Americana* is precisely the fruit of the internationalist character of political liberalism, and fundamentally, that is the most precious thing we stand to lose if we abandon political liberalism both at home and abroad.

The threats

The dual, domestic and international, character of political liberalism is evident not just in the way it is manifested, but in the way it has come under attack from both directions. Liberalism is an ideology that has to be internationalist in nature, not least because it recognises the equal dignity of all people, regardless of whether they are 'your people' (in whatever sense). That means that it blurs the distinction between domestic and international politics on principle. And, it appears, so does the anti-Liberal backlash. For that reason, the culture wars launched against liberalism, whether by the reactionaries at home or by Putin or Xi Jinping from abroad, are the very same conflict.

The structures that get utilised for this conflict, including the states, the media landscape as it stands, and so on, are incidental. So even if one part of this issue can look like a traditional interstate problem (admittedly in a very new form) raising the issue of how to challenge Putin's propaganda efforts in our own media landscape, the core of the problem remains the retreat of our broader political culture from universalism towards not just nationalism but often an ethno-nationalism many believed had been dealt with in the 1940s. Unfortunately, this has been a bit of a blind spot for liberal commentators so far and something we need to address—the threat is both an aspect of domestic politics and stems from international relations.

As academic subjects, domestic politics and international relations have traditionally been seen as related but separate disciplines. In practice, officials and experts tend to have concentrated on one or the other, and often politicians focus their career and personal interests into one field or the other. There are good practical reasons for this. Gaining expertise in, say, the countries of the former Soviet Union requires knowledge that is very particular, including the linguistic demands for example, and is different to having the skills to draft a domestic reform of, say, health care arrangements. Equally, within a state, there is a need to engage with various interest groups, but in the end there can be relative clarity derived from the legal system. The international structures do include legal mechanisms, but their application is rarely all inclusive, the need for alliances and negotiations is different, and the relative power of the interested parties is of considerable relevance.

So the difference between the disciplines is soundly based but leads to a major blind spot. We cannot see the current threat to the liberal international order as either just a matter of international relations or just a matter of domestic politics. The two are essentially entwined.

One thing that has been historically helpful for the United States was that the country's international policy has rarely been a focus for domestic electoral events in the post-War era. Policy elites debated the minutiae, but the US overall had broad, bipartisan liberal assumptions to its international stance until the Trump presidency. Sure, the US has always had an isolationist element in its electoral base, but since 1945 there was a consensus towards an engaged, liberal foreign policy. In the main this is true more widely across the Western world; a country's international orientation has often been widely accepted by the electorate but with little or no practical scrutiny. As another example, the French electorate rarely called into question the ongoing engagement with the Francophone countries of Northern and Central Africa except when it was clearly going very wrong, such as in Algeria in the early 1960s.

Yes, specific engagements, such as, for the US, Vietnam, have been subject to real contestation, but the broad features of engagement with the UN, with economic bodies such as the IMF, and with alliances such as NATO, were not matters of electoral debate.

This relative disengagement has not always been helpful. In the US, it allowed a policy of framing international economics towards maximum openness, not least because this helped US firms enter new markets at the same time as domestic economic policy pushed towards minimum regulation and the use of credit to offset the emerging problems of stagnant wages. The choice to tie in economic policy with political ideology was a mistake, primarily in the sense that it has made the political project of liberalism hostage to the fortunes of financialised capitalism. And that was a mistake, not least because the latter is just so inherently unstable.

After the ill-judged and poorly executed Iraq War, this general consent around foreign policy in America and elsewhere has been withdrawn. Since then, significant parts of the electorate have voted for candidates who say they are opposed to the 1945-2004 consensus, both in its economic and its political dimensions. Barack Obama won his 2008 election on an anti-war platform and increased economic interventionism at home. And so did Trump in 2016. Joe Biden in 2020 pledged to bring an end to America's involvement in Afghanistan. These are three very different presidents but they share some common themes and analysis of America's emerging role. This does point to a need for a systematic debate of how a liberal state should act both at home and abroad, especially in the context of the two-pronged attacks it faces. More generally, the profoundly dishonest case for the Iraq war has done much to undermine popular acquiescence in traditional foreign policy choices, as well as adding substantially to a widespread distrust of conventional politics.

So, as I will argue later in this book, this is one strand and it is clear that liberalism faces external threats; a significant part of the problem stems from the choices of politicians who would see themselves as broadly reflecting that tradition. However, in order to understand the threat, it is useful to try to summarise the issues, as:

- the philosophical rejection of the equal moral standing of all human beings, in favour of tribal, ethnic, or religious 'primacy' of some groups—typically the 'majority' identity of a given society or polity;

- the erosion of both civil and political rights of those deemed outside of the 'in' group;
- the corrosion of the rule of law, whereby the powerful are no longer equally accountable under the law, and thus the law becomes just a tool for the imposition of power on the powerless;
- the association of political liberalism with economic doctrines that have failed the majority of people and which are quickly becoming very unpopular—i.e. so-called 'neoliberalism' in economics; and
- the erosion of the scope and ambition of international cooperation.

The surface manifestation of these threats looks like 'populism' in the political discourse: the chaos in our cultural political landscape engendered by the unregulated media environment, skewed by the economic incentives of the attention economy, the financial interests of the owners of media outlets, and so on, which allow the unchecked proliferation of conspiracy theories and thus the erosion of a shared understanding of reality; the contestation and politicisation of all aspects of shared social realities, from health policy responses to a global pandemic to climate change, to the absurd trivialities of the raging culture wars; and perhaps most corrosively for the public good, the normalisation of gross, overt corruption at the top of politics.

However, I think the existing liberal commentary on these issues understates the threat and nature of the new right-wing populism. Larry Diamond's *Ill Winds* is a good example in that he places most of the blame on external actors such as Russia or the infrastructure created by the social media companies. That is to miss the level of agency of politicians across the world who have taken populist positions in their pursuit of power, and the loss of faith in our economic structures that has left many amenable to simple solutions to the problems they face.

The populist parties across the Western world are clearly not a single entity or movement but they have many elements in common. At one level or another, they all promote a form of ethno-nationalism, they tend to stress the right of the nation state to pursue its own domestic policies without constraints, they identify clear enemies (exactly whom varies but inevitably these are painted either as 'elites' or as 'outsiders', and include those in the relevant polity who are not true believers in the goals of the populists), and they are happy to propagate conspiracy theories. In addition, such regimes see themselves as the true embodiment of their nation, of the 'will of the people' and in consequence are very unwilling to risk losing power. So far, of these movements who have achieved power, only Trump has been electorally defeated and we see on a daily basis in the US the repeated lies that this only happened due to electoral fraud. And of course, they are, both in their own states and internationally, profoundly and explicitly opposed to the old liberal norms.

Domestically, one reason that the anti-liberal populist backlash has made such inroads since 2010 is because it appears to respond to the concerns of those who feel they have been let down by the 'old approach' to politics, economics and international relations. So to begin with, much of their electorate were not supportive of the wider ideology and the conspiracy theories of the populists. However, unfortunately, there is growing evidence of the scope for rapid radicalisation and the adoption of an internally coherent anti-liberal, and sometimes even anti-democratic world view, from this seed of discontentment and alienation grown from the failures of the incumbent orthodoxy.

Here we can see how the ideology behind populism, the lax attitudes of the social media gatekeepers, and hostile foreign disinformation, particularly from Russia, come together. One reason that the West failed to take action when Assad used chemical weapons in the Syrian civil war was that the electorates were suspicious of the claims of our governments, as a result of the Iraq War. This manifested itself as a sense that such interventions often ended badly and a lack of trust that any response to Assad would deliver the stated goals. However, there was also a concerted effort that went into constructing and propagating alternative theories as to what happened, particularly driven by Moscow. So people came to believe it plausible (or at least worth considering) that the anti-Assad rebels had set off the chemical weapons, and complex chains of evidence were curated by Russia Today, placed onto Twitter and Facebook and shared by individuals in the populist movements and their media outliers. This is a well-established technique drawn from the playbook of the old Soviet Union: no evidence goes unchallenged, however contrived the counter arguments may be, nothing is ever just true or false, everything is always contested.

This technique has also been used by others, especially those who seek to deny climate change or promote the smoking of tobacco. But we now have organised groups of political actors both at home and abroad, with no interest in truth or lies, and both the far-right propaganda machine in the US and the Russian state are more than happy to amplify any conflict, and profit off social division and the political fragmentation of the mainstream political discourse.

Internationally, the assault against liberal values comes from many quarters, from Hungary and Poland, to Turkey, Brazil and India. Nevertheless, Russia and China remain the main antagonists. Following the collapse of communism in Eastern Europe, the USSR under Gorbachev was seeking some degree of political liberalisation while retaining a socialist economy. Under Yeltsin, the state fragmented politically, and the economy effectively became a series of mafia fiefdoms. With the accession to power of Putin, the political model has become one of an authoritarian managed democracy, with the fragmented mafia fiefdoms now being organised and directed by the central state. It also saw the de facto return to power of the KGB with its old mindset about Russia's place in the world but now shorn of any need to adhere to a communist ideology.

China took a different path following the Tiananmen Square protests of 1989. The Chinese leadership had shown their ruthlessness in crushing domestic dissent and had no desire to end the one-party state. But they continued down the path of economic liberalisation initiated a decade earlier by Deng Xiaoping.

These different routes that Moscow and Beijing took from 1991 define the very different ways in which they are antagonistic to the liberal west today. Russia has never regained its status as a global military power. It still possesses a massive nuclear weapons arsenal, but it has struggled to dominate in the various wars it has entered in Ukraine, Georgia, Armenia, Syria or Libya. The main theatre where Russia remains a globally leading player is in information warfare: and that is the main avenue through which it seeks to attack what it sees as its main strategic adversary, the United States.

China, on the other hand, is now the dominant power in East Asia, and quite possibly has the conventional military power to challenge the US at least close to its own borders. But it would also prefer to avoid direct military confrontation with the US. Instead, it mostly challenges the US in the diplomatic, economic and increasingly in the cyberarenas. And here too, Beijing sees the 'Western' liberalism it associates with America as a critical ideological rival to be challenged and discredited, in favour of China-first, transactional modes of international conduct.

Thus, China has become increasingly abrasive, seeking to use its economic power to draw states particularly in Asia and Africa into its orbit, and willing to engage in state-to-state internet-based attacks, such as the cyberattack on Australia in early 2020 (and since then aggressive actions towards Australian naval assets). When challenged over Hong Kong, or about the genocide of the Uyghurs, it is uncompromising in its response. Unlike Russia, while China clearly meddles in the domestic politics of other countries, in some ways it either acts as a conventionally hostile foreign power or to maintain a client state within its perceived sphere of influence (such as its regular support for the regime in Myanmar). China thus acts mostly as a traditional state, one with a well-defined perception of its interests, one that can be hostile, but also one that is integrated into the global economy and is willing to cooperate where this is in its interest. It is never easy to deal with a powerful rival, but China will typically respond to the tools of conventional diplomacy.

Russia, for reasons of both current weakness and some of its recent (Soviet and Tsarist) history, presents a very different challenge. It has no real capacity to project military power, and its economy remains weak and (apart from in energy production) largely dislocated from the world economy. If the Putin regime has a structured goal, it probably is to draw the former states of the Soviet Union, such as Ukraine, back into the sphere of control of Moscow, either as a single state or so closely entwined as to make any residual independence notional.

However, it is clear that the Putin regime has a clear idea of who it considers strategic enemies, and the institutions and states it would like to undermine. This includes the UN Security Council, NATO, the European Union, above all the US, and more broadly also the values of liberal democracy that all these states and institutions represent. The problem in responding to Putin is that it is relatively easy to work out how to deal with a state that wishes to gain something. But dealing with a state whose aim is primarily to damage and disrupt is much harder.

The Russian role in instances such as Syria, Libya, Ukraine and in protecting its allies at the UN will be addressed later in this book. For the moment, what should be noted is that this is another place where international relations and domestic politics entwine. The old USSR built extensive capacity for spying, information warfare and destabilising states and institutions it saw as being hostile—as did the West at the time. It also had a network of Communist Parties that it could work through to influence domestic politics or to promote Soviet interests and propaganda.

State policy and preferred tools often survive notional regime change. Putin's Russia is not trying to foment a proletarian revolution any more, but it is using the toolkit it inherited from the USSR to try to dismantle certain multilateral institutions, weaken some states and generally undermine liberal democracy everywhere in the world where it is present. But where in the past its proxies abroad would have been those Communist parties, now their 'useful idiots' are the various populist parties and movements—some openly embracing the Moscow connection, others less so.

Moreover, populism is not just a matter of new parties disrupting the old electoral system; in some places such as the US it has seen the effective colonisation of existing traditional right-wing parties, and then we have seen systematic attempts by Russians close to the Kremlin to pay their way to influence within the Republic National Committee; even the National Rifle Association was getting Russian money at one point. This is not to say that groups as diverse as the Five Star Movement in Italy, the renamed National Front (now the National Rally) in France, and the Alternative for Germany are a new form of the Communist International. Indeed, some of the populist parties, such as the Law and Justice party in Poland, are very anti-Russian. However, those politicians in these movements who are not explicitly anti-Russian have gained from Russian largesse, will be backed by Russian social media disinformation, and have reliably supported Russia in any dispute with the West in return. The confluence of anti-liberal interests between Moscow and local populist parties in the West is the main threat to Western liberalism and our liberal democratic systems of government, and those ties must be attacked directly and unapologetically.

Unless we find a means to deal with that, the mix of conspiracy theories promoted by the populists, amplified by Putin's intelligence agencies, and disseminated by the social media algorithms designed only to maximise attention-grabbing, the situation will become increasingly precarious for the West's system of government and our way of life. Something of the order of 70% of those who voted for Donald Trump in 2020 still believe the election was 'stolen'. Even if we stop the circulation of the untruths on this issue, we need to face that problem: there are political actors in Western countries that are hostile to liberal democracy, and they will ally with hostile foreign forces to destroy the system of government and the moral foundations of the West's political culture. And an increasing number of voters are on board with this. We must surely dread what a rerun of the election in 2024 will do to the already fragile state of the American Republic.

Ideology: The return of 'Realist' states

It is worth restating why the re-emergence of a state-centred international system matters. One reason there was such a shift to multilateral bodies in the aftermath of the Second World War was the acceptance that some problems affect everyone (the emergence of nuclear weapons being an immediate concern) and that the solutions could not emerge from traditional bilateral modes of interaction. This mindset also underpinned the creation of a body of international law around human rights,[2] a focus on stabilising the international economy (to prevent a return to the policies adopted in the late 1920s and 1930s that tried to protect individual states at the expense of wider prosperity) and the hope that the United Nations could provide a forum for collective security and shared decision making.[3]

Running across this was a view that state-centred international orders had a major problem. They could generate periods of relative peace (such as in Europe from 1815 to 1850) but in the main tended to generate instability as different ambitions clashed (sometimes triggered by a rising power or new social movements).

If one driver to cooperation in a structured multilateral way in the 1940s was fear of nuclear weapons, we now face an equally massive threat in the form of the climate emergency. Our relatively rich societies are the product of a fairly short period of time of climatic stability, which linked to improvements in agricultural productivity, allowed many to escape subsistence living. The only way to deal with what is a global threat is via multilateral agreements,[4] given the risk of any response fracturing along the lines of some states accusing others of having caused global warming, the poorer nations in turn being most at risk and rapidly industrialising societies such as India and China wishing to achieve their own development goals. The global response is already probably too weak, and too vulnerable to states acting in their short-term interests, who then lose the ability to work cooperatively, making it likely that we will lose the climatic stability that underpins so much.

In this sense, the problem is not just whether Russia or China act disruptively over a particular issue, or seek to undermine liberal democracies; it is that as we revert to the ideology of the nation state (key to what passes for a populist ideology) as the only meaningful part of international relations, we undermine any capacity for cooperative action. And, if liberal democracy fails domestically, it will mean the end of any serious multilateral framework. We already see this; the states where the populists are well entrenched, from India to Hungary to the UK, are all increasingly dealing internationally on a zero-sum model seeking to maximise what they see as their advantage. Increasingly this is also seeing them renege on existing agreements making the chance of longer-term cooperative action that much harder.

So we have a situation where many international bodies are seen to have low legitimacy, some such as the World Trade Organization effectively moribund[5], the UN Security Council blocked by Russia and China, and agencies such as the World Health Organization struggling to function in the face of China–IUS disputes[6]. This may sound stark, but if the US voluntarily votes to bring ethno-nationalist populists back to power then that is deeply regrettable but could be seen as a choice that primarily affects the US;[7] if the attempt to rebalance the global economy to mitigate the effect of climate change founders on nationalism, then the resulting crises will probably make debates about the merits of liberalism, socialism or populism quite redundant.

So not only do the domestic problems of states like the US have an international dimension, our ability (or otherwise) to deal with global problems is in part a product of how we choose to order our domestic political systems.

How to respond to these attacks?

How the West responds to the challenges of today will matter as much for the rest of this century. After 1919, the US embraced isolationism—but then decided to act as the bedrock for the internationalist, multilateral international order after 1945. In Europe the period 1919–39 was one of a return to narrow nationalism, whereas the period after 1945 one of a steady growth of cooperation leading to the foundation of the European Economic Community in 1957.

The bitter experience of history is that a world dominated by authoritarian nation states is not one that is stable or peaceful. Equally, and here is the germ of sense in the liberal interventionism of the late 1990s, we now know that we all suffer if states fail their own population. Moreover, simple economic integration is no guarantee of peaceful relations. To give but one glib example: in August 1914 the firing pins used in French rifles were manufactured in Germany, and, as we know, this did not stop the First World War from breaking out.

Given the immediacy of the global threats of climate change, of environmental degradation, of increased global populations and of resource depletion, just the simple instinct of self-preservation would dictate that the response coming from the populist right should be off the table: the impulse to bury our heads into the sand, to assert that climate change is a hoax, to see the mono-ethnic nation state as some sort of desirable, or even viable future, would amount to national suicide.

On the other hand, the debate among serious commentators is currently limited mainly between two ways to revive the fortunes of the older liberal global order. One proposition is that what the US needs to do is to return to a modified form of the international politics and interactions that served it well in the past. This view remains painfully US-centric, but it is more mindful than we have been in the past that there are other powerful actors, and that even China is both threat and partner. The hope is that the Trump presidency can be set aside as a painful aberration, and that old links can be revived and reworked, and that the old Bretton Woods framework can be once again used to deal with the global challenges of today.[8]

The alternative proposition is to argue that Trump's undermining of multilateral institutions was unfortunate, but most of them were already moribund. The UN, especially at the level of the Security Council, cannot function when a client regime of China or Russia is the focus. The WHO may still do much useful work, but it has blundered during the Covid pandemic because of political interference from China, and to a lesser extent, from Trump. The WTO is increasingly irrelevant, and many other international institutions are equally impotent to fulfil their mission, for myriad reasons. The course of action for Western states should therefore be 'pragmatic' in a more Realist sense. It should focus on working primarily with liberal democracies, try to work with others such as China only on narrow issues of shared interests, but they should not be expending much effort on building universalist institutions or alliances.

These two propositions have much in common, however. They largely agree on the diagnosis of the problem, and mostly differ on how the West should readjust course, on just how broad the subsequent alliances can be, and the extent to which old institutions can be repurposed.

But their shared diagnosis is unfortunately flawed in a number of key respects. Yes, it would be helpful if politicians such as Trump, Modi, or Viktor Orbán stopped promoting falsehoods. Yes, we need to find a way to make the campaign of disruption more costly for Putin. But even if we could deal with all this, we are left with a disengaged electorate who no longer consent to some of the key pillars of the post-1990 liberal order, and have become suspicious of what democracy can deliver for them. Within this analysis, it is important to bear in mind the distinction between a growing scepticism of how democracy functions and a yearning for authoritarian rule. One important part to charting a way forward is to drop the distinction between international relations and domestic politics. The ideological war over liberalism is not constrained by this distinction. Our thinking should not be either.

A second important part is to draw a distinction between:

1. those who are attracted to populist politics;
2. those who lead populist parties; and
3. those who create the media and intellectual ecosystem that allows the conspiracy theories to thrive.

Most of those who voted for Trump (twice) want what is best for themselves and their community and are reacting against an economic order that has left them marginalised. The bulk of the 41% of the French electorate who voted for Marine Le Pen in 2022 are seeking a change that will deal with the deep problems affecting them and their community. By contrast, we can see Trump, Le Pen, Nigel Farage and the others as fundamentally dishonest demagogues who are not as interested in offering solutions to people's problems as they are in promising them to further their own interests.

If we are to promote liberal values abroad in a sustainable manner, we need to start with why the support for this agenda has waned domestically. And that has to start with answering why wages have fallen so much, while all the gains of the economic system have gone to a very small minority over the past forty years. In this period asset values have appreciated, investment in real estate or in obscure financial instruments is now so much more worthwhile than investment in productive enterprises. Equally, we all gain from open and free trade, but that does not mean allowing capital to become hyper-mobile. We have experimented with this for the last forty years and it is one reason why so many of our citizens see the current system as broken.

The domestic challenges reflect particular circumstances. In the US context, for there to be significant change the Democrats need to find the political will to fight the fights that need to be fought. But in any case, they must do so quickly, because the populist menace is still growing. In the UK, given the depth of the populist takeover of the Conservative Party, it is vital the Labour Party finds a clear voice. Elsewhere there are more promising signs. The Dutch electorate has largely marginalised their far-right populists and recent elections have been dominated by the conventional centre-right.

Rebuilding the liberal order internationally, however, will be more difficult. America is no longer the sole superpower in the world, able to act unilaterally and have the rest of the world merely reacting to its will. China and the EU are almost as important to global geopolitical dynamics already. In time, India may rise to a similar status.

Of these other players, the EU is in many ways a natural partner to the US. There is the overlap in membership between the EU and NATO (with this becoming closer with Sweden and Finland now planning to join NATO), there are the shared values and institutional cultures, there is the desire for structured global rules for trade, and it is in the main composed of liberal democracies. But in other respects, the EU is also a competitor, not just in being an alternative economic centre, but also in the ways in which its rules and regulations affect US firms, notably in the technology sectors. Then, the EU comes with its internal political complexities, with some member states such as Hungary, Poland and increasingly Slovenia, having turned their back on liberal forms of governance in favour of reactionary politics and a form of 'managed' democracy more reminiscent of Russian or Turkish authoritarianism.

Another complexity in dealing with the EU is that it lacks a coherent geopolitical stance—unsurprisingly, given the range of states it encompasses—and so it has an institutional bias towards focusing on issues where there is more agreement, such as trade. There have been huge differences between the attitudes towards Russia, with Germany in particular being more dovish while Poland and the other Eastern members are much more hawkish. These differences are clear in the way the EU is trying to construct a response to Putin's invasion of Ukraine. And on China too there are differences; though the block as a whole has been more positive about economic ties with Beijing, at least until the 2020s.

For the purposes of putting international liberalism back on the front foot, the West faces three linked challenges. First is one of institutions and structures. Can organisations such as the UN be redeemed or are they going to fade into some ceremonial role? There is no point making a fetish of older structures but how they are renovated or replaced will matter. One temptation (and at times this will be necessary) is to work only with states or organisations that are aligned to the West's own values and share the wider goals of liberalism. The problem here is that the global agenda is and will continue to be dominated in part by issues such as climate change, where nations will not have the luxury to only work with their friends. Equally a given regime may be an ally on one issue and a rival on another. Even essentially liberal bodies such as the EU can also be both cooperator or competitor to the US.

As far as foreign players hostile to liberal democracy, we can separate them into three groups. Some, such as Iran, can be seen as regional powers that are authoritarian and antagonistic, but who nevertheless also have relatively well-bounded goals, which means negotiations will be possible. Others, mainly Russia, do not offer a structured alternative to liberalism and are effectively playing a spoiling game. Even so, the US will need to work with Russia in some instances, not least as it is the only other major global nuclear power. Finally, there is China. Beijing does offer a structured political and economic alternative to the West, and remains the main geopolitical challenger to the US. China deliberately seeks out poor authoritarian states that possess key resources or geopolitical assets, because it has something like a 'competitive advantage' in making deals with such regimes, compared to the West. Yet its assault on the norms of liberal democracy is less about undermining consent in the West, and more about ensuring that this model of governance it is not attractive to their own population. For this reason, China will be more reliable in discussions with the West than Russia ever could be. The final issue is how to deal with multinational problems such as climate change, Covid and other potential future pandemics, refugee crises and the imbalances of the international economy. To some extent, how the West frames its response to the domestic and international factors set out above will help determine how these major problems can be dealt with.

In any case, the response we must mount to the ongoing woes of liberal democracy must start with at least the following steps:

- the robust and explicit rearticulation and defence of the philosophical foundations of liberalism both at home and abroad, including the clear and deliberate separation of political liberalism from any economic project that may call itself 'liberal', so that the moral values underpinning the political project do not get tarnished by the fortunes of any economic project;
- the reinvigoration of existing liberal institutions where possible, or their replacement by new institutions where not, both domestically and internationally; and
- conscious and active conflict management with the anti-liberal forces, again both domestic and foreign. We cannot simply play defence against these attacks and hope for the best.

If we hope for liberal values to continue to thrive among our populations, we must respond to all attacks, ideological, political, military, etc., in kind and at least in equal proportion, against enemies both foreign and domestic. This book sketches out a plan of how to do just this and is designed to explore the domestic and international problems that the US and its democratic allies now faces in terms of retaining a broadly liberal world. As is clear, there is a need to hold both strands in mind at any one stage. It also develops a set of practical steps that at least will allow us to stabilise the situation.

For countries like the US and UK with a political system that has two major parties and a degree of separation between gaining political representation and the number of votes cast, this means asking what do we do if one (or both) of the British Conservative Party or US Republicans is captured by undemocratic populists. It is unlikely in the short term that this will lead to electoral failure (in the sense of absolute collapse of their vote); narrow defeats are readily turned into material for conspiracy theories. Both countries have political systems that were structured long ago and in both there is a long overdue need for a debate on what sorts of political structures can cope better with pluralism of views. There is no absolute correlation, but broadly European proportional voting systems seem to allow populists to emerge more readily and in most cases (Germany, the Netherlands and Scandinavia are all good examples) marginalise them as their electoral appeal hits its limit and they have to defend their arguments in open debate. Even in Italy, where populists have a long history, the relatively proportional voting system has made it harder for them to consolidate power along the lines of Orbán's Hungary. They have regularly come to power and then lost it since Berlusconi exploited this mode of politics after 1991.

In a way, how to recover the conventional democratic centre-right is going to be a major part of the challenge to securing a democratic future. That both British Conservative Party and US Republicans have non-democratic wings is now all too clear; the problem is that in both, that populist wing is in near complete control. If the right disengages from democracy, as has happened in, say, Germany in the 1920s (and substantively in France at the same time), then it is unlikely that that state has a democratic future. This is not to say that domestically populism is just an issue for the right, but in the main it is manifesting itself as an electoral vehicle on the political right and its immediate threat is to the more conventional centre-right parties. In non-proportional electoral systems, how they respond now matters for us all.

This in turn gives a US bias to aspects of this book. Like it or not, the US is central to the Western world and the growth of political liberalism since 1945. It may not always have been the most considerate custodian but its importance is clear. The extent to which right-wing populism is able to entrench itself in the US does have profound implications for us all.

2

LIBERAL AND MANAGED DEMOCRACIES

We hold these truths to be self-evident: that all men are created equal; that they are endowed by their Creator with certain unalienable rights; that among these are life, liberty, and the pursuit of happiness.

Thomas Jefferson, The Declaration of Independence

What makes a liberal democracy?

Equality and a shared basis of fundamental rights for all human beings are the core philosophical concepts behind liberalism and form the basis from which democracy emerges naturally as a political system. From these truths it should follow that democracy is the system of government that is most conducive to human well-being. Yet in the grand scheme of history, democracy is still a very recent political experiment and remains a relatively untested idea. And even among the leading democracies in the world today, attaining the ideal of democracy is still work in progress.

The core argument of this book is that liberal democracy is the system of government most aligned with our fundamental human nature and desires, that it therefore is the most likely to produce good governance at the national level (even if it is not always guaranteed to do so), and that, at a global scale, liberal democratic states tend to produce a cooperative, rules-based international order that is the most likely to help humanity meet global challenges which affect us all: from pandemics to environmental crises. At its best, it allows debate, dissent, plurality of voices and to ensure that most citizens feel they belong and that their voice matters in setting policy.

If we are to defend the notion of democracy, however, we need to give it a more precise definition. Readers of a certain age will remember that the Soviet satellite states in Eastern Europe called themselves 'People's Democracies', and to this day, North Korea formally titles itself the Democratic People's Republic of Korea. Neither of these examples are what we usually have in mind when we talk about democratic societies.

In history we also find a number of polities which claimed to be democracies, but would equally fail to match our modern understanding of the term. The Athens of the fourth century BCE is often cited as the first democracy in the world, but the recognised citizens with full political rights numbered only 10,000, out of an estimated 400,000 total inhabitants. Women, slaves, freed former slaves, foreigners, and even men who failed to meet certain requirements of birth or property had no formal political rights or representation, and therefore had little input into the governance of the state.

In the medieval period, assemblies such as Iceland's Althing are sometimes cited as early examples of democratic government. In fact, the Althing had no electorate, and the members of the assemblies were just local chieftains who assumed for themselves the right to speak for their entire community (although they had to secure some consent for this role). The English Magna Carta or the Scottish Declaration of Arbroath are typically cited foundational documents of democracy in the United Kingdom, but in reality, these were treaties between the monarch and the leading nobles of the land, negotiating their relative balance of power. Neither side in these disputes had the slightest interest in the views of the bulk of the population. The voice of the people in the medieval period was almost always expressed through the peasant revolts that were a regular feature of late medieval and early modern history in Europe and Asia—not through the treaties of aristocrats.

Various revolts against monarchical government, and especially against absolute monarchical authority, occurred in parts of Europe in the seventeenth and eighteenth century. Here and there, the outcome was a Republican form of government, but yet again, as in the Netherlands,[1] these republics invariably represented only land owners and the wealthiest urban merchants—what today we would call an oligarchy, not a democracy.

The latter years of the eighteenth century brought three new approaches to political thought and practice. At one end of the scale, authoritarian regimes such as Austria moved to an economic model of cameralism (basically that allowing individuals the chance to build up their own assets would lead to greater social wealth) leading to increased liberties but in a political framework of an absolutist monarchy.[2] This ended the forced labour (the *Robot* in Austrian-German core of the regime) that had been a feature of feudalism and allowed urban communities to gain rights at the expense of the previous feudal landowners. On the other end of the scale were thinkers such as Voltaire and Paine, who had more recognisably democratic views on individual liberty and the rights of man, which in turn inspired the political structures first of the new American Republic and then of the French Republic. In between, states such as Great Britain were developing a new power sharing arrangement between the previously absolutist monarchy, the old landowners and the newly expanding middle classes.

The liberal-democratic approach has had examples of both success and failure. While the American Republic enjoyed relative peace, for the eighty years after its creation the First French Republic never escaped domestic conflict[3] and an unceasing set of wars before collapsing back into dictatorial rule and then morphing into the First Empire. Both the American Republic and the French Republics saw themselves as embodying universal liberal and egalitarian truths, yet both were sparing about who should enjoy full political rights. Both tolerated slavery, and the first French Republic deliberately set out to undermine the new republic established by ex-slaves in Haiti.[4] Both expelled a substantial sub-section of their population for lack of loyalty to the new regime. And, of course, neither gave women the vote.

What was new, and a critical factor for the eventual evolution of truly democratic polities, was that both the Americans and the French envisaged a direct connection between the electoral system and the governance of the country. In this, they opened the door to something different to the earlier developments in the English and Dutch Republics and the various extensions of the franchise and tentative steps towards democracy that were part of the wider nineteenth century in the various Monarchies and Empires—at least in Europe and the Americas.

The struggle for genuinely universal franchise, which today we recognise as a necessary feature of genuine democracy, was long and arduous. No country achieved it until the twentieth century. And indeed, even in many modern, established democracies, we still witness legal exclusions and structural efforts used to deny the vote to many citizens. So when is a country a genuine democracy?

The existence of an electoral system, and even a widespread franchise, is clearly not sufficient. If the extent of the electoral franchise were a determining parameter, then Germany in 1914 would have been far more democratic than the UK or France. Yet Germany at that stage separated out its government from the outcomes of its electoral system: the government was appointed by the Kaiser, and the elected assemblies were there to pass the proposed legislation. Conversely, the French and the US Republics, and even the UK monarchy, were led by the elected government, even if the franchise did not extend nearly as broadly as in Germany.

Today we can still see clearly that the formal trappings of regular votes, an assembly, and even the existence of multiple political parties, can exist in manifestly autocratic countries.[5] A definition of democracy, therefore, evidently does not reduce to just the presence and good functioning of these common political structures. These structures are important, but they are not sufficient.[6]

We must also see that the electoral process actually determines the makeup of the government and the policies that the government produces. The system must also allow for political power to reside in the various organisations of a lively civil society, consisting variously of other representative groups, trades unions, an independent press and so on. The legal system must be entirely separate from executive power.

These tests do not all need to be met[7] and a given state may emphasise some over others. But it is essential that the system overall mitigates against crude majoritarianism: an electoral majority does not grant the government unlimited power to impose their will and whim upon the fundamental rights of anyone in the political minority, even if this inconveniences those currently placed in power by the electoral process. How this pluralism is achieved varies substantially, reflecting national traditions and how a democracy is structured. The US, as an example, opens up many posts to direct election that in other democratic states are removed from the political process—such as, for example, judges—and with this distinction seen as an essential safeguard on both sides of the approach. However, a common thread, and a theme that is developed later, is of a wider civil society that interacts with the state, can challenge it, and can sometimes be a constraint.

This is why democracy, as we understand it today, is a political system, and moreover a political culture that has been centuries in the making. And it is also why democracy remains a work in progress, even in its heartlands.

One reason to start this discussion with a review of the emergence of democratic systems is to offer a workable definition as to the kind of society that we must defend and promote. The other is to make a simple point: genuine democracies predicated on continuous contestation between those in power and civil society really are a recent political phenomenon.

We can identify a long-held aspiration and draw on various ancient, medieval and early modern writers and movements as looking towards some form of genuinely democratic governance, but as an established political practice, fully functioning democracy really is new. The historical norm for human political systems, to the extent to which such a norm could be defined, seems to be towards autocratic rule, typically tempered in some way by the wider participation of a national elite. Outright unmediated tyranny or totalitarian rule is rare, because such a political order is expensive to enforce, and brittle in the face of sustained popular revolt (and vulnerable to the population simply disengaging). But this wider participation was often limited to an oligarchic elite who act as enforcers for the overall regime, or it might take the form of some kind of direct engagement with the broader public in a way designed to defuse discontent, for example, by allowing some form of electoral dynamic.

Against this historical background, I worry that the period between 1945 and 2010 may not have been a new dawn for an enduring model of domestic and international governance, but more of a historical anomaly. If we leave it at that, then I believe we will lose something truly precious, something that many earlier generations of humanity dreamt about, and something that future generations will dearly miss.

Liberal politics, liberal parties and liberal economics

To further define what it is that we stand to lose, and what we should seek to protect in our societies when we talk about liberal democracy, it is also essential to clarify what I mean by liberalism in the context of this book. And we must also understand how liberalism differs from the politics of self-identifying liberal parties and from (neo-)liberal economics. The definitions that follow will give the reader an idea of how liberalism diverges philosophically from the policies and attitudes espoused by notionally liberal parties, and in particular how certain, unreasonably narrow, definitions of what liberalism is about that have emerged since at least the 1980s have planted the seeds of the existential crisis in liberal democracy we witness today. And we will subsequently explore the ways in which these issues have played out since the 1990s in the next chapter.

Liberal politics

Building on the definition of a functioning democracy outlined in the previous chapter, we can say that a liberal political system is one that seeks to represent and to govern for all who live within its borders, accepts the core of the post-1945 human rights settlements, and does its best to avoid discrimination on the basis of characteristics, such as ethnicity, religion, race, gender, disability or sexuality.[8]

A defining feature of how a liberal political order achieves this broad representation and empowerment of everyone who lives within its borders is the way in which it can cope with dissent, and indeed, the way in which it finds value in dissent, taking it as feedback to help it improve decision making and enable necessary social change. This is one of the main strengths for liberal political organisations when compared to regimes that lack this positive attitude to criticism. The latter typically run the risk of ossification, as the impulse to dissent among the people first becomes passive disengagement, then later alienation, which then leads to the loss of commitment to the political system as a whole.[9] By contrast, free speech,[10] freedom of information, protection for whistle-blowers,[11] critical independent journalism[12] and other means by which state decisions can be criticised, are not a systemic threat to the political order in a liberal system, but they are essential pillars of the political order.

However, it is crucial to recognise that neither free speech nor freedom to dissent are absolute ends in themselves. They are the means through which the safety and well-being of everyone is maximised.

For this reason, in the classical philosophy of the founding fathers of liberalism, like John Locke or J.S. Mill for example, free speech has never been an unabridged right to say anything, anywhere. Liberalism, properly understood, has never argued that anyone should have the right to shout 'Fire!' in a crowded building, for example. Moreover, it shouldn't need to be said, but in the era of social media this seems to be misunderstood: your right of free speech is not matched by an obligation on anyone else to listen to what you are saying, and much less by an obligation of private parties to amplify your speech to the detriment of wider society. In the US, you may have a First Amendment right to use your voice to demonise political opponents, but Facebook and Twitter are not therefore obliged to carry your message to 300 million people.

Equally, there are obvious limits to dissent. Dissent that peacefully seeks to reform society is very welcome. Dissent that kills people in the name of some political doctrine of opposition to the political order is not. In some instances, this is fairly self-evident: if someone uses terrorism as their means of dissent, no society, liberal or authoritarian, should accept this. But sometimes things are much harder to adjudicate: for example, both in the context of radical Islamism and the new far right, what should a liberal society do about those who hold the same views as the terrorists, but who do not themselves take the extra step to violent political action?[13] Equally the UN's human rights structure retains the right to resist tyranny, with violence if that is the only solution.[14]

There is no self-evident solution here. What should be clear, however, is that even a liberal society must have limits in the kinds of dissent it accepts. We must have a clear and principled understanding of what these limits should be, and once defined, those limits must be defended robustly and unapologetically.

What we must understand about the politics of liberalism and liberal democracy in the twenty-first century, however, is that there is no principled reason to tolerate intolerance that is incompatible with the fundamental human rights upon which liberalism is predicated, and there is no principled constraint on the right of the liberal political order to defend itself against existential threats from forces that might want to destroy it. It is not illiberal to crack down on political forces that want to overthrow liberal democracy; it most certainly is not illiberal to name them for what they are.

Liberal parties

Most modern democratic countries have a liberal party—often not called 'Liberal' explicitly—even if few are electorally that popular these days. In one guise or another, the governance of most of Western Europe and North America in the nineteenth century was a contest between Liberals and Conservatives. In the United States, this remains the main political fault line to this day, even if the ideological orientation of the historical political parties in the country has shifted from time to time.[15]

In Europe, the historical liberal parties were mostly superseded by Labour or Socialist political parties in the early years of the twentieth century as the main opposition to the enduring Conservative parties,[16] and by the end of the Second World War these liberal parties were often electorally irrelevant, appealing only to very narrow sectors of the urban middle class. The flip side, however, is that on the spectrum from the social democratic centre-left and the Christian democratic centre-right, all major parties have subscribed to most aspects of liberalism wholesale, at least until the last decade or so.

The explicit torchbearers of Liberalism (in its party-political sense) in Europe today tend to govern as part of coalitions, and mainly align to the centre-right. The German Free Democrats, for example, perhaps Europe's most influential liberal party, have regularly featured as minority partners in coalitions with the conservative Christian Democrats, pulling them towards a greater degree of social liberalism, while agreeing with the conservatives' fiscal stances on reducing the size of the state and greater deregulation of the economy. It is only in the US that the main liberal party stands on the centre-left of the political spectrum, in part reflecting the historical electoral failures of social democratic parties to gain an electoral foothold. Conversely, the Liberals of Australia are staunchly right wing, closer in orientation to the US Republican Party than to any European liberal party.

So when we talk about liberalism we must be clear that we are not interested in the historical political meanderings of any party that bears the name 'Liberal', or any party that might have at some point aligned themselves with this political vision. Nor are we interested in the particular policies that such parties happen to be advocating for today. What we are concerned with is the essence of a liberal vision of society: universal human rights, equal political rights and representation, the rule of law, and cooperative politics both domestically and internationally. These are the values and the political principles that have given us the best societies in human history so far, and it is these societies that we are trying to protect and promote. Political parties are, at most, just the vehicles through which we might achieve such societies.

Liberal economics

One of the more contentious parts of liberal democracy as it is understood today is the way in which it has become conflated with a particular form of economics since the early 1990s.[17] The problems that have emerged from this conflation will be discussed in more detail in chapter 4. But it must be noted that up to the early 1990s, the economic models of many typical liberal democratic states varied substantively.

Countries like France, for example, had adopted a level of central state planning in the 1960s and 1970s that in some ways echoed the Soviet model.[18] Northern Italy saw the introduction of a distinct economic model based on family-run SMEs, partly funded by the local governments, and that sat within a wider social and economic framework explicitly directed by regional governments.[19] This may sound unremarkable, except that electorally this region was also dominated by the Italian Communist Party, and they were the main supporters of this form of economic governance as an alternative to a fully-fledged capitalist economy. And this Communist Party-led system nevertheless thrived in the Western free market, and was perfectly compatible with the wider norms of the then European Economic Community. Sweden, at one stage, experimented with a plan to slowly draw large firms under the control of their workers by share acquisition,[20] while states such as the UK directly controlled major industrial sectors such as coal and steel.

From the late 1940s and onwards to the 1950s, virtually all liberal democratic states adopted some model of Keynesian economic management coupled with an expanded social welfare system.[21] These models may have worked more or less well, may have been more or less appropriate to the demands of a particular set of circumstances, but despite the more hysterical claims of some economists—most notably the likes of Hayek[22]—such economic models were perfectly compatible with the norms of liberal democracy. Indeed, some have argued, plausibly, that this kind of active management of the macro-economy was actually essential to a political system predicated on mass participation, and on shared assets and costs.[23]

Still, even in the heyday of the Keynesian era, there were dissenters who insisted that the economic and social models of the pre-war era were not flawed and that they had provided the basis for secure development, as proven by the success of that model in the emergence of the Western capitalist countries to global dominance.[24] And their moral insistence that their view of classical economic liberalism was essential to a free, liberal, society,[25] while the common Keynesian practices of the day would be a step on the path towards Soviet-style authoritarianism, did have a narrow, if dedicated following.

These ideas remained initially on the fringes of centre-right European Christian Democracy, but they did inform the views of some of the smaller Liberal Parties. The turning point for these ideas, however, came following the apparent breakdown of the post-war economic model in the wake of the oil crisis and stagflation of the 1970s, when they came to dominate the economic thinking of both the US Republicans and the British Conservatives.

From 1990, this liberal economic model, now typically referred to as 'neoliberalism', came to be associated with American liberalism, just as the US was finally winning the Cold War. Against this background of American geopolitical triumph, this historically contingent association between a certain set of political values and institutions on the one hand, and a certain set of economic arrangements on the other, came to be seen as the ultimate way to run a society. What happened to be 'the American model' at that point in time came not just to dominate Western economic thinking, but to muscle out any consideration of alternatives.

Thus, strict limits on social welfare, free movement of capital and finance, deregulation and the privatisation of state assets, and so on, had become the only 'sensible' way to run an economy both in developing countries[26] and in economically mature countries.[27]

Yet from the beginning, some of the trends that this model would set in motion were apparent. The empowerment of shareholders at the expense of ordinary workers was always going to have predictable consequences. And part of those consequences would be the slow erosion of trust and support for 'the system' overall among the masses of workers, with attendant consequences for incomes and ownership of assets. As I will argue in later chapters, this is essentially unsustainable if we wish to see the great majority of citizens accept the ebb and flow inherent in a liberal democracy.[28]

Then this economic model only went and blew up spectacularly and very publicly during the 2008 financial crisis. The damage from that very public collapse extended beyond the public's faith in the model. Having implicitly conflated the neoliberal economic model with the political values and institutions of a liberal society, substantial parts of the public started to sour on liberalism and liberal democracy itself, prompting something of a backlash.

Unfortunately, even among educated political commentators, let alone most of the public, the historical precedents which showed that liberal democracies can adopt just about any economic model have been forgotten. Conversely, the contemporary examples which show that neoliberal economics works just as well in illiberal, non-democratic states are ignored. Because both the economic and the political models have 'liberal' in their name, they are now viewed in the minds of many as inextricably linked.

Which of course poses the critical question: if substantial parts of the democratic electorate perceive the economic structures of society to be out of bounds of the liberal democratic political process, what are they to do if they no longer have faith in the economic model? Put another way, if I wished to see a different economic model put in place, and the democratic process seemingly cannot be used for this goal, then why should I engage with the democratic process? I may have no desire to overthrow democracy, and I most definitely have no desire to live in a tyranny, but equally, I will lack any reason to accept the economic outcomes of the current political processes. And that leaves me very open to politicians promising a different approach.

Liberal internationalism

Liberal internationalism emerged properly as a meaningful force in international relations only in the post-war settlement, and for most of that period it only really applied to Western countries' dealings with each other. Yet even that slow evolution scarcely had much to do with nominally liberal parties, and certainly not in Europe.

The last period when liberal parties dominated governance in Europe was at the end of the nineteenth and early in the twentieth centuries. In the UK, for example, three Liberal prime ministers were influential across the period from 1880 to 1920. Yet in terms of international relations, their mindset was that of narrow state interests, competition between states and a willingness to threaten or engage in warfare. At various stages between 1880 and 1910, Britain came close to war with Russia, France and Germany, and even indulged in a border dispute with the USA that could have spiralled into a full war. The swansong of this political tradition on the international stage was the peacemaking that ended the First World War.[29] There is a case to be made that the ensuing attempts to set up the League of Nations were an early effort towards a more liberal mode of international politics; this drew together statesmen (and they were all men) trying to do their best in difficult circumstances, but the reality of the League of Nations was still one of naked national self-interest and great power politics, only moderately cloaked under an institutional guise by the desire of the Western winners of that war to maintain their wartime alliance of Britain, France and the USA.

Otherwise, the interwar years were in many respects a reversion to economic mercantilism, even going as far as efforts towards autarky in some states, and with scarcely any new or meaningful mechanisms for international agreement or cooperation.

There were some successes, such as banning the use of chemical weapons, that would hold even during the Second World War. But for the most part, international diplomacy was a series of conferences designed to address a given discrete crisis, and there was no ability to deal with states that either never joined, or that quickly left the League of Nations. Thus crises were dealt with at conferences of the main powers with the solutions handed down to those involved; in other instances changes to the various post-war treaties were imposed by state power.[30] The nascent Soviet Union was initially excluded and by the 1930s both Italy and Germany had been expelled (the Soviets in turn were expelled in 1940 after their invasion of Finland). Whatever the merits of this or that instance, it is not a happy reminder of the last time international affairs were handled on the basis of sovereign states.

As noted above, the policies of liberal parties in governance have often been markedly at variance with the expectations of a liberal order, either domestic or international. It was left to the winners of the Second World War and in Europe to Social Democrats and Christian Democrats to finally challenge these older modes of international relations, and institute some of the values of liberalism at the international level. This mostly came in the form of setting up legal and institutional structures underpinned by liberal values, and with a liberal geopolitical outlook.

New rules of war, and new human rights in times of peace were developed from universalised liberal principles.[31] The goal was to stop any more genocides[32] and to ensure that minorities (however defined) were protected. It also found time to start to address the problem of corruption as a barrier to economic development and good governance.[33] The United Nations was instituted as a global body where issues could be raised, and disputes settled with the Security Council (led by the main victorious wartime powers) designed to allow rapid response to emerging crises. To many at the time, a structured global institution was seen as essential given the new, existential, threat of nuclear weapons.

In terms of economics, the political energies of the time were focused towards regional integration[34] and a global economic order based around easing barriers to trade (what became the General Agreement on Tariffs and Trade—GATT—and is now the WTO[35]), financing of economic development (the World Bank) and ensuring stability of currencies (the IMF). All this was made easier due to the relatively rapid recovery of the

European economies outside the Soviet bloc due to the US Marshall Plan. The explicit aim of all these policies was to make war always economically more expensive than ongoing economic cooperation, thereby disincentivising conflict.

It is easy to critique this settlement both in its aspirations and even more so in its practical application. The end results have often fallen well short of the initial lofty aspirations, and the leaders of these institutions have frequently compromised on the foundational principles in practice.

However, the achievements of several decades of multilateral collaboration through a clear legal framework are also hard to deny.[36] Peace in Europe has been achieved, and in Western Europe at least, the return of overt military conflicts is today genuinely inconceivable. This may be wishful thinking given the wars that marked the implosion of Yugoslavia and Putin's invasion of Ukraine in early 2022 but generally the idea that a dispute between states would end up as a military action makes little sense given our expectation that multilateral institutions would seek to mediate in such a crisis.

Globally, there have been plenty of human rights abuses since 1945. Wars, human rights abuses, and even genocides still abound. They have done all through the post-war period. But throughout this liberal era of international relations, things really have been better than at any time in history. War came to be seen as abnormal and rare, not as a normal part of politics. That innocents are hurt in war used to be understood, throughout earlier history, as a normal part of conflict, and the wholesale extermination of civilian populations was thought of as a pragmatic, if unsavoury, way to 'pacify' regions. Now both of these actions are rightfully reviled by everyone, and therefore even the worst tyrants began to think twice before they set off down such a path.

The recent fraying of this wider consensus, as populist parties and politicians push narrow nationalism, has led to authoritarian rulers feeling they can act with more impunity. After the conflicts in Yugoslavia in the 1990s, NATO intervened to end the war in Bosnia and to help the International Criminal Court to bring those guilty of war crimes to justice. This created a brief moment where anyone who carried out war crimes could reasonably fear being brought to justice.

These remaining norms, and these achievements, are also very much a target of the illiberal nationalists who are seeking to subvert liberal democracy in this age. Putin, Modi, Xi, and a growing cadre of other leaders, are resenting these norms as a constraint to their power and their methods of control within their own countries. They describe these norms as 'undermining national sovereignty'. As these states increasingly try to reclaim their 'sovereignty' from the post-war liberal order, it is their citizens, especially the more marginalised citizens, who will suffer at the sharp edge of their countries' newfound 'autonomy'.

Disagreeing in a democracy

Dissent is a key aspect of democracy, and our tolerance to accept those who profoundly disagree not just with our particular policy preferences but the entire system is one thing that marks democracy from other forms of governance. The supposed benefit of liberal democracy is that it does better at listening to and engaging with dissenting opinions—even if in the end, the democratic majority ends up disagreeing respectfully. But this only helps hold a democratic society together for as long as even those who lose this or that political argument agree that the difference of opinion we have on the issues is legitimate, and that the processes by which we decide, as a society, which way to go on any given issue, are fair and effective.

An ability to agree to disagree is thus the necessary virtue that liberal democracy demands of most of its citizens, if it is to function. And most adults are quite capable of doing this. In practice many of us accept things we disagree with—for example, many of the decisions of our parents, of our employers or of our fellow citizens in an electoral process. Our dissent maybe vocal, perhaps to the point of leaving a social group to register this[37] but by and large, that does not send us reaching for a gun to go and overthrow society.

So when does dissent go from a normal and expected behaviour in a democracy, to a threat to social order and the laws of the state? Insights from Social Identity Theory[38] might provide an answer: what is necessary for us to accept something we disagree with is that we believe the process that went into making that decision was fair. So if our parents tell us we cannot go out tonight, their authority seems fair, since we live in their house and they get to make the rules. If an employer tells us to move to a different office, that seems fair, since they are paying our wages, and they get to determine the conditions under which we continue our employment with them. And if a free and fair election results in a candidate we loathe being elected to govern our country, we are still bound to let them do so by the commitment we have made to the electoral system when we signed up to vote—we might grumble about it, but this is what we signed up for.

This shared view of fairness is critical. If our chosen outcome is seen as being broadly fair, that too leads to an (unwilling, quite often) acceptance. All these are judgements, driven by how attached we are to those making such decisions. If we really do not like our job, and the new office requires a long commute, our dislike of a decision may lead to us looking for a new job. Equally if our employment contract specifies where we should be working, at that stage, we may well dispute the decision (and not just by grumbling). But the issue of fairness is critical; we will accept decisions we don't like if the process is seen to be fair.

One problem for authoritarian regimes is that by supressing low-level dissent they tend to be faced by people who secretly opt out or who seek to leave, or, in many cases, dissent ends up as open revolt simply as it has nowhere else to go.[39]

At the same time, language demeaning our political opponents is not just a product of populism. Winston Churchill, during the 1945 election campaign, described the Labour Party as 'like the Gestapo' due to its social welfare plans. His opponents were equally robust, one describing the Conservatives as 'vermin'.[40] But among the rough and tumble of electoral politics, what neither said was that the voters or leaders of the opposition were anything but members of the wider polity in the UK. They might be wrong, perhaps dangerously so, in their preferences, but that's part of politics, especially when big issues are under consideration; but no one was suggesting they should lose the right to vote or their citizenship—not least because politicians on both sides had just had first-hand experience of where those attitudes can lead a nation. And this goes beyond political debate: free and fair elections, with as wide an electorate as possible, are what underpins a democratic system—and that includes acknowledging that our preferred outcome is not endorsed at the end of the process.

Modern populism always contests the existing political order on the fundamental grounds of fairness. Their foremost argument is that the interests of the people are being ignored by elites, and that therefore a system that allows the people to be ignored in this way is inherently not fair, and should not have the support of the governed. Usually this is overlaid by allegations that the elite cheats, engages in conspiracies, secretly controls the real sources of power.[41] This argument has the rhetorical advantage that it gains even more potency if the populists lose in a fair election: after all, in their world view, they represent the real interests of the people and the only reason they fail to gain (or retain) power is due to some malign conspiracy.[42] This is the essence of the threat they pose to liberal democracy: democracy is a system of government where any political actor should expect and accept that voters could disagree with them just as well as they could agree. If your political ideology does not allow you to accept that voters might prefer the other guy, then your political ideology is incompatible with democracy.[43]

It is equally important for the citizens of a liberal democracy, and doubly so for the political leaders of a liberal democracy, to yield to the decisions coming out of the democratic process, even when we do not understand why people make the choices they do. Political discourse inevitably has some element in incomprehension: 'Why can't they see that?'; 'How can they vote against their own interests like that?' But it should be obvious to any mindful adult that most political decisions involve the weighting of multiple criteria[44] and it is unreasonable to expect that everyone should be responsive to the same criteria, in the same way, consistently over time.[45] In a given political choice, for example, we may share an understanding that there are, say, five key criteria that will determine our personal preference: even then two or three of us can come to radically different views as to which is the most important, and the diverse weightings that we give to each criterion can drive each one of us to vote in radically different ways.[46] Thus we may vote for a party or an individual whose policies are against our interests on one issue, if we expect they will give us what we wanted on our more important criteria. In the UK referendum on leaving the EU, for example, some of the voters voted in favour of Brexit even if they believed that they themselves would pay some economic cost in the aftermath of the vote. Or in other words, other criteria trumped personal financial gain.[47]

Here again, populists attack the choice of criteria, or the preference ranking of the criteria, that go into the decision making of anyone they disagree with, typically with 'moral' outrage: 'Only weak and traitorous people could prefer a peaceful, prosperous life, over the glory of the nation' (as Putin was suggesting to Russians at the start of the war in Ukraine in 2022). But in a democracy, we must respect the intellectual autonomy of other citizens to make their own decisions about what they care about. And we must be vocal in defending this principle any time a populist uses rhetorical tricks to attack this fundamental principle, just as readily as we should be vocal when a neoliberal economist tells us that we are could only possibly want to have unfettered free markets, even if they prove harmful to our other political priorities.

The challenger: managed democracy

The main alternative to liberal democracy in the world today is an approach to government we typically call 'managed democracy'. These are regimes that take the formal aspect of democracy, with regular elections, *de jure* independent institutions, and so on, but which are in practice tightly controlled by a single political organisation or party, with an explicitly illiberal political philosophy. And after the receding threats of Soviet communism and global jihadism, these regimes are emerging as the main challengers and threat to liberal democracy on the world stage.

This mode of political organisation has long antecedents in places like Germany, Austria and Italy in the nineteenth centuries and Russia in the early twentieth, where the electorate was steadily expanded but the electoral system had little real effect on state governance. Unexpectedly, over the past decade or two, this mode of governance has returned, and is becoming entrenched in an increasing number of countries.[48]

While there are still some totalitarian regimes around the world, most countries that now diverge from liberal democracy are practising some form of managed democracy. The specifics of implementation vary from country to country, but the common features they all share is a veneer of a mass franchise, regular elections and some form of parliamentary system. Some are explicit in doing this. Iran, an early pioneer of this mode of governance, has a constitution that deliberately sets out the limits of what the electoral system is allowed to influence, so as to protect the theocratic core of the state. Most, especially those who have previously had more contested democratic politics and whose systems are officially supposed to be liberal-democratic, are more subtle. Rigged elections, fake opposition parties, closing down dissenting media and so on, are the hallmarks of Putin's Russia and Orbán's Hungary. Others seek to limit the electorate to exclude those who are deemed no longer to be a rightful part of the polity—Modi's India stands out for this.

These approaches are easily recognizable. Limited franchises, careful monitoring of which political parties were allowed to compete, and representative systems that lacked real powers, were the norm in countries such as Austria and Prussia from the 1850s onwards. The movements and political parties that are currently using this approach to maintain power are for the most part right-wing nationalist in their political outlook, but there are exceptions in places such as Venezuela. All share a common mindset, however. They think of themselves as representing 'the will of the people' axiomatically, and therefore deem opposition as only possibly representing forces and interests fundamentally opposed to the polity as a whole. This mindset often results in attempts at political exclusion on ethnic or religious grounds, on attitudes or occupation, or even just on voting for opposition parties. They tend to not see democracy as a politically neutral process of gaining power, enacting a program basically in line with manifestos and negotiating with the other power structures in the state. The institutional constraints of liberal democracy are seen as a legacy, or sometimes even a foreign imposition, that frustrates their efforts to 'voice the real will' of the people. In government, even Orbán or Recep Tayyip Erdoğan cannot be described as totalitarian, but these echoes of Fascist and Stalinist thinking are very evident in their political language.

Because they purport to embody 'the will of the people', their opponents cannot therefore be merely wrong: they are traitors or should never have been part of the polity in the first place. That their political opponents might ever be right is a logical impossibility in this mode of thinking too. And that 'the people' might prefer another party to govern them is unfathomable. So far, most of these populist governments in places such as India, Turkey, Hungary, Poland, and Brazil have not yet been challenged by the loss of power. Only Trump in the US has actually lost power in an electoral contest. And that fact has been incomprehensible to the adherents of the movement, as it has been to their leader: the only way for them to make sense of this event is to put it down to some kind of conspiracy or fraud. Ceding power in an orderly and peaceful transfer of authority after an election would therefore also be tantamount to betraying the nation. 'Real patriots' therefore organised an insurrection to 'defend the will of the people' from the 'fraud' perpetrated on them by the actual election results.

To the extent to which there are rival centres of power in the country that might challenge the 'will of the people' as embodied by the leader and their party, for example, critical media, non-partisan institutions, or NGOs that might take a different view on a particular issue than the government, these too can only be actors maliciously hostile to 'the people' and 'the nation' as a whole. It is therefore the moral duty of such a government to fight and suppress any other centre of power at the first sign of disagreement. Independent media, 'unelected judges', the 'faceless bureaucrats' in the electoral commissions overseeing elections, to the extent to which they deviate one iota from the party line, they can only be conspiring against the 'people' for some reason or another. The conspiracy theory as to why they are doing what they are doing may still be a work in progress, but the 'truth' will inevitably 'come out'.

In the emergence of these movements that are challenging liberal democracy in the West, and their coordinated, cross-border mutual support in opposition to liberal-democratic authorities and institutions, we also see one of the defining geopolitical dynamics of our times, and how domestic and international politics entwine. And we also see the role of new media and social media as an essential battleground in twenty-first-century information warfare.

To understand the power of these movements, for example, we must understand particularly how they gain adherents online, and indeed how their efforts are directly and explicitly supported by authoritarian, anti-liberal regimes in states such as Russia and China. Between the battle tactics deployed on nominally neutral platforms such as Facebook or Twitter, and the closed ideological systems of alternative 'facts' and ready-made narratives, liberal democracy as we have practised it in the twentieth century is ill-equipped to respond. Deliberative representative democracy underpinned by a faith in the free exchange of ideas may have worked in a world where the ideas being exchanged were being subjected to slow, systematic analysis and critique by media institutions which had an unshakeable faith in truth and a real, if flawed, commitment to political impartiality. That world does not exist anymore. And if liberal democracy pretends that it does, it risks digging its own grave.

The end point of these anti-democratic phenomena is fragmentation of the electorate, not just into contested ideas, as would be right and proper, but into irreconcilable reality bubbles that simply cannot communicate with each other through earnest democratic dialogue. Once that is achieved, democratic governance for the public good becomes virtually impossible. And on that front at least, Russia is certainly the most consequential state actor, with its demonstrated expertise at exploiting contentious issues within our open democratic discourse to sow irreconcilable differences between our citizens. But it is apparent in the USA: Fox News basically refuses to show the hearings into the 6 January (2021) attack on the Senate. Its viewers are not just seeing a particular news slant or interpretation of the findings, they are not seeing the findings in any form.

For these reasons, I believe that managed democracies are not just a lesser alternative to liberal democracy, or some transitional form along the path towards full democracy. All the emerging evidence is that these kinds of regimes become readily entrenched,[49] are politically stable, and explicitly hostile to liberal democracy. In the world as we have it today, they are the de facto antithesis and main geopolitical and ideological rivals to liberal democracy. If liberal democracy is to survive, we must recognise this fact, and respond to them as such.

3

TRIUMPH AND HUBRIS

1991 saw the collapse of the Soviet Union at a time when China was of little global relevance. It was to many a comprehensive triumph of Western models of liberal democracy and capitalism over authoritarian, or totalitarian, political systems and managed economies. There is much that is true in this analysis but it was not as complete as some of its enthusiastic proponents suggested. Even in Western Europe and North America there had been a wider range of political structures and economic systems than could be readily fitted into a single model of economic management. But it was a single model that was now proposed for all, an economic system based on minimal regulation, the importance of shareholder value, and with democratic intervention pushed to the margins. In effect, the Soviet Union collapsed because fundamentally it tried to force reality to fit a narrowly defined ideology—an error that was to be repeated in the West as a single economic model was prescribed to be the only acceptable approach.

For some time, this core framing of both politics and economics seemed to work—especially by comparison to the stagnation of the 1970s. Regardless of substantial shifts in the distribution of social wealth, most citizens of the Western states gained in the decade after the fall of the USSR and slowly, other states did become more open, both democratically and economically. However, enthusiasm for the model that 'had won the Cold War' blinded its proponents to this system's own frailties. These frailties would therefore go unaddressed for over two decades, and would build up to eventually undermine the entire foundation of this economic model, as well as, unfortunately, the political model that had championed it.

Internationally, the focus tended to fall on those states still outside this new consensus. Some, such as North Korea, were marginalised, but still posed a serious problem due to their nuclear weapons programmes (and sales); others, such as Saddam Hussein's Iraq, were a residual concern—subject to stringent sanctions, but also seen as a useful counterbalance to an emerging Iran. Whatever these states were seen as, it was not an alternative political or economic model. When post 9/11 President George Bush started to identify his axis of evil, the list contained states that were essentially domestic tyrannies, not those that aspired to offer a political or economic model to the wider world.

The fundamental issue is that both international relations and domestic economics were too easy for the United States and their allies in the 1990s. That made them complacent, and let ideology capture their imagination, unchallenged by dissenting facts. The 2000s would not be so lenient, and by the late 2010s this system would appear in terminal crisis.

The model started to fray from 2001 onwards—slowly at first, and then at an accelerating pace. Crises such as the 'dot-com' bubble of the late 1990s were easier to see as a classic overinflation of asset values and the inevitable correction. The first significant warning that history was not yet over came with Al-Qaida's assault on the US in 2001. This was an unwelcome reminder that not all revolts have material goals, and sometimes a contrarian ideology is all that is needed. The lies that underpinned the 2003 invasion of Iraq were to haunt a generation of politicians in the US and the UK and diminish trust in the political system even in these mature democracies, with long-term implications for the health of their political cultures. The fallout of the 2008 financial crisis devastated many people in the real economy, while the financial sector that had caused the crisis emerged mostly unscathed. And to add insult to injury, the government policies that aimed to keep the economy going also led to an explosion in economic inequality, especially as a result of the economic rewards going towards the owners of assets, as opposed to ordinary workers. This left many, in the US and UK, starting to feel they were not gaining from the only acceptable political and economic model. In effect, by pushing the idea that there was only one acceptable model of economics and governance, faith more widely in liberalism and market capitalism started to seep away

But before getting to the challenges of the subsequent decades, it is also important to quantify in detail the Western triumphs of the 1990s, to see why it was so easy for Western policymakers to be seduced by their own propaganda. If there is one big lesson in this for the reader, it must be the importance of intellectual humility in those who make the big decisions in our societies.

No alternative left standing

The collapse of communism

By the 1980s the Soviet economy was clearly in decline. The short-term boost in the 1970s from higher oil and gas prices had long evaporated, and the costs of modernising their armed forces was stretching thin an already weakening economic base.[1]

Their ill-fated intervention in Afghanistan was producing a steady stream of casualties, sapping political morale as much as it did the coffers of the state.[2] And then the Chernobyl nuclear disaster happened, shattering the already fragile political fabric by the way it laid bare the serious lack of competence and probity at the heart of the system. The Soviet Union did not collapse immediately after Chernobyl, but the state and its foundational ideology appeared already mortally wounded.

This series of events pushed Gorbachev to renew Andropov's limited reforms[3] to the fundamental pillars of the Soviet state apparatus, most notably Glasnost and Perestroika. But these reforms would serve only to further lay bare the rot at the heart of the system. In any case, Gorbachev was not given the opportunity to try and salvage the hollowed husk of the Soviet state edifice. Hardliners opposed to his reforms attempted to stage a coup to stop their implementation. When their coup failed however, the USSR swiftly collapsed in a matter of days in August 1991,[4] breaking up into its constituent republics.

The fragmentation was immediately disastrous for the economy of the entire former territory of the USSR, as the long-established supply chains and trade patterns that made the republics economically interdependent were broken overnight.[5] To make the situation worse, the now unviable managing companies running the big sectors of the economy were either closed down, or sold at huge discounts to their previous managers. Under the shock of rapid industrial collapse, and with the loss of key parts of the previous administrative structures which might have served as a check, a politico-economic elite arose from the still-smouldering ashes of the former industrial conglomerates, based on managers of previous assets, individuals with connections to the KGB, and elements of the existing mafia system. And this new elite then proceeded to enrich itself with the looting of the remaining state assets, by any means necessary.[6] Russia itself, was thus balkanised into the personal fiefs of this new elite, and slipped into something akin to a crypto-feudal mafia state.

The Central Asian republics, on the other hand, lacking the economic diversity of Russia, were quickly captured by the dominant economic interest in their respective regions. Domestically the old party bosses mostly seamlessly reinvented themselves as rulers of their respective Republics, retaining overtly authoritarian rule, while also seeking to update their approach with some elements of the Chinese model, most notably a certain degree of economic liberalisation.[7]

In this way, the collapse of the USSR in 1991 removed from the world stage the only coherent alternative model of economic and political governance at the time to Western-style democracy. Most surviving communist states, such as China and Cuba, were then effectively forced to opt for a hybrid approach, based on economic liberalisation, while trying to retain political control of the single Communist Party. But at that time, even those with great economic potential, like China, were far too weak to have any real influence outside their own borders.

Holdouts who refused to liberalise economically, like North Korea or Myanmar, became more isolated than ever, and practically faded from significance on the world stage beyond the threat of violence they still posed to their neighbours—and their own citizens. All in all, it seemed history had settled the debates on governance and economics, and there was only one political and one economic system that anyone anywhere in the world could reasonably aspire to: Western-style liberal democracy.

Lessons to be learnt

But those who jumped to that conclusion did so prematurely. We now know that the collapse of the sclerotic Soviet model and the loss of confidence of much of the social democratic left in the West did not, as some claimed, mark the end of history.[8] And yes, war was still very much possible between two states that both had McDonald's restaurants[9] despite some optimistic claims. And in no small part, the problem would turn out to be precisely because so many people jumped to the triumphalist conclusion, that the main debates of politics and economics had now been settled.

Yes, a system based loosely around democracy and free market capitalism had triumphed over one based on authoritarian governance and a state-managed economy. But the lessons 'learnt' by the winning side were often the wrong ones. Instead of learning from the Soviet experience what happens when a political and economic system emphasises ideology over reality, many of the winners, especially on the centre-right of Western politics, had convinced themselves that it was their ideology, rather than the realism of their system, that had won the Cold War. Thus, the triumphalist winners now moved in unison to amplify the characteristics of economic liberalisation, without any regard to common political sense or empirical evidence. With quasi-religious zeal, the simple solutions that were preached for any economic problem, however complex, had to be less economic regulation, less constraint on market capitalism, more globalisation of the economy and, to some, a need to export a form of democracy to the few international holdouts. This policy framework rapidly came to dominate, but, as I argue in the next chapter, it missed the point.

Moreover, it is in fact possible to argue that the opposing system had not been 'beaten'. Instead, an equally reasonable reading of events is that it had in fact collapsed, under its own weight, and for reasons that had not been predicted by the winners, or their ideological outlook. The sequence of events in late August 1991 in the USSR was more a comedy of errors than a coup, and the actual outcome was neither intended nor expected by any of the participants. A handful of decisions made differently at certain critical junction points could well have left the USSR standing, in the same way that the Chinese managed to effectively suppress the pro-democracy movement in Tiananmen Square in 1989. And out of that, the Soviet Union could well have survived with some form of state-directed socialism, especially if Gorbachev's reforms had worked.

Nevertheless, the Western triumphalist interpretation of events came to capture the imagination even of the former centre-left of the political spectrum in our own countries. So much so, that the Clinton presidency in the US and the arrival of New Labour in the UK also brought a more overt and militarised commitment to globalised free trade, as well as to 'spreading democracy' to the whole world. This materialised in a willingness to challenge the few regimes that were seen by the US and the UK to be at variance with the new norms of liberal economics and a plural political system, even with direct military confrontation, regardless of notional UN approval. Thus by 1997 the US and NATO had intervened decisively to end the fighting in Bosnia and again,[10] in 1999, to end Serb control over Kosovo. In this period, the British Prime Minister, Tony Blair, spoke of liberal interventionism,[11] a willingness to intervene to protect the citizens of a state from their own government.

This is not to say that any and all such interventions were bad, and should not have been pursued. Quite the opposite: the world had a moral obligation to step in stop the nascent genocides in the Balkans in the 1990s, and when the world failed to coordinate and intervene as a whole through the UN system, it was morally right that the West assumed responsibility and stepped up to curb the human rights abuses. The problem, however, is that once they had won these conflicts, the US and its allies would often simply impose their own notions of how a state and an economy should be run, without any reference to the local circumstances, and how the local people thought they should be governed. And even worse, the early successes in these conflicts gave especially the United States a sense of righteous entitlement, and a faith in the inevitability of their own success, that would lead Washington into the disastrous decision to wage two simultaneous wars in Afghanistan and Iraq, without any long-term plan as to what they might do, or would need to do, after they toppled the tyrannical local governments.

The rejection of social democracy

Another oddity of the era is that the collapse of the Soviet economic model was also taken to have somehow discredited the social democratic economic models that were still very successfully practised throughout most of western continental Europe. Neither in theory, nor in practice, had these models anything much to do with the Soviet approach, except perhaps the belief that the state did still have responsibilities in the running of the economy.

But unfortunately, these otherwise successful variations in the practice of capitalism had nevertheless now come to be seen as somehow compromised forms of capitalism, somewhere in the middle of the spectrum between the 'obviously correct', completely deregulated, Anglo-Saxon neoliberal model, and the 'obviously failed' Soviet model. These forms of capitalism thus ceased to be understood as pragmatic, situational responses to varying national circumstances and the outcomes of the democratic political process, and instead were viewed through the ideological prism of neoliberalism as 'impure' capitalism, that should, in time, conform to the 'true' American model.

The triumph of the neoliberal ideology of the centre-right was most quickly seen in the United States, where the notionally centre-left Democratic administration of Bill Clinton adopted this economic outlook wholesale, and pushed through a sustained reduction in existing welfare systems and the outsourcing and privatisation of previously state-delivered services, with the same energy that might have been expected from a Reagan Republican. This same path was soon followed by the notionally centre-left Labour Party in the UK under Tony Blair, when they came to power in 1997. And in time, much of the traditional European centre-left followed. By the 2010s, even the French and Spanish Socialists were trying to balance budgets with welfare cuts, while simultaneously seeking to lower taxes.

Before the fall of the Soviet Union the debate between the centre-right and the centre-left of Western politics was essentially about how best to regulate capitalism to maximise public good and economic growth and how to use social security systems to redistribute wealth and assets to benefit society as a whole. Afterwards, it became about how quickly to deregulate, and how to prevent social security systems from being a barrier to a 'flexible labour market'.

Enduring dissent

Yet dissent against the neoliberal vision of politics and economic practice still remained. Merely removing a system that had sought to offer a structured alternative did not change the fact that there were principled and practical reasons why some still opposed the now hegemonic model of globalisation and unregulated capitalism.

Soviet Communism presented itself as an alternative model, and was thus a useful foil for the ideological defenders of neoliberalism, and especially so after that alternative was seen to have failed. But not all critiques of a system need to be so structured and intellectually coherent: objections to a system can also be just negative revolts against the status quo.

A more careful reading of history would have remembered that not all revolts are for a pre-defined, positive programme. Eighteenth-century France, for example, was rocked by a series of peasant revolts, the *Jacquerrie*, that had no realistic goals but instead were the violent (and self-destructive) outbursts of those with nothing to lose.[12] Similar peasant revolts had in fact occurred all throughout Europe in the seventeenth and eighteenth centuries, and, for more contemporary examples, many of the revolts against colonial rule in the nineteenth century were marked by a combination of brutality (on both sides) and a lack of any realistic goal to the uprising.

Thoroughly destructive revolts that can even bring down a whole system need little more than a dash of fantasy and mysticism[13] to get going, and the promised rewards do not even have to all be attainable in this life. The first manifestation of a revolt against the triumphalist hegemony of neoliberalism came with a militant form of Islam, a movement that first came to believe that it brought down the Soviet Union in Afghanistan,[14] and now decided that it also needed to bring down the hegemonic United States too.[15]

But that would not be the only challenger to 'Western liberalism' for long. Because there were plenty of people in our own countries who had good reasons to dissent against the ideology and the social and economic effects it produced, and most of them were not Muslims. Before long, many Americans and Europeans would find solace in another similarly non-liberal source of identity that was supposed to be under threat from the prevailing liberalism of the state: ethnic and racial identity. And in time, illiberal ethnic nationalism would build into a seemingly more coherent, and certainly more potent, ideological challenge to the liberal status quo, especially as the crises of liberalism, most notably the crises of the economic system associated with liberalism, mounted up.

The New World Order

Domestic economics in the West

A simple example can illustrate the diversity in economic norms across Western Europe and North America up to the late 1980s. Insurance in the US and UK was essentially a transaction between the individual and a financial institution. In West Germany by contrast, each state provided a set of prescribed insurance products. The market for insurance in West Germany was therefore less efficient, with some products being more expensive than might have been expected, the surplus premium being used to subsidise many more products at the lower end that were widely available, in a cheap, relatively easy to understand form.

As part of extending the EU's single market to financial services, however, the UK successfully pushed for this arrangement to end across the EU, to allow other financial service companies to enter the various national markets.[16] Which of these models is the better one is beside the point here—though it should be noted that the old West German system was never blighted with the mis-selling of financial products so common in the UK or the US. Rather, in this example we can see how the ideology of a particular form of market economy and globalisation crowded out the alternatives, and denied the local electorate any political agency in the matter. The long-term consequences were that German motorists gained cheaper car insurance, yes, but on the other hand German financial institutions like Deutsche Bank were now able to accept the logic of the international markets to start engaging in the sorts of risky lending and other high-risk, high-reward financial operations that would turn out to be so destructive during the 2008 financial crisis.

'Neoliberalism' is an overused framing for the new economic norms, but the label does capture some meaningful aspects of how policymakers' approach to economic matters shifted from the 1980s onwards: deregulation, privatisation, cuts in state provision of services, and the introduction or extension of market competition in areas where it had been previously absent.

Which is not to say that every particular instance of implementing one of these policies was ill-thought out or economically unadvisable. The problem, rather, is that this set of policies became the only acceptable package of responses to literally any situation or problem, just as the very specific form of economic theory that underpinned them became the only acceptable basis for public policy.[17] To the extent to which the resulting policies still reflected national variations and past experiences, the diversity of implementations was increasingly cosmetic. The space of acceptable public policy narrowed across the Western democracies with very similar approaches being adopted across the board[18]—and as we came to learn in the financial crisis, that left all Western democracies with the same kind of economic, social and political vulnerabilities.

One of the more pernicious effects of this ideological shift is becoming especially apparent in the 2020s in the context of the Covid pandemic and the ever-increasing threat of climate change. These are challenges of the 'global commons'—the set of public goods both within nations and internationally that are necessary for complex societies and economies to function sustainably. But under the influence of the neoliberal revolution, economic policy, especially in the US and the UK, increasingly lost any distinction between activities that added value to the wider economy, the wider society, and the commons that underpin them both, on the one hand, and activities that merely generated easily quantifiable profits for the organisation or firm undertaking them on the other.[19] The core debate in economics for over 250 years about value in macroeconomic policy, running from the French physiocrats to Adam Smith, Riccardo, Marx, Keynes and all the rest, was declared redundant. If an activity made someone a profit, it was deemed valuable. Any other criteria of value were deemed superfluous.[20]

Such a framing significantly reduces the field for acceptable public policy. And critically, it pushes policy aimed at sustaining those absolutely essential public commons outside of the field of practical discussions. The result is an economic ideology increasingly blind to its own existential needs, indeed an ideology that is explicitly hostile to any government intervention at all, even those interventions and 'regulations' aimed at helping the economic system not destroy itself by depleting its underlying physical basis.

Few people who live in Western Europe or North America would disagree with the core assertion that a combination of liberal democracy and free market capitalism has broadly delivered greater social wealth since the end of the Second World War. But if this kind of strong ideological framing is the only politically acceptable basis for policy, then we must hope that it is entirely correct, that it serves all people better than any alternative system, and that it is sustainable within the physical constraints available on our planet. If any one of those things does not obtain, then the ideological edifice will, sooner or later, run into the wall of reality, just as the ideological edifice of the USSR did.

What is more, those increasing numbers of discontented citizens appear to be right.[21] The neoliberal approach to the economy writ large has suppressed their incomes since the 1980s, has pushed them into ever-increasing levels of household debt,[22] and has shifted the overall economy away from industrial production and towards financialisation, suppressing long-term productivity, and therefore long-term growth. And to top it all off, the financialisation has enabled almost all the gains of growth since the 1980s to accrue to investors and asset owners, with ordinary workers being left with nothing to show for their longer working hours and increased productivity, except depleted state services.[23] Since wages in the US broadly stagnated, while those with capital or existing assets saw substantial gains, the result was not just growing income inequality but the steady erosion of what had been the large American middle class.

This is an issue across the Western world but the situation in the US is instructive. Not least, it offers a ready explanation for why Trump's claims and policies found such a ready audience. In the US, the period 1980–2018 saw the real earnings of the richest 0.1% increase by 340%, of the richest 1% by 158% and the bottom 90% by 24%.[24] The differences really are that stark and the gap only started to rapidly widen after 1990. This also broke the historically relatively close correlation between productivity gains and the resulting wage rates—the link started to weaken around 1980 and this has accelerated since.[25] Since 1980, worker productivity in the US has increased by 70% and wages by 11%. In contrast between 1950 and 1980, productivity increased by 109% and wages by 93%. If we want to understand why so many are now turning to the populists for answers, this loss of any connection between intensity of labour and wages sits at the core.[26]

The natural consequence of all this was that, as of 2020, the average US household has debts 105% of their net disposable income,[27] a sum that can never be repaid unless the income distribution trends noted above change rapidly.

The consensus in international economics

The other crucial pillar of the new consensus was the way international 'free trade' became an item of ideological conviction, leading to a belief in globalisation as a goal in itself, as opposed to a pragmatic economic policy that should aim to benefit the citizens of all parties. Instead of asking whether a new trade deal would actually benefit everyone, this was more likely to be assumed out of hand, because our leaders stopped being able to imagine that this might not be the inevitable outcome.

There is no argument that trade between diversely specialised partners is of benefit to all partners, but the real world is not a realm of perfect economic simulations devoid of political constraints. The political aspects of trade are at least as important, and depending on how those are handled, trade really can be the boon economists say it is, but it can also be a disaster.

The best example of trade done right, with the politics of it thought through carefully, is the Single Market of the European Union, where from the late 1980s all people and all businesses across the member states have operated as if national borders do not exist.[28] Especially because this was allied to freedom of movement for workers, to match the freedom of movement for goods and capital, this broadly worked as intended, with lower costs, greater efficiency and greater levels of economic activity as a result, but also with the economic gains being more broadly distributed. Some of this came from matching freedoms for capital with freedoms for workers but it also derived from the wider political and social arrangements put in place. In effect, regions that were at a disadvantage then received additional support, something that was to prove valuable when the former Soviet bloc states began to join after 1991. This is not to argue that the package was ideal, or that all the related decisions were well made, but it is an acceptable example of what was once called 'political economy'—accepting that the economic structures are derived from political and social choices. This is not to claim that all of this was handled perfectly in practice in all instances, but the general approach has worked, even if it has steadily frayed in the aftermath of the 2008 financial crisis.

The US model has been different, mainly seeking either bilateral trade deals with other states or trading blocs or taking the form of the North American Free Trade Agreement (NAFTA) with Canada and Mexico building on existing trade agreements.[29] In each case, the US approach has focused on the ability of US firms to enter other markets, to relocate and gain access to cheap labour, and to improve access for US finance, but without the single market framework adopted within the EU: specifically without free movement of people or politically directed investment in areas that lose out from the economic shifts—not even in the US itself, as we can see in the 'Rust Belt'.

This distinction matters as the evidence suggests that how globalisation is delivered is as important as the generic benefits that can follow from trade liberalisation.[30] The immediate effects of NAFTA have been limited for Canada, as most of its trade with the US was already covered by other agreements, but Mexico did benefit from US businesses investing in the country and relocating facilities to take advantage of the cheaper labour.[31] President Trump was later to present this as evidence that the deal was flawed, but at the time when NAFTA was originally envisaged, the hope was that by stabilising and growing the Mexican manufacturing sector and creating a reliable tax base for the Mexican authorities there would be less pressure for illegal migration to the US.[32]

The wider impact on the US is complex. Some point to the loss of jobs to Mexico but other work suggests that being able to base part of the manufacturing process in lower-cost Mexico has enabled US automakers in particular to deal with competition from China,[33] while also being able to retain other, higher-value jobs in the US itself. The people who did less well from this deal were the well-paid, unionised blue-collar workers in America's former industrial heartlands. And due to the dominant 'free market' ideology of the US governments of either party, commensurate government investments into those communities to repurpose them for other industries or other productive activities would never take place. NAFTA may well have improved the resilience of some industrial sectors, but also accelerated large scale de-industrialisation in some areas of the US, and above all in the Mid-West. The appeal of Trump in the Rust Belt states is an inevitable conclusion of that.

Even for Mexico, NAFTA has had mixed outcomes. The hope of a broad boom in foreign direct investment driving wider economic gains has not happened, leading to the emergence of a two-tier economy. The Mexican economy outside of the sectors serving US corporates has seen relatively little in the way of spillover benefits. And that also causes political strains in the domestic politics of the country.

This is not to say that free trade is not beneficial in principle. It is merely to point out a brute fact that the ideology of neoliberalism normally demands we ignore how trade fits with the domestic economy, and that inevitably has political consequences.[34] In a democracy, affected citizens should have both an understanding of, and a say over, how trade is done. It is extremely unwise to engage in trade liberalisation without giving any thought to how the expected gains from it are to be allocated and how those who lose out are to be compensated.[35] In a democracy, the leaders implementing such policies also have the moral responsibility to account for how trade deals affect their citizens. But economic ideology has prevented political leaders in the US from engaging with any such thoughts. This is not to argue for a Trumpian narrow nationalist approach, but if a deal will cause hardship (alongside the wider benefits) then a state has to seek to mitigate those consequences,

What is worse, ideology also does not allow (at least some of) our leaders to learn from past mistakes. For the true believers in economic liberalisation, the failure of US policies to reduce income disparities is down to a lack of zeal in the prosecution of globalisation[36]—they argue that the way to solve the ill effects of globalisation so far is to double down and do more of it, until all the problems will solve themselves by the magic of the free market. As we will see, similar arguments were advanced in the aftermath of the 2008 financial crisis. According to this view, what had gone wrong was not insufficient regulation of the financial sector, or that the overall policy framework had been flawed, but that there had been too much regulation left in place since the 1980s.[37] Axiomatically, the ideology demands that the 'freer' a market is, the less imperfections it has, and, therefore, any market failure can only be due to still lingering regulations.[38]

In the US, this axiomatic mindset meant the response to the 2008 financial crisis failed to find bipartisan support, and was passed with only Democratic support, while the Republican opposition at the time was promising to remove the new regulations at the earliest opportunity. More generally, there was very little appetite to improve the regulation of the financial sector and most of the requirements imposed in the 2008–10 period have long since been rolled back.

This leaves the financial system still vulnerable to the exact same kinds of shocks it experienced in 2008, but it has had palpable effects farther down the economic ladder as well. The impacts of globalisation and financial deregulation have intersected with other laissez-faire choices around the relative rewards for wages as opposed to assets, and the steady dismantling of social security mechanisms. It did take a while, but increasingly large swathes of the electorate have already caught on: this economic system is failing them, and both the mainstream parties were only able to argue for superficial variations of more of the same. When someone came along who claimed to offer solutions, however dishonestly,[39] desperate people voted for that alternative, even if it might cost them their political freedoms. This is a well-trodden path in so many developing countries. The past six years in the US shows that the same dynamics can work there just as well.

The developing world

The narrowing of the acceptable field of economic policy has had even more disastrous consequences in the developing world, especially in the context of the fall of the Iron Curtain, and the desire of so many former Easter Bloc countries to start developing economically and catch up with the West.

By 1991, both the previous Warsaw Pact states and the constituent republics of the former USSR were seeking external capital and advice on how to modernise. Under the aegis of the World Bank and the IMF, the policy prescriptions were universally the privatisation of virtually all state assets (even economically viable ones which would have otherwise shored up the balance sheets of the countries in question), significant reductions in social welfare programmes which had direct effects on health and education provision with long-term negative economic impacts, and a programme of 'shock-therapy' market liberalisation designed to rapidly restructure the economy. The result was invariably high unemployment, poverty, and emergence of large, mafia-style informal sectors. Those who had (usually politically endorsed) access to resources quickly snapped up anything worth owning at knockdown prices, while the majority of the population were left to adjust to the 'shock' without any state support.

In the wider world, the same 'development package' continued to be prescribed to the Global South: in exchange for modest monetary aid, poor nations, especially in Africa, South America and South Asia, were expected to open up their domestic economies to international competition as rapidly as possible. This had some successes,[40] but the dogmatic approach took little account of local differences or the politics of each particular country. What became known as the Washington Consensus[41] expected all nations to transition quickly to full exposure to the global markets, without allowing them the chance to develop their own infrastructure and competitiveness so that they could actually thrive in those open markets. This would inevitably lead to the hollowing out of even the little industrial base that these countries had inherited from the colonial era, and it was the best-case scenario when local manufacturing facilities would then be taken over by multinational corporations that might then try to exploit the cheap local labour.

And of course, the best-case scenario occurred only rarely. The more frequent scenario was the complete devastation of locally owned industry, and the reverting of many of these countries' economies to low-value primary extraction. Then, the local political elites who had the authority to grant access to multinationals to these primary resources would pocket huge sums of corrupt kickbacks, while all profits from the primary extraction would be accrued by Western investors.

When challenged on the failures of this development model, the free-market ideologues would therefore have corruption to point to as an explanation for why their free-market dogma was failing to serve the people of these countries. And plenty of focus was therefore placed on improving accountability[42] and reducing corruption—with at best modest amounts of success. But the fundamentals of the ideology that underpinned this development model were never questioned, despite the glaringly visible fact that virtually all the countries that had successfully developed since the Second World War had explicitly rejected this model. All the successful East Asian economies, for example, from Japan to Taiwan and South Korea, were built on protectionism and state-led investment, tolerated by the United States for geopolitical reasons.

To be completely fair, the application of the Washington Consensus model of development was less uniform in practice than it was in theory. In part, there were differences between the various sponsoring organisations. In Eastern Europe for example, the EU was an important counterweight to the World Bank and

IMF policy platforms, as the former Warsaw Pact states started to move towards accession from 1992 onwards. Equally, the old East Germany was a special case as it was now part of a unified Germany, with economic integration directed by the government in Berlin towards a nation-building goal. Some resource-rich countries were able to pick and mix in terms of how they sought to develop; in particular the Gulf Cooperation Council region could lever its substantial oil and gas revenues, and sovereign wealth funds, to set its own approach. But the Washington Consensus model of development was prescribed widely, and it was hugely damaging to both the economic fate, and the political stability, of most countries where it was imposed.

The post-1991 zenith of American power affected how the US was seen around the world, but also how the US saw itself. America briefly became the uncontested global hegemon, unconstrained by the existence of any other contender, and unchallenged by any other coherent ideological rival. In the new unipolar[43] world, the US appeared to be the only global actor who truly mattered.[44] It could be said that other Western powers colluded in this view. Most dramatically cut military spending with the end of the Cold War, and multinational groups, such as the EU, always had a natural focus on internal economic dynamics.

The removal of alternative sponsors to emerging economies not only closed off options in terms of development models, but it also influenced how the US interacted with its allies, and, more importantly, how it interacted with those states that stood outside the new consensus.

No one now had the ability to challenge the US overtly, so the resistance to American power went underground. During the following two decades, the main challenges to the American-led world order therefore came from terrorism, and the proliferation of weapons of mass destruction.[45] The few states who still resisted American power would frequently try to use these means against

American assets, particularly through non-state proxies—the sponsorship of terrorism by countries like Libya, Iran, Iraq and Afghanistan are illustrative examples. Others sought, or gained, nuclear weapons as an insurance policy: possession was believed to confer a degree of immunity from US response to their actions.

This is what initially prompted the willingness to use force to end the ongoing civil wars and ethnic cleansing in the former Yugoslavia by Bill Clinton and Tony Blair. By 1999, Blair was quite explicit that regimes that were seen to be flawed were a risk to all—and should be dealt with.[46]

During the same decade, Al-Qaida had started to create a global network of resistance to American power, and became involved in almost every conflict in the Middle East and North Africa. It then went on to launch a series of direct attacks on US and European targets. The attacks on the US in September 2001 were taken as evidence that the assumptions underpinning Blair's 'liberal interventionism' had been correct: failing states could indeed be a threat to more than their own population, and the fears about the proliferation of weapons of mass destruction, in particular, were well founded.[47] There was therefore almost no domestic opposition to the decision to drive Al-Qaida from its bases in Afghanistan. And at least in the policy-making circles in Washington, there was also very little opposition to the later decision to invade Iraq.[48]

But as the saying goes, 'when all you have is a hammer, everything starts looking like a nail'. The indisputable military supremacy that the US enjoyed at the global level meant that it was too inclined to reach for military solutions to every problem. In time, the US would learn the hard way that not every form of dissent or resistance can be quashed with aerial bombardment. But at least during the 1990s, the United States did indeed solve a number of thorny international issues with blunt military force. From that, America's political leaders learnt that military force could be used to solve any international challenge, and that increasingly diminished America's understanding of what threats could look like, and how not all threats could be addressed in the same way. Militarism thus became ingrained in the ideological outlook of America's leaders. And, as noted above, most other Western states colluded in this, at least in so far as many retreated into a form of insularity in their international outlook.

The beginning of the end: Iraq and the 2008 financial crisis

Iraq—a loss of trust

In the US, the Bush administration that came to power in 2000 initially offered little different to Clinton in terms of foreign policy. They were perhaps more determined to stamp America's authority upon the corners of the world that stood outside the new, narrowly defined, norms, and key figures in the Bush administration had produced a plan for what they called an American Century.[49] The plan, initially formulated by the Project for a New American Century (PNAC) think tank, advocated a foreign policy aimed at forcefully imposing 'US pre-eminence' to 'secure and expand the 'zones of democratic peace' through, if necessary, the forcible removal of hostile dictators, not least Saddam Hussein[50] from Iraq.

Al-Qaida's murderous attack on the US on 9/11 gave this framing a fresh impetus. The US response was, unwisely, dubbed the 'War on Terror',[51] leading to an approach that saw the US increasingly ignore international law (especially around human rights) and an increasingly paranoid suspicion that any and all poorly governed states might harbour terrorist groups like Al-Qaida, either intentionally, or by lack of state power to crack down on their safe bases. This unlimited 'war' on 'terror' would prove an expensive and self-defeating exercise in futility.[52]

When the Bush administration came to power, Iraq was of little concern. Clinton had earlier signed the Iraq Liberation Act calling for Hussein to be removed from power and this had backing from some of the neoconservatives who had influence over the new administration. However, other senior officials had had substantial dealings with the regime in the 1980s during its long war with Iran,[53] and argued against intervention. Post 9/11 this shifted and a case for war was constructed on the basis that Hussein was both linked to Al-Qaida and possessed (and looked to use) weapons of mass destruction[54] At times, the issue of regime change was added to this list and then dropped as it violated the UN Charter.

As the US and UK headed towards a war of aggression against Iraq, they sought the support of the UN, leading to the public presentation of many of these claims and the attempt to link them into a coherent narrative. Both in the US and UK, there probably was majority support for an invasion, not least as the major media outlets gave the case a sympathetic hearing. But the domestic scene was far from unanimous. Considerable minorities were opposed to the war, and highly engaged by the issue. Especially on the grounds that the *casus belli*, as presented, was so flimsy. The UK government, for example, produced a dossier that claimed Iraq could hit the British bases in Cyprus within forty-five minutes with a nuclear weapon. To those who already had doubts about the war, this was evidence of mendacity by those in power. But in retrospect, even those who had been initially convinced to back the invasion felt they had been deliberately deceived. Iraq was not just a failure of policy. It led to a profound breakdown in trust in the US and the UK. A lack of trust that has not yet been recovered two decades later.

Moreover, major Western allies did not buy it: France and Germany were sceptical, and did not want to participate in the military offensive.

The initial invasion itself was launched on 20 March 2003, and by 1 May President Bush felt able to announce 'mission accomplished'. Yet by the end of May, the US had already planted the seeds for its ultimate strategic defeat in Iraq: the defeated Iraqi army was disbanded wholesale, and the majority of civilian government officials had been sacked on account of having been members of the ruling Ba'ath party.[55] What followed was insurgency, the collapse of central state government and the ascendency of a myriad of militias, the eventual Iranian control over the new Shi'a government, and, by 2012, the emergence in the north and west of the Islamic State.[56]

The case for war rapidly fell apart even as the occupation of Iraq bred a vicious insurgency. By early 2005, a Presidential Commission declared that 'not one bit' of prewar intelligence on Iraqi weapons of mass destruction had been accurate.[57] Responsibility was in the end put at the feet of the CIA, who were supposed to have mis-advised President Bush, but nobody in government, not the individuals, nor any of the agencies, escaped with their reputations intact for their conduct in the run-up to the war—least of all, President Bush. In the UK, the long running Chilcott Enquiry similarly found failures at all levels, and ultimately painted a picture of the public being misled by the case for war, both in deliberate and non-intentional ways.

The invasion of Iraq might have had a less profound impact on the domestic electorates of the US and the UK if their leaders had not made such public efforts to make and sustain their case for war, and if they had not presented it in such convoluted, implausible forms.

In later years, the effects of this mistrust would be seen again and again, when our leaders called for intervention in other places in the Middle East, even on humanitarian grounds. When the Libyan civil war broke out in 2011, the US and the European members of NATO[58] did intervene with aerial bombing to arrest a possible massacre in Benghazi, but that limited intervention ultimately only produced a failed state.[59] In Syria, attempts to respond to the use of chemical weapons against civilians by the Assad regime floundered due to a lack of support.[60] Brutalised civilian populations around the world cannot rely on protection from the West to this day, because Western electorates do not trust the motives of their own elected representatives in matters of foreign interventions. But that mistrust has only grown wider since the failures of Iraq. I will come back to this instance in later chapters as it offers an early example of what has become the standard Russian and populist play book: raise the intelligence failings over Iraq, obfuscate what actually happened and present it all as a bizarre Western plot. An interview by Jeremy Corbyn, who was to become the leader of the British Labour Party, on the Russian state broadcaster, Russia Today, is a classic of the form[61] and indicative of how Russian propaganda and the views promoted by populist politicians can so closely align.

The 2008 Financial Crisis—a failure of an economic model

Following the deregulation of finance in the late 1980s across the Western world, the banks developed a business model in which they were lending money they didn't really have in order to earn more. At the core of the system was a small flow of real income, derived from insurance premiums, repayments of loans (including student loans) and mortgage payments. This core was then leveraged to sustain lending of up to 100 times that actual income. The increased risk that was compounded by this huge leverage was supposed to have been controlled by an increasingly arcane set of financial instruments that broke these income streams into more or less secure elements. This produced supercharged profits for the banks involved in these operations, but financial arcana aside, the visible result for the real economy was house price inflation (and asset inflation more generally) divorced from wages, interest rates or even population demand. Yet blinded by their free market ideology, the regulators barely noticed that anything was wrong, never mind any suggestion that they should intervene to prevent any of these developments. But this was treated as completely normal, with financial institutions simply lending more (and obscuring the risks). Lehman Brothers alone saw its long-term debt increase from $207,106,000 in August 2007 to $349,765,000 in May 2008.[62]

The system eventually crumbled because those arcane financial instruments which were supposed to be controlling the risk as the levels of leveraging increased ultimately did no such thing. They did successfully spread the risk, yes, and that was good enough for the purposes of any given firm in this system. But in aggregate, the pervasive use of these instruments did not have the same effect: the real assets and income streams that were at the foundation of this edifice still had the same risk characteristics as they had always done, but the pervasive use of those risk instruments now made the balance sheets of all the market players look like all the systemic risk had effectively vanished. The true risks of the underlying real economy had been magicked out of the balance sheets of the insurers and the banks. And when house prices started falling in the United States for exogenous reasons, that rendered all those balance sheets obviously inaccurate, sending the entire system of financial accounting into tailspin. This spread across the Western world due to the interlinking of the financial sectors and that asset (especially house price) inflation had become widespread. New Labour in the UK had built its entire fiscal model on being able to impose limited taxes on the proceeds of the City of London and was in no position to ask just how real those profits really were.

In the short term, a bailout of the financial system became necessary. That bailout would be coordinated on a global level following the G20 meeting in London in 2009.[63] But the recession caused directly by the financial crash led to many people losing their homes and jobs. And, at the same time, governments were reducing their social safety nets at the time when they were most needed, in order to pay for the banks' bailouts. Farther down the line, a combination of the recession and the political choices made by politicians led to the acceleration of the trend towards insecure, low-paid work for many. On the other hand, financial asset values skyrocketed, as some of the measures taken to shore up the financial sector, most notably quantitative easing, overshot their initial goals. Workers saw their lives become noticeably worse, and at the same time they also saw those who triggered the crisis, and those who owned assets, gain more than they had done before the crisis as asset values quickly recovered.[64]

However, the way the bailouts were structured had profound consequences. First of all, they increased government debt levels substantially. In 2007, US Government debt had been 86.2% of GDP, but it reached 125% by 2010 and remained over 130% till 2018. Then Trump's 'tax cuts' and the impact of the Covid pandemic pushed it to 161% in 2020.[65] These headline figures for public debt were common across the OECD and, in turn, led to calls to bring these numbers down—a debate that was reframed[66] by the usual neoliberal suspects as a problem caused by overspending on social welfare and social infrastructure.[67] Meanwhile, the debt-driven consumption model for households remained unchallenged and continues to suppress effective demand as well as leaving households vulnerable to any more financial shocks.[68]

In the US, the limited measures to rein in the banks and stimulate the real economy were reversed once the Trump administration came to power in 2016. In the UK, the Conservative-Liberal government that came to power in 2010 cynically and deliberately framed the financial deficit as a product of systemic overspending on social welfare by the previous Labour government. Their solution was a radical programme of austerity that choked off the small economic recovery that was taking place, reduced the fiscal transfers that might have sustained effective demand[69] and ran down investment in the public realm, leading to significant long-term problems of state and personal finances and reduced robustness of the UK to cope with any new problems.

Drawing together the consequences

While this book is about the wider dynamics facing the Western democracies, in some respects it is the US experience that is central. Some of this, quite simply, reflects the relative power of the various actors but also the extent to which the threat to the survival of democracy in the US is of concern to us all. The problem was that the response to the fall of the USSR became manifested in intolerance towards diversity of political and economic thought, as well as towards divergent policy options. The wider policy prescription of reduced state intervention in the economy, limits to social welfare and less regulation was widely adopted. Internationally, emerging economies had to adapt rapidly to these same prescriptions, while states seen as being outside the new norms were considered potential threats to all. But there was a particularly American aspect. America was number 1. And clearly, what was working for America had to work for everyone else. Who could think otherwise? And what sinister motivation might those who think otherwise have?

And why was America so exceptional? Here, Americans reverted to the exceptionalism of their foundation myth: liberal democracy. At the time of the founding of the Republic, the relatively democratic political character of the United States really was unique in the world. But now, in the latter days of the twentieth century, America was also the richest and most powerful country in the world. In the minds of many Americans, that progression had been inevitable: it was their political constitution that made them exceptional, their 'freedoms', which begot their economic system, which begot their military strength, which begot their international power. America's economy, their military and their politics had to be inextricably linked—never mind that the particular economic model they espoused at the time was less than twenty years old, and the US had also been dominant economically and geopolitically under a very different economic system in the 1940s, 1950s and 1960s.

The problem with linking the domestic political institutions of liberal democracy so closely to a specific form of economic policy and a specific international order, and especially to American supremacy in both of those areas, is that if any of the latter suffered, then liberal democracy itself would come into question.

The first unforced error, driven by sheer hubris, was the invasion of Iraq. The US and its allies were already waging a war they were not winning in Afghanistan. Moreover, the justifications for war against Saddam Hussein were tenuous: that he had nuclear weapons or was in close alliance with Al-Qaida stretched credulity for many even at the time. Over time, various enquiries, especially in the US and the UK, exposed the level of deceit used by our political leaders to justify the war. To say nothing of the calamitous handling of the post-conflict phase.

This seriously undermined trust in electoral politics in both countries. If they lied to justify a non-essential war, what else would they lie about? In time, the Iraq War also showed that while America and its allies could still win any war, they had little capacity to win the subsequent peace. America's military supremacy could no longer guarantee that America could have its way in the world unchallenged. With subsequent failures in

Syria, Libya, and ultimately the shambolic withdrawal in defeat from Afghanistan, Americans cannot, and no longer even seem to desire to, be the global hegemon.

At one level this is an inevitable, perhaps even welcome, correction to several decades of hubris and overreach. The wider issue is that America's global posture, which had become so closely associated with its liberal democratic politics, is now very much diminished. And with it, the appeal of liberal democracy all around the world.

On the side of the economy, the 2008 financial crash exposed the flaws of the deregulated markets that were meant to bring prosperity. Not only did we see flagrant instances of outright criminality, but further revelations showed the role of many banks in money laundering[70] for some of the most corrupt regimes in the world, while many of our own economic elites were repeatedly revealed to able to arrange their affairs so as to pay little to no tax.

The policy response to the financial crash in many countries had been to bail out the financial sectors, and this was paid for from austerity imposed on the rest of the population, many of whom were already struggling[71]. The impact of this was variable in terms of domestic opinion, but in those states where this led to a greater loss of social welfare, there was a subsequent loss of legitimacy of the democratic system that had imposed these hardships on ordinary people.[72] Nor did the democratic system offer these people any alternatives, as both the centre-right and the centre-left supported the same austerity measures for the benefit of the financial system, for the same reasons: neoliberal economic dogma accepted nothing else. With no democratically available avenue to dissent, many disengaged from normal politics. If there was no way to affect economic policy through the electoral system then why bother with the electoral system? And really, who can blame them?

In the short term, across most of Europe, the centre-right gained electorally in part as many of the social democratic left were now seen as responsible for the economic mistakes—they were in power at the time of the 2008 crisis, and they did try to support the bailouts of the financial system with austerity measures. Equally, and often mendaciously, many centre-right parties framed the crisis not as one of financial institutions out of control but of excessive state expenditure that now needed to be reined in. The problem, as we will explore in later chapters, is that the wider loss of democratic legitimacy was to be worsened by the impacts of austerity. Those who suffered as a consequence of these political choices were given little choice: the only politicians who seemed to hear their cries were the new wave of populist parties. And before long, neo-fascist political movements moved in to capitalise on the political crisis, taking aim squarely at the liberal democratic system for the failures of the liberal economic system. If ideological blinders would prevent even the centre-left from offering an economic alternative, people would now be looking for their alternatives elsewhere.

Almost fifteen years on from the 2008 financial crisis, the liberal-democratic centre of politics still has no convincing answer to an ever-worsening economic and political outlook. Not one that is convincing to the people who they are failing to serve, and seemingly not even one that is convincing to themselves. This must change, and soon. Because liberal democracy is running out of time. We are already repeating too many of the mistakes of the 1920s, and if we do not manage to correct course within the liberal-democratic strand of politics, people will look to solutions in the conflict-based approaches to politics proffered by the populists. The reason this matters is that the new populists quite deliberately hark back to the domestic politics and international norms of that period—and there is no reason to expect it to produce different results the second time around.

4

WESTERN POPULISM

Populism is now an international phenomenon, strongly entrenched in places like Brazil, Turkey and India where previous democratic systems are being eroded. Despite this wider context, this chapter primarily focusses on how it is manifesting in Western Europe and North America. My argument for this narrow focus is that this wider region can be seen as the core of mature democracies and as, or if, these fall back towards what we earlier called 'managed democracies' then liberal norms become increasingly untenable at an international level.

Populist parties have become an increasingly prominent feature of domestic politics in many democratic countries. Yet this trend is, for the most part, not the result of a single event, or political shift across the world. Rather, all these parties have very different histories, traditions and trajectories, emerging largely from local circumstances. What unites them in the present is their way of appealing to voters by claiming to be channelling 'the will of the people' in opposition to 'the political establishment', and their typically hostile attitude towards the rules and institutions of liberal democracy—though their respective critiques of the 'rules of the game' might be very different, especially, for example, between the right-wing populists and the left-wing populists. The other common thread is that they make a deliberate appeal to those abandoned by neoliberal economic doctrines or disenchanted with conventional politics due to the perceived mendacity of mainstream politicians.

Many of the 'older democracies' have equally had old, anti-liberal traditions dating back to the nineteenth century and renewed between the First and Second World Wars. Equally the early half of the twentieth century saw the emergence of communist and fascist traditions running along in parallel to the liberal-democratic mainstream, but the communist movements have either collapsed or receded from public consciousness following the end of the Cold War. In contrast, the fascist traditions have typically endured, and in many cases, they have evolved to take the form of modern right-wing populism, usually by a deliberate process of whitewashing their histories[1] and mainstreaming themselves by slowly lurching to the centre, at least in terms of rhetoric and presentation. The French National Rally is perhaps the best-known example of such a party. It has roots in the pre-Second World War authoritarian, catholic, anti-Semitic parties that had opposed the existence of the Third Republic,[2] but has sought to reinvent itself as a modern party with its leader now regularly being one of the final two candidates for the French Presidency.

Its component parts are instructive as to one way a populist party can emerge. In this case Le Pen's (the father of Marine) NF was a fusion of various right-wing elements; some of these had links to the collaborationist Vichy regime, others took part in the wider resistance to German occupation giving them some post-war credibility. The NF gained some electoral support in the 1980s and 1990s due to a series of corruption scandals among the Socialist and Gaullist governing parties. It also gained a new electorate as the previously pro-Soviet French Communist Party (PCF) collapsed; its voters found themselves readily supporting the NF's nationalistic narrative about immigration and the EU, and very responsive to the conspiracy theories that were a staple of both the PCF and the NF. In effect one version of the interaction between populist and traditional far right parties is for the latter to move into the space vacated by the collapse of its former rivals.

Elsewhere openly fascistic parties have had brief spells of electoral influence but often fallen apart under closer scrutiny. In the UK in the 1970s the openly neo-Nazi National Front certainly found a ready audience on the right of the Conservative Party (and in sections of the British media) for its views on race, immigration and British membership of the European Economic Community (now the EU) but had little electoral appeal due its open fascism. By the early 1990s, one of its successor parties, the British National Party, had some electoral gains as it tried to obscure its fascism and instead promote Islamophobia and racism. The balancing act failed and the rise of the UK Independence Party (UKIP), notionally a single-issue party with a focus on withdrawal from the EU, absorbed its electoral base. In reality, UKIP was a right-wing populist movement that exerted considerable influence over the mainstream centre-right Conservative Party without ever forming an electoral threat in itself.

By contrast, in the young democracies of Eastern Europe in particular, parties like Orbán's Fidesz in Hungary, and the Polish Law and Justice party of the Kaczynski brothers have their roots in the nationalist elements of the opposition movements to communist rule. Though sometimes these parties also hark back, at least rhetorically, to interwar ultra-nationalist movements, or figures. For example, Fidesz deliberately draws on the iconography of the pre-War authoritarian Horthy regime.

Yet in other instances, both in new and old democracies, some of the populist parties have sprung up from entirely new mass political movements that emerged in the febrile political atmosphere post-2008. Some examples of this are the Five Star Movement in Italy, and Podemos in Spain. But there are also a number of other, slightly older radical parties formed in the 1990s and 2000s that also came into their own in the same wave of populist upswelling, and which most closely resemble Five Star and Podemos: among those would be the likes of the British UKIP.

Populist movements, however, do not always manifest in the formation of new political parties. Some movements have successfully taken over an existing conventional political party. This has tended to happen especially in electoral systems with very high barriers to entry, like in the US, UK, and Australia. By now, the US Republican party seems to have been entirely taken over by the radical right-wing movement that started life under the banner of the Tea Party, but now lives on as 'Trumpism'. In the UK, the Conservative Party was seen by some as being quite thoroughly colonised by the Brexit movement, while even the Labour Party had come under the sway of populist sentiment between 2015 and 2019 under the populist tone of the Corbyn leadership. And in Australia, the right-wing Liberals have also increasingly tried, with varying degrees of success, to emulate the playbook of the radicalised US. This type of takeover can happen if a party has a strong electoral appeal and is often part of governance but is perhaps small in terms of actual membership and exists in an electoral system that favours two major contenders.

In continental Europe, the rise of the populist parties outside of the old social democratic–Christian-democratic spectrum has mostly emerged as older parties collapse. Winners in this respect on the left were the Greek *Syriza* and the legacy party of the old East German regime, the Party of Democratic Socialism (this later merged with a previously West German leftist party to form *Die Linke*). Both gained from the absolute (Greece) or relative (Germany) collapse of the old Social Democratic alternative. In these instances relative plurality in the electoral system allows new parties to emerge but also often acts as a limit to their ability to translate an electoral presence into gaining political power.

Yet in the US and the UK, something different happened. Because of the entrenched two-party systems, it was the old parties that would become bastions of populist radicalism. And this would happen on both sides of the political spectrum.

In the UK, an ill-judged promise at the general election in 2015 by Conservative Prime Minister David Cameron to hold a referendum on the UK's membership of the European Union would soon upend the entire political scene. The Conservative Party would go on to win that general election on the back of that promise. Labour's electoral failure in that election led to them electing an old populist socialist as leader in Jeremy Corbyn later that year, taking the party sharply towards the populist left—and with initial electoral gains in the 2017 election. The Brexit referendum in 2016 would eventually go against what all the political leaders, including David Cameron, wanted, and set in motion the descent of the Conservative Party into the populist nationalist party that it is today—and which won a stunning majority at the 2019 general election on a mandate of populist nationalism under the figure of Boris Johnson. By 2022, the somewhat incoherent electoral coalition that had been forged by a series of populist promises is threatening to tear the Conservative Party apart as it tries to balance populism with more conventional centre-right politics.

In the US, the Republican Party took a sharp turn to populism, with the selection of Donald Trump as the party's presidential candidate in 2016, and then with his success in that year's election. The United States is still reeling from the political consequences of those events, and what Trump has done to the Republican Party and the republic overall since that time. In the 2020 presidential election, the election of centrist Democrat Joe Biden to the White House offers some respite but with obvious problems as they still have no answers to the clear systemic failures of the economic system that they have championed as their own since the Clinton era.

In 2020, the American electorate voted for a pause in the insanity of the Trump era. But the reasons why they voted for Trump in the first place in 2016 are all still there. And the centrist liberal wing of the Democratic Party is not doing anything to fix any of that. If the Democrats are to have any chance in the electoral cycles of the mid-2020s, they may well have to take the populist turn as well. More worryingly, there is no sign of the Republican Party having any interest in reconstructing itself as a conventional centre-right democratic party.[3]

Common themes

Regardless of their historical differences, these movements have ended up with much in common, both in terms of methods, and in terms of their ideology: authoritarian inclinations, a penchant for conspiracy theorising, viewing the world as a binary struggle between 'elites' and 'we, the people', and little regard for political plurality and the diversity of opinion that liberal democracy is sworn to protect. The problem is that they use a kernel of truth and manipulate real concerns. We either move into a future where such parties regularly achieve power (and as we are seeing, they are very unwilling to risk losing it subsequently) or we actually challenge the basis of their claims and address the deep-seated issues they manipulate.

Early forms

In many ways, populism seems to be a recent phenomenon, working off the growing disenchantment of many with the post-1991 political and economic orthodoxy and offering simplistic solutions. There is a strong case to say its current incarnation is relatively unique but it draws on older roots. As the modern nation state emerged in early modern Europe, rulers sought to ensure often ethnically, linguistically and religiously disparate social groups identified with the new nation state. Some regimes, such as the Habsburg Empire continued to focus on the regime as the unifying strand[4] and even into the late nineteenth century accepted its multinational, somewhat fragmented, nature.[5]

Others, especially Britain and France, sought to create a concept of the nation as the focus. Benedict Arnold classically referred to this as a process of creating imagined communities[6] that in turn give a logic to a shared community bounded by one of the new nation states. States such as Germany and Italy that emerged in the nineteenth century in turn looked to both narratives drawn from the past and somewhat tendentious arguments about historical structures and ethnic alignment to the new regime's borders[7] as they justified the consolidation of existing states and disputed the boundaries of the new unified regime.

The extent to which the concepts of citizenship, ethnicity, religious identity, nationality and state boundaries were interlinked has always varied. Some regimes, usually those that are also authoritarian, seek to draw these boundaries closely. So, the military regime in Burma from 1962 onwards sought to define 'Burmese' as meeting all these criteria, and seeing any variation in religious or ethnic identity as a threat.[8] Nazi Germany was obsessed with ensuring those who were allowed to live under its rule met clear criteria. On the other hand, post-war Germany has an open citizenship policy where those with historical links (including Jews who fled Nazi persecution) can claim dual nationality and generally gaining German citizenship is relatively easy if someone has lived there for a few years.[9] Equally, a key feature of the EEC and now the EU is how citizens of one member state can readily move, work and live in another.

One variation of this was how the French revolutionaries conflated 'people' with the new state—a view reflected back by their opponents[10]—giving what was in some ways a universalist, non-nationalist ideology a strong national identity. Out of the chaos of the First World War came a conflation of nation with linguistic or ethnic group[11] as states were created out of what had been the Tsarist and Austro-Hungarian empires. In turn, while often seeing themselves as the natural representative of a particular ethnic group, they found they had contested borders where overlapping historical claims often conflicted with the ethnic mix of the disputed region.

Again, a great deal of myth-making went into bolstering the legitimacy of these new states and their borders. In some this involved ignoring ethnic differences, in others denying smaller groups any agency and, at worst, seeking to remove all rights from those who did not form the desired part of the new population. The steady spread of right-wing authoritarianism and fascism in Europe amplified this last part as states such as Poland and Hungary both sought control over regions that had, in the past, belonged to them, and sought to deny any rights to the ethnic or religious groups who now lived there. As fascism spread, this focus on who was an acceptable member of the polity became ever more murderous in its interpretation and implementation.

Modern-day populism is thus a hybrid. As above, it encompasses fascist parties, ex-fascist parties and politicians who are clear in their support for fascism involved in the wider network of such organisations. Sometimes, these dominate such as in France in the vehicle of National Rally. In Italy, the relatively new Brothers of Italy, formed as a series of splits from more conventional right-wing populists such as Berlusconi's Forza Italia, are fast becoming a key part of the constellation of right-wing populist parties. In turn they have merged with traditional parties that long formed the Italian fascist right tracing their lineage back to Mussolini's post-1943 regime. Most populist parties do not carry this direct connection to fascism but happily import its basic analysis of who is, and who should not be, an acceptable member of a given nation state.

Another point of similarity is that many have been found to be taking money from Putin's Russia, and parties such as the French NR then back Russia in any dispute (taking on the older mantle of the consistently pro-Soviet French Communist Party). In Europe their shared distaste for the EU tends to leave them supporting Putin in many disputes. But this is not consistent. The Polish Law and Justice Party is part of the wider grouping of populists in Central Europe but for reasons of geography and history is extremely anti-Russian. Some have sought to downplay this since Putin's invasion of Ukraine but others have carried on amplifying Russian propaganda about the reason for the attack, the make-up of the Ukrainian government and responsibility for war crimes.

The ideological core that binds together all these movements is the same thing that sets them in opposition to liberal democracy: the repudiation of political pluralism, based on the premise that only they represent 'the people', however 'the people' happens to be defined by their particular ideology, and that anyone else is, by definition an 'enemy of the people'.

When these movements gain high political office within a country, this authoritarian logic drives the movement to quickly subvert the checks and balances that liberal democracy has built in to protect political pluralism and minority voices, so that the state rapidly takes an authoritarian character, as the state apparatus is turned to marginalise or even outright exclude all those not considered a 'proper' part of 'the people'.[12] In turn, this sets in train a self-fulfilling electoral logic where state power is used to favour the main client group and the electoral and civic rights of others are steadily curtailed: a phenomenon usually termed 'majoritarianism'. Thus, even where a particular populist movement is not explicitly or intentionally fascist, the effects are similar to what a fascist might argue for, especially among right-wing populists who define 'the people' along ethnic or religious lines. Critically this rejects the drive towards inclusion of all who live in a polity that sits at the core of universal human rights. In practice, populism rapidly diverges even from the most basic democratic norm of free elections, never mind the openness that we would see as the feature of a liberal democracy.[13]

Hungary also illustrates very well what this comes to mean in practice. Once in power, the populists will close down every alternative source of legitimate political action that opposes their views or their aims. State funding is used to reward key client groups and the independence of both the press and judicial system will be rapidly undermined. Not only does this reduce the likelihood that the electoral system might yield a different governing majority at the next election, but it also amplifies the determination of those in power to stay there. On the one hand, ideologically, if they lose, this can only mean that the will of the people is being undermined. More prosaically, all those moves to undermine the checks and balances of liberal democracy will, very likely, at some point have involved illegal actions, and senior leaders in the movements will be desperate to avoid losing parliamentary immunity and face legal repercussions.

Electoral strategies and political ascendency

The emergence and ascendency of the populists within three very different political and electoral systems can illustrate both the ways in which they are local responses to local concerns, and also how and why they have come to have so much in common across borders in recent years.

Italy

Italy emerged from the Cold War with a broken political system. The exclusion of the Italian Communist Party (the PCI) from national government (despite it being the second largest party with over 30% of the vote) after 1945 led to decades of domination by the highly factional Christian Democrats and their allies. Such governments were often corrupt and had no particular interest in addressing Italy's wider political and economic problems.[14] All this was made worse due to the long-running problems of far-left and far-right terrorism in the 1970s and the power of the Mafia and similar groups; (in part their impact was amplified due to their links to factions in the Christian Democrats). The result was a distrust of the state, views that this or that terrorist group was being manipulated or funded by the secret services and a widespread belief that a series of bombings such as at Bologna station in 1981 were being carried out by part of the state. None of this mistrust was eased when the Italian government finally admitted to the actions of the NATO-organised Gladio movement[15] in 1990; when the Prime Minister for most of the 1980s fled to Tunisia to escape corruption charges, or when the five times Prime Minister, Andreotti, was found guilty of collusion with the Mafia and ordering the murder of a journalist (he was eventually released on appeal).

1991 saw the effective collapse of the two parties that had defined post-war Italy. As with many communist parties, the Partito Comunista Italiano (PCI), the main party of the left, dissolved as the Soviet Union was falling apart, but significant elements of the party did reform into a more centre-left Party of the Democratic Left (PDS), in effect completing the ongoing shift of the PCI into a conventional social democratic party.[16] Once the PCI was out of the scene, however, the centre-right Christian Democrats also lost their unifying enemy and thus their *raison d'être* as a broad-church party, and collapsed into their component factions. Meanwhile, many senior politicians at all levels of government were found to be mired in the corruption scandals. In fact, almost the entire political scene, across the spectrum, was finding itself tainted by corruption investigations, alleged Mafia ties, and so on, leaving hardly any political continuity into the 2000s from the pre-1991 era in the Italian republic.

And so Italy was to become a trial run for the populist politics we would see elsewhere in the West in later decades. As the Christian Democratic-led coalition system from before 1991 fell apart, a new centre-right coalition emerged in 1993 built out of three unlikely partners. The xenophobic Northern League, (who saw southern Italians as the main problem and had an ideology suffused with a belief in the previous existence of a noble Celtic north before its conquest by Rome), the National Alliance, a direct descendent of Mussolini's Fascist Party with electoral appeal in central and southern Italy, and Forza Italia,[17] a celebrity/personality-led new political movement around Silvio Berlusconi. In this arrangement, the Northern League and the National Alliance brought the fascist pedigree, and Forza Italia brought the new populism to power for the first time,

The latter relied on substantive control of the media to project an image of a supposedly self-made billionaire, Berlusconi, (whose wealth had suddenly appeared in the early 1980s and who had been part of the P2 Masonic lodge which was the core of the political and economic scandals of the 1980s[18]) as embodying a 'fresh', dynamic type of Italy, in opposition to the sclerotic image of the old establishment. This new Italy was at the same time opposed to the elite represented by the old Christian Democrats, as well as railing against the 'Communist' judges who were investigating the various corruption scandals (not least, Berlusconi's own scandals), both of which were supposed to be threatening the livelihoods of decent Italians. Does this sound familiar yet?

How about this? Forza Italia was systemically light on policy, but heavy on conspiracy theories and insinuation, mostly appealing to voters who had independent, but otherwise entirely good reasons, to be disgusted with the old political order. The party presented itself as liberal on economic issues, but conservative on cultural issues, trying to disentangle what it saw as the Christian roots of Italian society from the political legacy of Christian Democracy.

The mercurial character of Forza Italia, and of Berlusconi himself, as well as the awkward fit with the other coalition partners produced an unstable coalition that gained power, fragmented in infighting and then reconstituted to reassert its grip on power a number of times over the next decade and a half. And if nothing else, this provided the base with entertainment, even as their living standards continued to stagnate.

Berlusconi himself was eventually caught out by the corruption investigations, some of them stemming from his earlier business activities, some from his conflation of personal financial interests and government decisions when in office, and was finally sentenced to prison in 2013. Yet Italians were to be presented with a new variant of the populist spectacle. If Berlusconi set part of the electoral template for populism, the next incarnation in Italy developed it even further.

Founded in 2009, the Five Star Movement led by the comedian Beppe Grillo railed, correctly, against corruption and the extent to which Italian politics ignored the needs of ordinary people. Their first innovation was moving political discourse mainly to the online space, with what *seemed* like a model of direct participatory democracy, at least in internal party politics—though certain things were beyond democratic contestation, like for example the position of Grillo himself as head of the movement.[19] Moreover, using the internet as the main platform of political discourse had extra benefits, like bypassing the old media gatekeepers (at this point still dominated by Berlusconi's interests), but also, crucially allowing policy to be vague and messaged on the basis of form and emotion, without having to face serious scrutiny.

Another innovation, in some ways refreshing, in other ways problematic, was that in terms of practical policies, the movement and their representatives when they were in elected office either nationally or in cities such as Rome, have veered casually between policies from the centre-left to the centre-right. The seeming positive of this was an apparently non-ideological, pragmatic approach to politics. The rather more unfortunate reality it betrayed was that neither the party nor the individuals it elevated to positions of responsibility had much of a grasp of the policy issues they were dealing with, nor a coherent programme to address the needs of their constituents.

Broadly, Italy can be seen as offering one model where populism can come to dominate. The electorate had every reason to be repelled by the actions of the pre-1991 political elite: the Italian economy has failed to produce decent living conditions for many[20] and it is a polity where conspiracy theories (that sometimes turn out to be true) have long been part of public discourse. Berlusconi capitalised on this by creating a new political party, relying on a compliant media (which he partially owned) and placing the ills of Italy on 'others' (the target varied but 'Communist' judges featured often, especially when his own wealth was under investigation). Out of the wreckage of his project, the centre-right of Italian politics is now in the grip of a range of populist movements. In some ways, the reasons for this are unique; Italy was the only West European state to see such a rapid collapse of its traditional political order in 1991, but the approaches developed first by Berlusconi and now his successors have been adopted elsewhere. In ideological terms, the main grouping, derived from the old Northern League, is a perfect fit to the European populist right, talking about representing the 'people' against elites, obsessed with immigration, anti-EU and happy to support Putin's goals (and to accept his funding).

The populists were right to rail against the corruption and ineffectiveness of the old governing elites in the 1990s, but in thirty years of dominating public life in Italy, they have never proven to be any more effective at governing, and have frequently proven to be just as corrupt. Even when they asked the right questions, they were unable to offer any better answers. Not in Italy, and so far as we have seen in other places in the world, not anywhere else either. Indeed their implicit rejection of the democratic norms means they tend towards corruption and the allocation of funding to their chosen client groups.

The UK

Traditionally the political alignment of the far right in the UK outside the Conservative Party has been openly fascist. In the 1930s this took the form of the British Union of Fascists, which despite playing a significant role in British domestic politics at the time never gained more than 16% of the vote in any election. Post-war, sympathy for this ideology declined (not surprisingly) but by the early 1970s the openly neo-Nazi National Front sought to exploit racial tensions. It gained about 10% in a few small elections but never more than 3% at a general election. The next iteration, the British National Party, sought to play down the neo-Nazi ideology, focus on practical issues and stress its opposition to immigration, Islam and what it saw as Cultural

Marxism. Nationally it had little impact (gaining under 4% of the vote in 2005) but built strongholds in local government in areas such Burnley and the East End of London. Thereafter it rapidly imploded. In effect, there is a pattern here of a far-right party briefly gaining some traction (though at a minimal level) and then falling apart. However, in each instance its influence was probably wider than the raw numbers suggest as they gained sympathetic coverage in parts of the right-wing media[21] and their approach to race and immigration[22] was shared with individual politicians on the right of the Conservative Party.

An optimistic reading of this sequence is that the UK's electoral system kept such parties marginalised when they briefly gained some wider traction and their failure to make electoral progress undermined their appeal. As outsiders, they could be incredibly dangerous to individuals of the wrong religion, skin colour or politics but they offered no systemic threat. For parliamentary elections, the UK uses a first-past-the-post electoral system with the country broken down into 650 constituencies (for the 2019 election), with the candidate with the largest vote in each becoming the local MP. At times, such a system can work out to be quite representative in practice. For example, in the 1950 election 98% of the votes were for either the Labour or Conservative Party, so the winner of that election had a reasonable claim to be representing the will of the majority of Britons. This has steadily broken down, and by 2005 the same two parties gained 58% of the votes but claimed 86% of the available seats. The system can also produce large majorities with a minority of the vote. So in 2019, the Conservative Party had a majority of 80 over all the other parties, with less than 44% of the vote. This can work the other way: in 1983 the Labour Party only gained 28% of the vote but still retained 32% of the seats.

At the other end of the scale, the Green Party gained over 800,000 votes (around 2.6% of the total) for just one MP. This matters, especially when the two main parties can only claim around 75% of the vote (as they did in 2019—and some of that would have been given unwillingly by people who would have preferred to vote for an alternative). Practically it is only parties that have a specific geographical logic to their vote that can gain representation reflecting their actual vote share; and this only really happens consistently for the nationalist parties of the smaller nations, i.e. Northern Ireland, Scotland and Wales.

So we end up with parts of the electorate feeling excluded with this usually leading to a disengagement with the electoral system. This is made worse when, as between 1990 and 2015, the two main parties shared much in common, leaving those looking for alternatives excluded. So if there is no electoral route to representation outside the two main parties, an alternative strategy is to capture one (or both) and the 2019 election was contested by populists on both the left and the right as they had gained control of both main electoral options.

In past decades, the ways in which this system fended off the representation of extremist parties in parliament was held up as a virtue. What was not appreciated by the defenders of this system was that though populist sentiment remained underrepresented in parliament up 2015, it was still growing just the same within the electorate. If anything, the evident systemic exclusion of their voice from the official platforms of political debate might have even lent credibility to their conspiratorial and anti-system screeds in the growing spaces for political discourse online. On the right UKIP was increasingly seen by Conservative politicians as a serious threat, drawing off potential electors and proving to be popular when the UK used a proportional system (which it ironically did for elections to the European parliament). UKIP never had a defined set of policies (apart from leaving the EU) but led by Nigel Farage it sought to capitalise on right-wing discontent with the direction of the Conservative Party under David Cameron (and that between 2010 and 2015 it was governing in coalition with the Liberal Democrats).[23]

In an attempt to end this threat, David Cameron promised to hold a referendum on the UK's membership of the European Union should he win an outright parliamentary majority in 2015. Cameron expected to be returned in coalition with the Liberal Democrats, and with this in mind he included policies in his manifesto that he suspected would then need to be traded away in subsequent negotiations. When Cameron won a clear majority, he felt he had little choice but to proceed with a referendum, in part to appease his own right-wing MPs. He personally did not want the UK to leave the EU and clearly did not expect that the people of Britain would vote for Brexit in the event that they actually got their referendum. He was wrong, and in the referendum held in 2016, people voted against continued membership of the EU.

UKIP's campaign for the UK's departure from the EU used all the arguments and approaches typical of populist movements. A framing of their opponents as an 'elite' (despite many of their senior supporters having been in government for many years), an obsession with migration, misleading claims as to the benefits of departure, pro-Putin arguments and generally presenting their opponents as dangerous traitors.[24] The campaign to leave the EU was classic populism. A lack of policy (there was no work done on how to leave the EU in the event of victory), deliberately obscuring what the goal was and ready use of racist tropes. Less well noted at the time, it also made substantial use of social media to stoke support, provide arguments and, more cynically, to obtain data on their potential supporters.[25] This primarily relied on data extracted from Facebook to target adverts to specific individuals and to influence their voting intentions. However, the campaign to remain in the EU made its own set of mistakes in the way it promoted the status quo as a desirable situation.

During the 2016 referendum on leaving the EU, the argument by the official campaign to stay in, that house prices would fall if the UK left,[26] to many sounded less like a threat and more like a long-overdue correction.

When the UK voted to leave, the senior politicians involved in the successful campaign tried to gain control of the Conservative Party and many of the individuals behind the Leave campaign became senior policy advisers. Instead the relatively establishment Theresa May secured the leadership but shaped her policy to meet the views of those who had promoted Brexit and wished to see an extreme version of it, with the UK cutting most ties with the largest trading bloc in the world. Theresa May briefly tried to manage the UK's exit in a way that satisfied some of their agenda but also sought to minimise the economic losses. She failed to find a solution to this tension and was replaced in 2019 by Boris Johnson, who had been one of the leading figures in the Leave campaign, and who steadily drove out the remnants of the more traditional Conservative MPs in favour of those who shared his views on the UK's future.

From then on, the Conservative Party has been occupied more and more by the Leave populists who had argued for a hard Brexit, and those members of the parliamentary Conservative caucus who were most open to playing the game of populism were the ones that would increasingly take over. By late 2019, even some of the most respected of the 'old guard' who challenged this populism, like the grandson of Winston Churchill, Sir Nicholas Soames, had been actively purged from the party by the increasingly assertive new wing in the party: led from the top by a biographer of Winston Churchill and former close friend of Soames, one Boris Johnson.

The Labour Party also travelled on that same path but in substantially different ways. The roots to this shift lie in the 2010 election in the UK. This was unusual in that it produced a coalition government between the Conservatives and the Liberal Democrats. Labour's response to losing power was broadly to align itself to the policy choices of the new coalition, in part as they shared much of the analysis[27] and in part as the existing senior leadership felt they needed to move to the right to reflect the views of the English electorate.[28] This left those hit by the austerity agenda,[29] and anyone hoping for a progressive discussion on issues such as migration or asylum or a defence of the welfare state voiceless. Following Cameron's shock win at the general election of 2015, the party receded into a period of introspection, during which time they also had to elect a new leader. The party ended up taking a sharp turn away from the 'soft-left' embrace of the economic neoliberal consensus that had characterised it since the early 1990s, and chose as leader an old socialist, with impeccable bona fides for everything anti-capitalist, anti-imperialist, and anti-NATO that had existed in the 1970s.[30] In other words, Jeremy Corbyn.

Many of his supporters were hoping for a change in economic and social policy but what they had elected was a perfectly predictable populist agenda.[31] In so far as his leadership of the Labour Party produced a coherent policy agenda it was one of economic nationalism, greater sympathy towards Putin's Russia than other leaders (initially demanding more evidence for authorship of the Salisbury poisoning), and opposition to Western intervention in Syria—all overlaid by deep-seated anti-Semitism. His electoral defeat in 2019 led to a new leadership election and, effectively, the marginalisation of his supporters (who had always been a small minority of Labour MPs even if they had support among the party membership). Elements of the economic policy put forward would have been unremarkable a few years previously and represented a useful correction to the post-2010 austerity economics. However, this was lost in public concerns about other aspects of Labour policy.

The 2019 election campaign became a contest between left and right populism with Corbyn's unpopularity giving the (now very different) Conservative Party a large majority. The Conservative government continued with the full populist playbook, using public funds to reward client groups, attacking civil society institutions, curbing the influence of those sections of the press not sufficiently supportive, labelling its opponents as 'enemies of the people' and with a ruling party awash with funds supplied by Putin's allies. If there is a coherent policy framework it is one driven by ethno-nationalism, a disdain for expertise and a casual, and deadly, approach to handling the Covid pandemic.[32]

Here the Labour Party did something unusual. Corbyn had never been popular with his fellow parliamentarians and when he resigned the party shifted back to the centre with Sir Keir Starmer. The strength of this shift is that it restores Labour as a conventional centrist party; the risk is that those who wanted the economic changes identified by Corbyn will be alienated. Whether this new drastic shift will bear fruit at the next parliamentary elections remains to be seen. This move certainly goes against the populist mood of the age, but perhaps by the time of the next election, the British electorate will have lost patience with the Conservative government. The practical fear is that as with Biden in the US they will fail to generate the sort of social and economic policies needed to address real concerns as they seek to promote the virtue of competence around a prosaic set of policy choices.

As elsewhere, the fallout of the Iraq War and the 2008 financial crisis (plus a major scandal around how MPs were claiming public money for dubious personal expenses) all combined to reduce trust and allegiance to the standard model of politics. The populist capture of the Labour Party was relatively brief, in part as the bulk of its elected members were opposed to the man who became their notional leader. The capture of the Conservative Party appears to be profound. The policies espoused are a close fit to the wishes of the small, elderly membership; those MPs with a different perspective have largely been removed; and it has built an electoral base that is broad (if weak, in that different parts actually want different things). That this electoral base is essentially located just in England is placing the wider union with Scotland, Wales and Northern Ireland under considerable strain when the national government effectively only addresses the concerns of its own supporters in the wider electorate.

The UK tends to allow ready concentration of power if one party can win enough votes (usually around 40%) for this to become a clear domination of the House of Commons. While the US has some similarities, the wider range of electoral processes makes winning the Presidency less of a guarantee of being able to act without many constraints. At the time of writing, Trump lost the last election in part as many on the traditional centre right voted against him, but at the same time he has consolidated his hold over the Republican Party. In the UK, Johnson won the 2019 election but had to resign as Prime Minister when elements of the traditional centre-right electorate started to turn against him. The problem is that this might remove one populist but the Conservative Party itself has seen a profound change in the last five years.

The US

Aspects of modern populism actually have long-established historical precedents in American political history, going back to the American Revolution: in particular reflecting periodic concerns about immigration and attempts to limit who can be an American citizen. While a regular part of US political debate, this has only slowly come to dominate the process. Part of the reason why populism has been held in check in the past in the US is similar to the structural reasons why it was suppressed in the UK:

the electoral system really only leaves room for two main parties on the national stage, which in turn means that these parties are both forced to become relatively broad (sometimes uneasily so) coalitions. Each of these parties will have their populist wings, but so long as the respective party bureaucracies, or 'establishments' if you will, keep true to the liberal democratic principles outlined by the constitution, the populists will struggle to gain a critical mass of support to seriously challenge the system. However, again it does leave those seeking an alternative to 'politics as normal' unrepresented[33] and, as argued in earlier chapters, this becomes more important as the status quo increasingly fails the bulk of the electorate.

However, the Republican Party has been increasingly aligning itself towards populism for many years. It has quite deliberately sought votes from the religious right and tried to use cultural conflicts as a tool to mobilise its voters.

The reasons for this fundamental shift in the Republican Party is to do with the party's base: whereas in the past, populist sentiment was either a minority of the electoral base of each party, or was actively resisted by the leadership of each of the parties whenever it seemed to be in the ascendency, the populist wave in the Republican base is now overwhelming both in terms of numbers, and in terms of political energy. And this radicalisation of the party's base has taken place over decades, at times actively and consciously encouraged by at least some of the party's leaders over that period. In effect, Nixon's decision to adopt his Southern Strategy meant the party was actively seeking votes using racist arguments and stressing cultural issues. Over time, this became more important as issues such as abortion were used to seal an alliance with the evangelical right. The consequence was that, to many party members, it was these issues that defined why they supported the Republicans as opposed to the party's traditional platforms.

The Clinton presidencies in the 1990s coincided with the growth of a populist right-wing media in the US (some formal such as various radio shows and Fox News, some informal and based on the fast-developing internet). At the core of this coverage was a steady stream of conspiracy theories about the administration (admittedly fuelled by revelations of what was actually true). In turn the contested Bush victory in 2000 led some Democrats to reject the legitimacy of his administration. By the time Obama came to power in 2008, the ecosystem of right-wing media, conspiracy theory and the internet led many on the Republican right (and outside the Republican Party) to question his right to be President.

In effect, even before President Trump captured the Republican Party with a populist agenda, many Americans (mainly but not all on the right) had lost faith in its political institutions.[34] This produced an electoral bloc who took their news from a closed set of sources, who shared a view that the US today was not the country they remembered (or wanted) and who were open to Trump's economic nationalism. Themes such as race and migration were also part of this mix but their relative importance varied across his electorate.[35] Some observers placed substantial emphasis on the importance of 'culture wars' in cementing this coalition, and, in the view of outsiders, leading people to vote for a right-wing, minimal state, minimal regulation vision of the economy that was at variance to their own interests.[36]

The motivations to vote for populists are similar across much of the world. A yearning for a reform to the economic system (with economic nationalism being held to be the best corrective to excessive globalisation) and a degree of alienation from the conventional political system—because it either does not reflect particular views or offers no solutions to real problems. And this is where the recent trends towards populism in the US feel different from the past: for the first time, the populist wing of one party, the Republicans, seems to be steadily colonising the whole governing structure of their host party.

In the US, Trump harnessed these aspirations to launch an ongoing takeover of an existing party. Unlike the earlier Tea Party, or the 1992 Ross Perot presidential campaign, this embedded populism as the formal alternative to the Democrats in the US political system. The fallout continues to be deeply concerning. His presidency was marked by a sustained undermining of the institutions of US democracy, corruption and an aimless weakening of America's international defence posture. Since his electoral defeat, the majority of his electoral base continue to believe the election was stolen, with devastating impact on the legitimacy of the US political system.

In some ways what has happened in the US reflects the UK experience. A populist takeover of one of the traditional parties, which is often in power, has left the liberal basis of society in the balance. The problem is how to correct the situation.

Different forms, similar threat?

The three case studies above offer different paths by which populism can become entrenched in a political system. In Italy, Berlusconi emerged and flourished in an utterly devastated political system where the historical power bases had self-destructed by the time he fully came onto the scene. But then the internal dynamics of the populist movements themselves also made them quite unstable, so their effective control over the political path of the country waxed and waned, as the movements variously coalesced, collapsed in internal infighting, and then coalesced again. His populist successors have developed an approach based around nativism (sometimes still aimed at Italians from other regions), railing against elites, increasingly using the internet both to avoid internal party democracy and to try and dominate political debate as well as backing Putin's regime in disputes (and taking his funding). Despite this fertile ground, Italy's electoral system has prevented them retaining control, with a regular cycle of them winning power and then their usually fragile coalitions falling apart.

In the US and the UK, populism may have had frequent grass-roots representation, but has only managed to take hold in high-level politics by capturing established major parties. Going via this latter route comes with many complications, as the incumbent structures (the old party bureaucracies, the other institutional checks and balances like the courts, etc.) will resist the ascendency of the populists in various ways. But once established, their presence is both difficult to dislodge, and also likely to permanently influence the political agenda, whoever ends up being in office.

So the form of the electoral system matters in how populist politics plays out. In a first-past-the-post system, it is hard for emergent political movements to translate even substantial support into electoral gains. However, if they can capture one of the dominant parties, this dynamic is flipped: populists like Trump can hold and wield the power of the executive branch, for a long time, with as little as 40% electoral support.

On the other hand, systems that allow a more proportional representation of multiple parties make it easier for populists to gain their first elected members. In Europe, most states have recently seen the emergence of right-wing populist movements, who then established a permanent presence in the parliaments of their respective countries. But in most countries, these new parties have tended to stall at 10–15% of the electorate. This allows the old social democratic and Christian democratic parties of the liberal middle-ground to institute large effective 'cordonnes sanitaires', to keep these movements from capturing the political agenda. So in most places, allowing the populists early representation ended up constraining the threat they pose to liberal democracy in the longer term. Yes, they have some public influence, but the electoral system also helps limit that influence.

In the main, contemporary populism is a movement of the right. There are left-wing versions; some have held power, such as Chávez in Venezuela (his successor is best seen as an old-fashioned autocrat). Others, such as Corbyn, have briefly captured traditional social democratic parties. But broadly none of these seem to have managed to articulate a policy framework that mimics the interests of an electorally feasible portion of those eligible to vote.

In power, some of the new populists appear to take very reactionary stances on social issues, whereas on economics, their positions are much more interventionist: basically a perfect inversion of what it meant to be on the centre-right, even a mere decade ago. This raises one important question: is right-wing populism just the reformation of the centre-right conservative consensus because of the economic failures of the old centre-right model? Are we seeing this new ideological consensus and this new electoral coalition only because economic (neo-)liberalism is no longer an appealing electoral offer, so instead the centre-right is coalescing around cultural conservativism and economic protectionism as the political platform of the right wing?

If that was all that was happening, it would probably be fine. We might have different opinions about this or that policy, but we could debate about each issue through the normal processes of democracy. I, perhaps you, might have serious concerns that such a mindset would produce poor public policy, even seeing aspects of deep concern, but it is a recognisable configuration of traditional, democratic, right-wing politics.

The reason things are not so fine in actuality, however, is that this populism has adopted explicitly anti-democratic[37] tendencies. This is especially apparent for right-wing populists who will eagerly exclude people from their majoritarian 'democracy' based on race, ethnicity and religion. But for all of them, once any political actor or movement starts to claim a monopoly on representing 'the people' and 'the will of the people', any of the processes of liberal democracy, and any of the protections that liberal democracies afford to minorities become illegitimate obstacles to majority rule, and anyone who dissents from the party line, whether political opponents, or apolitical judges or journalists, becomes an 'enemy of the people' and a traitor. No populist government acts in the interests (perhaps badly, perhaps well) of all who live in a particular polity. Every one of them quite deliberately draws boundaries and those outside—for reasons of political beliefs, social attitudes, ethnicity, religion or sexual orientation—are not really part of the valid portion of the people. And from that comes the language of traitors, out-of-touch elites, public health experts who want to impose 'socialism' when discussing how best to mitigate the effects of a highly contagious pandemic.

France has had a regular problem in its presidential elections of one of the Le Pen family challenging an often disliked centrist politician (this has happened three times in the first twenty years of this century). So far, each election has seen a robust rejection, but the risk of a more able Le Pen (or an even less likeable centrist) will see a victory for the far right. In the US, the Republicans are traditionally a party of power (similar to the British Conservatives) so the chances of a populist-led Party winning again is substantial. As of the early 2020s, the Democrats (and the British Labour Party) seem to have the same attempted solution—competence and a return to civility and normality. This worked for Biden in 2019 but has not laid the grounds for either a change in the Republican Party or for the creation of a stable electoral coalition.

I will return to this dilemma in the final chapters.

5

CONSPIRACY THEORIES AND SOCIAL MEDIA

Populist political movements, like their authoritarian and totalitarian forbears, tend to rely very heavily on myths as a core part of their appeal. At its most extreme, this can see groups like the Italian Northern League inventing a polity that never existed (Padania) and seeing themselves as the descendants of the Celtic tribes overrun by a decadent Rome. To some extent, every political and national movement needs some degree of myth-making[1] and this can have a positive aspect. There are plenty of examples where the myths emphasise tolerance and openness as 'national characteristics', orient their understanding of the purpose of politics as improving the lot of its own citizens and offer a model to others. But the ethno-nationalism that sits at the core of especially right-wing populism is not benign in this way. Rather, their chosen myths about the identity of the 'real' inhabitants of a given polity are always exclusionary, and moreover, 'the real people' of the country are always under threat, whether from migration (both immigration and emigration), from 'foreign' cultures and religions, usually Islam, but also political enemies within, typically the liberals who are open and tolerant of others.[2]

Yet modern populist parties go far beyond the typical foundation myths we see in most political projects, and instead try to augment their world view with an oppositional, almost Manichean, struggle between good (represented by themselves and their 'people') and bad (everyone else). And when the 'forces of evil' are not easily identifiable, populists have no trouble inventing them outright: hence the endless theories about the 'bad people' and what they are trying to do to keep the 'good people' down. The nature of the conspiracy theory may vary, but the intent is consistent. Whether it was the assassination of J. F. Kennedy, the moon landings, the Clintons, 9/11, Obama's birth certificate,[3] 5G phone masts, or that the British Royal family really are shape-shifting lizards. In a way the actual form is unimportant, the takeaway is that there is some kind of 'they', some kind of malignant 'elite' who has virtually infinite power, who therefore almost inevitably controls the government, and that therefore anyone in elected government always lies to you.[4] That this regularly slips into anti-Semitism and invokes anti-Semitic tropes is no accident either.

As a consequence, populist politicians must necessarily paint themselves as 'outsiders', people who are not part of the malignant elites who lie to you, but people who will 'go to Washington to shake things up' or 'drain the swamp'. And the success of Trump in the US, or someone like Nigel Farage in the UK, at wielding this kind of narrative has compelled a whole host of new, ambitious political operatives to emulate them. But in the US we now see veterans of the Republican Party establishment and their supporting media infrastructure following suit, so Tucker Carlson, heir to the Swanson family fortunes, presents himself as the champion of those ignored by the social elite (of which he is very much a part). In the UK politicians of considerable inherited wealth like to promote their outsider credentials as they seek to appeal to populist sentiments.

So now we see how on issues like the validity of the US 2020 election results, or the efficacy of Covid vaccinations, we see little difference between what elected Republican politicians say on mainstream media and what the most deranged conspiracy theorists like Alex Jones say—with usually as little as one week's delay for the most extreme claims to be mainstreamed by even establishment Republicans. This has led to a disturbing trend, among some US Republicans, to decide that protecting the polity they wish to support (defined often in racial and religious terms) is indeed worth dismantling American democracy.[5] And this is not just a US issue. Members of the 2020s UK Conservative government have claimed that 'cultural Marxism' is a real threat, and every deranged theory about Covid has found some members of the UK's ruling party happy to repeat it. In effect, there is a very close match between conspiracy theories, populism and the social media architecture used to spread them.

The synergies between conspiracy theorising and populist politics

Typically, populist parties tend to be rather weak at practical governance. In part, this is because they lack serious commitment to policy formulation, and typically disdain the experts who might help them devise and implement good policy. But they are also not under the same political pressure to perform well in office as the traditional parties would normally be, at least in terms of the expectations of their core group of supporters.[6] Because of the peculiarities of their political outlook, and the tendencies of their electoral base, their practical failings at the job of public administration are readily blamed on secretive elites, treasonous opponents, or foreign interventions. Conspiracy theories therefore serve a dual purpose for populist politics: they are both part of the initial sales pitch to the electorate, as a tool to explain their goals and gain converts, but also immensely helpful in helping to rationalise away and excuse their frequent failings while in power.

The idea of there being a secret conspiracy that explains everything bad is probably as old as the existence of complex human societies where the members of the social order do not all know one another, or at least do not know one another well enough. And it is probably an effect of the same kind of cognitive mechanisms that compelled our ancestors to ascribe intentionality, an inherent spirit with a will of its own, to things like thunderstorms and earthquakes and all the rest. Where we do not understand the mechanical processes of why something happens, we find it cognitively compelling to construct a narrative. So when we do not understand why our societies are failing to function as well as we might want them to, sometimes it is easier to imagine that this is the design of some malevolent intentional force, typically in the form of some kind of hidden organisation or cabal of people with their own secret agenda, than it is to imagine that things are going badly because we ourselves are not doing the right things to make society function as well as we want it to.

Besides giving a shield for incompetence to populists, this is also dangerous because the populist penchant for conspiracy theorising also compels them to be constantly on the lookout for those secret enemies. And when they cannot find any actual enemies, they will invent them: meaning in practice that they will both initiate conflicts both against random groups within their own society, and also start wars against imagined foreign threats. In effect, the more alienated people have become from their own society, the more they feel the entire system fails them, and the more likely they are to find conspiracy theories compelling.[7]

Conspiracy theories seem to emerge for different reasons. During the Reformation and the religious turmoil of Europe in the sixteenth and seventeenth centuries, adherents of this or that Protestant sect might adopt conspiracy theories, especially the more fundamentalist sects,[8] as they sought to explain why the world failed to respond as they expected. In other instances, conspiracy theories are deliberated curated by the state to target particular groups or shore up support. So, the Tsarist anti-Semitic forgery, the Protocols of the Elders of Zion, had relatively wide distribution quite simply as a state published and disseminated them. Soviet claims of conspiracies against the regime were regularly constructed to explain policy failures. More recently, there has been a living to be made for obscure figures writing books based on conspiracy theories. So books suggesting that the British Royal Family are really shape-shifting lizards, for example, used to have a small audience prior to the advent of social media, because one had to physically go into some random, obscure bookstore to even find books with such theories.[9] But they no doubt generated a useful income for the author.

In effect, we have believers constructing conspiracy theories to explain why their beliefs fail to survive contact with reality. We have states curating conspiracy theories to attack parts of their population or to explain away policy failures. Finally, we have the fairly cynical construction of conspiracy theories as a means to personal income. Traditionally, there have been relative limits to the spread. One needs to join the given sect, one needs to be minded to believe the state or go to a bookshop and wish to buy a particular book. Anti-Semitism seems to be the one form of conspiracy theory that steps outside these limits, at least in notionally Christian countries, probably because it has been promoted since the early Middle Ages.[10]

The prevalence of anti-Semitic conspiracy theories in medieval Europe owes just as much to visible cultural difference, and the propensity for self-segregation of Jewish communities (even when this was as a reasonable effort to maintain their particular religious traditions, and not least, their norms of 'ritual purity' around food and prayer), as it did to religious animosity. Jewish communities were experienced by most who came in contact with them from the point of view of outsiders, and what they could see was often remarkably vibrant and successful communities. From that kernel of truth, it did not take a huge leap, especially in the minds of people already given to superstition and xenophobia, to invent all manner of deranged conspiracies about Jews, from the Blood Libel where Jews were presumed to be using the blood of Christian babies for their own ritual purposes, based on the fact that they were ignorant of Jewish religious traditions, to the political conspiracies that Jews controlled all the money and therefore all political events, based on the fact that Jewish communities had been forced into becoming merchants and professionals by laws barring them from owning land, but which in the end had the effect of making their communities relatively more affluent.

Social media makes this kind of material readily accessible, including the wildest nonsense, by removing the constraints of respectability and probity that had previously developed in the traditional print media industry. Under the guise of democratising information, all manner of peddlers, both the genuinely insane and the cynically exploitative, encourage audiences to 'do their own research', as a shorthand for 'the opinion of someone who has spent years studying a complex or highly technical field is no more valid than your own'. This too is a form of populism, and that is why these developments in the information marketplace dovetail so neatly with political populism: to hell with knowledge and expertise, to hell with peer review, and anyone who tells you otherwise is 'undemocratically' trying to take away your opinion, your voice and your 'freedom' to choose what you want to believe. 'The elites' are coming to get you, and they will impose the 'thought police' on you. And those hostile elites include the people who run the very social media platforms—ironically, the same people who created this conspiratorial ecosystem to begin with, for the sake of 'engagement', and the profit they hoped to make from that engagement.

The nature of conspiracy theories

Conspiracy theories tend to need three elements to become widespread. First, they rely on a small core of truth (or an argument that is believable); second, they are more accepted in periods of social or economic crisis; third, they tend to target already marginalised or distrusted groups.

Like propaganda, a conspiracy theory has more plausibility if it can build on elements of truth. For this reason, extravagant claims about self-serving elites become much more plausible when it is evident to the naked eye how at least some parts of that elite are indeed self-serving. Theories of a rich cabal engaged in child abuse gain plausibility when the crimes of Jeffrey Epstein are widely known and people can wonder why so few of those associated with him have been prosecuted.[11]

Beyond this, an environment with low levels of wider social trust in governance and the fairness of wider society is thus bound to be fertile soil for the emergence and spread of conspiratorial thinking. There are many points throughout history where this can be seen well. The witch crazes in northern Europe in the sixteenth and seventeenth centuries coincided with a period of economic pressure as a mini ice-age arrived.[12] Not surprisingly the combinations of political, social and economic pressures created an audience for conspiracy theories in the 1920s and 1930s.

In our own time, the fundamental dishonesty of the *casus belli* to invade Iraq in 2003 haunts us.[13] Anyone looking for evidence of dishonesty by elected politicians in modern times only needs to start there. After that absolute debacle, in retrospect, it was no longer so incredible that the Bush administration might have orchestrated the 9/11 attacks themselves as a 'false-flag' operation: and so, one of the defining conspiracy theories of our time, the '9/11 truth movement', became entrenched.

Finally, many conspiracy theories need a villain, a group that 'really' is in control. Anti-Semitism appears here very often but any group that is different to the rest of society will do. One key issue is to argue that their primary loyalty is not to the state they live in but some strange international elite. Thus, divorced from membership of the polity, their real allegiance then lies with their own group.

Psychologically, three factors seem to make people more generally willing to listen to conspiracy theories.[14] One is lacking the ability to distinguish between the validity of information sources, usually as a consequence of failing to understand the process by which knowledge is created. This can be (and depressingly often is) a wider failing in the education system, but is also more common for those with lower levels of relative educational attainment.

The second is the extent to which people feel that they lack control over their own lives and their immediate surroundings. When this happens, they are more likely to look for explanations— however nefarious—and more likely to accept conspiratorial hypotheses. In turn, this can give individuals a sense of at least psychological comfort, that they at least understand 'what is going on', and why things are going so badly for them. And in a sense, this has some benefits for the individual from the point of view of their psychological well-being.[15] When groups form around such beliefs, however, the conspiratorial nature of their unifying beliefs makes for very strong 'Us versus Them' dynamics, which in turn can be socially and politically dangerous.

Linked to this is the sense of fairness. If society is seen as being fundamentally unfair, or to not work as it should (in theory), then conspiracy theories become more acceptable. After all there must be some explanation for these failings? Thus the 1930s Soviet show trials had ever more elaborate conspiracies to explain why socialism was not delivering for the people and why long-standing members of the Communist Party had really been spies of foreign powers all along.

Once formed, such belief systems can be robust.[16] Often this is because their claims are unfalsifiable, either in principle or even just in practice: how are you supposed to prove that the British Royal family are not shape-shifting lizards, for example? It is a proposition that is so wild that you would not know what kind of evidence the believers would accept to refute it.

The belief systems are also typically very mutable in the details: the evidence the theory calls up and the logic it uses. The only persistent core will likely be that there is a 'they', and 'they' are doing something malign. That is the essence upon which you can hang any other social issue or broader political grievance. And indeed, you can recruit followers to your cause almost without end on the basis of perfectly sensible wider social concerns. Like, for example, who is not worried about child abuse? QAnon will take your concern for the well-being of children as its entry point, and then present you with ad hoc evidence, some real, some fabricated, to suck you ever deeper into the world view it espouses.

Given all this, it should therefore not be surprising that there are other social activities where 'Us versus Them' dynamics commonly avail themselves so readily of conspiracy theories, not least politics. And the more populist or extremist the political movement we are talking about, the more abundant and wilder the particular conspiracies.[17]

As I wrote this chapter in the summer of 2022, two different conspiracy theories were being peddled. One was related to politics in Scotland; the other was an attempt to deflect responsibility for the latest mass murder of school children in the US.

In late May 2022, the hashtag #BalmoralHotelIncident went viral on Twitter, first in Scotland and then across the UK. As more people shared this, or searched for it, then social media made it more widely accessible. It was a conspiracy theory aimed at Scotland's First Minister, Nicola Sturgeon, that she had caught her secret lesbian lover—a high ranking diplomat—in bed with another woman in the posh Edinburgh hotel. As with all conspiracy theories, the details vary, and are more or less lurid, but of course the 'truth' has been hushed up and measures are put in place to stop newspapers, hotel staff and police from telling the truth.

The story seems to have originated from supporters of an alternative nationalist party (Alba) which mostly exists as an online community. It was picked up by various Unionists who are also opposed to Nicola Sturgeon's gradualist approach to Scottish independence. As with Trump's attacks on Hilary Clinton, it uses a conspiracy theory based on a lie to undermine a senior female politician. And most definitely not on the grounds of their practical policies or competence in government.

Gossip about a political leader being a secret homosexual is a classic piece of disinformation. Especially on the new populist right with its definition of 'traditional family values' and a desire to limit the rights gained over the last fifty years.

Depressingly, trying to use misogyny and prejudice to smear our opponents can be seen as part of the rough and tumble of electoral politics. But generating conspiracy theories around the mass murder of school children really is not defensible at any level. But hours after the murder of nineteen children and two of their teachers at the Robb Elementary School in Uvalde, Texas, Republican Congressman Pete Sessions told the BBC that the killer 'wore eye-shade and sometimes wore dresses'. This was a lie, but shows the links between elected US Republicans and the far right. 4chan's notorious /pol/ board had posted an image of a trans woman who slightly resembled the killer, along with a link to her Reddit profile, and, without evidence, claimed she was the gunman. Once this idea started, others joined in as conservative activist Candace Owens claimed there were photos of the gunman 'cross-dressing', and claimed this was evidence that 'there were plenty of signs that he was mentally disturbed'.

Sessions is a lifetime member of the National Rifle Association, and a key part to that organisation's approach is to ensure no debate over the spread of automatic weapons in US society. Their preferred approach is to offer 'thoughts and prayers' rather than engage in a the discussion about gun ownership after the massacre of a classroom full of 10- and 11-year-olds by a man armed with two assault rifles that he'd bought just days after his 18th birthday.

So a simple conspiracy theory that in some way blamed the transsexual community was far more attractive. It usefully placed the killer into a group demonised by Congressman Sessions' supporters, and who most definitely did not fit the 'traditional family' model they wish to promote. And of course, this fits with a playbook of the NRA, and the far-right, response to every school shooting. Conspiracy theories not only distort political debate, they can kill.

Case studies: QAnon and Covid

These disparate themes can be usefully studied by looking at the two most popular and politically relevant conspiracy theories of our times: the Covid-related conspiracy theories, and QAnon which is steadily spreading from the US more widely.

Given all that, of course populist politicians will want to lean into just about any conspiratorial-sounding claim that gains even a moderate amount of traction on social media. We saw this dynamic at play very transparently as it related to the Covid conspiracy theories. But increasingly something like a genuine political movement, the conspiracy movement, is coalescing around the QAnon conspiracy theory. QAnon has risen to prominence as a kind of grand unified conspiracy theory that incorporates almost every popular conspiracy theory in recent *centuries*: from a repackaging of the Satanic scare of the 1970s and 80s in the US, to modern incarnations of the Protocols of the Elders of Zion aimed at 'George Soros and the globalists', to Blood Libel dug up from medieval-era conspiracies and moral panics, to the very recent Big Lie that Donald Trump did not in fact lose the 2020 presidential election. And because this conspiracy theory has an explicit bent against especially the Democratic Party, ambitious new Republican candidates can scarcely resist embracing it. In this way, the party turns more and more towards populism, and is becoming increasingly radicalised in turn by the conspiracy theories popular among their base.

QAnon

Research indicates that if someone believes in one conspiracy theory, they are very likely to adopt others. The QAnon conspiracy theory is remarkable in the extent to which it leverages this fact, by trying to bring together under one unified ideological edifice, all the most popular conspiracy theories of the past, in order to create an entirely parallel description of reality. In effect it becomes a separate reality with an answer for almost every question or event. In this it has become closer to an ideological or religious system as much as a conventional conspiracy theory.

QAnon is also distinct among conspiracy theories, in that it also advanced a single person, the then President, Donald Trump, as the one who will fix all the evils of the world as they see them. At its core, the theory argues that there is an international group of paedophiles who have effectively taken over most Western governments (and the media), but who will be dealt with by President Trump in the 'Storm'. The core focus on child abuse both reflects earlier conspiracy theories, such as Alex Jones's 'Pizzagate', where the Clintons allegedly ran a child abuse ring from a pizza restaurant in Washington, and also makes the underlying narrative attractive to those who do not share the wider far-right framing of the overall theory.

Somewhat unusually, QAnon goes beyond the vague assertions that are typical of conspiracy theories, and has regularly made firm predictions on future events, sometimes even with specific dates. None of the predicted arrests, terrorist attacks or the second inauguration of President Trump have actually happened. In theory this should have weakened the influence of the conspiracy theory on its adherents, but in practice most of them have adopted coping mechanisms designed to avoid confronting the possibility that their theory had been fake all along. One strategy is obviously to double down on the presumed hidden powers of the malignant forces at play, such that the 'deep state' were able to evade justice or prevent President Trump taking action. The other, familiar from the history of failed predictions about the Second Coming of Christ in the Christian tradition, was to return to a 'more careful textual analysis' of the past claims made by QAnon on 4chan, or by Trump on Twitter, in order to discern the real underlying meaning. Many adherents use techniques honed in the literalist study of the Bible in order to interpret QAnon messages.[18]

There are other strong religious parallels between medieval Christian millenialist traditions and QAnon, not least the promise that a cataclysmic ending is just about to befall this corrupt world, and this will then be followed by a promised golden age.[19] As with many millenialist movements, this leads to a propensity to resort to violence[20] in pursuit of such a clearly desirable goal. There have been regular reports of adherents turning to violence as early as 2019, with the FBI warning that

QAnon could 'very likely motivate some domestic extremists, wholly or in part, to commit criminal and sometimes violent activity'.[21] Since a 2021poll suggests that some 14% of the US population (and 25% of Republican voters) believe in QAnon's ideas, this is deeply worrying,[22] especially as a further 55% of Republicans disagree with the more extreme claims but believe they had some element of truth.

This is a very dangerous cocktail, and overall a recipe for the kind of upheaval and social strife that we have not seen since the wars of religion in Europe in the seventeenth century. And the situation seems to be only getting worse as the time goes on. The QAnon movement continues to grow, and its adherents continue to become more radical as time passes. Variants are now to be found in other Western states: in part as a direct import of the core beliefs but also then adapted to local concerns and political discourse.

Covid

The Covid pandemic has given rise to a number of conspiracy theories, and this situation illustrates very directly how conspiracy theories can hamper effective public policy formulation and implementation. The impact such claims had on policy can be most clearly seen in the claims firstly on the role of the Chinese state, and secondly on the safety of the vaccines. The pandemic started in Wuhan and there is no doubt that the early response of both the Chinese authorities and the World Health Organization was woeful.[23] The Chinese authorities sought to cover up what was happening, they did not provide samples for analysis, and their initial response contributed to the early spread of the disease.[24]

Some Western commentators jumped on these facts to spin a tale of deliberate malfeasance, claiming that China was not just negligent but deliberately engineered and released the virus.[25] President Trump was quick to adopt the narrative for his own purposes, as he was expecting the pandemic to affect his chances of re-election later that year. This was no longer a natural disaster; it was China deliberately sending a virus to the US to ruin his election year.

In response, the Chinese started promoting the counterclaim that the virus had really been engineered in a US military lab,[26] but then released near Wuhan in order to undermine China on the international stage. These latter claims seem to have been aimed purely at the domestic audience in China, but the material was often in English, and made widely available across social media.

However, Covid-based conspiracies have not just been a matter of US-China disputes. There have been constant conspiracy theories generated that have undermined the effectiveness of attempts to mitigate the effects of the pandemic. Some can be seen as a form of policy debate. Elements on the British right (both politically and in terms of the media) have constantly claimed that 'lockdowns' were a mistake and that people should have carried on acting as before.[27] At one level, this is an instance of poor policy but has regularly merged with claims that the state is using the pandemic to strip away liberties, that the virus is 'no worse than flu' and that the health impact is vastly overstated. This line of reasoning readily merges with conspiracy theories that the virus doesn't exist, that it is caused by the presence of 5G phone masts and that the vaccines are attempts at social control with all sorts of secondary health problems.

Vaccination campaigns have long been associated with conspiracy theories.[28] For example, the introduction of compulsory smallpox vaccinations in Germany in the 1870s saw the emergence of conspiracy theories linking this to a Jewish plot against the purity of the German nation (the link to the current claim of the unvaccinated to have 'pure blood' is, of course, obvious). Al-Qaida and Taliban-linked Islamist militants have attacked vaccination programmes claiming they are a cover for US spying operations. As expected, vaccine hesitancy has been found to be more common in social, ethnic or other groups that have a long-standing, and often well-founded, lack of trust in the state. In general, belief in these conspiracy theories is correlated to accepting other conspiracy theories,[29] and with relative social and political disengagement or marginalisation[30].

The scientific data, however, is crystal clear: large-scale vaccination offers our best chance at the social level to escape the constraints imposed by the pandemic, while for individuals it can be a life-or-death issue.[31] The political movements that have risen from the conspiracy theories supporting vaccine hesitancy have thus had dire effects both for individuals, and at the social level. The number of individuals who have died, and who would not have died had they taken the precautions recommended by the health authorities of their own countries, are likely to be at least in the hundreds of thousands. And this is before the needless death toll caused by the incompetence of populist administrations in places like the US,[32] UK and India.[33]

And socially and economically, we have seen that those countries where the populations have been the most understanding and cooperative with the measures mandated by the authorities have also been the countries that have suffered the least: they had the most early and stringent lockdowns, but in turn that meant that in the longer run, their economies suffered relatively little. The clearest examples of this are countries like New Zealand and Taiwan. And the performance of Taiwan is particularly remarkable for having been one of the countries to first get infections outside of China, at a time when the severity of the virus was yet unknown. Two years into the pandemic, Taiwan had only a total of 80 deaths per million people, and a total of less than 1,000 dead. The United States, by comparison, where the conspiracy movement adopted all these theories and grew into a political movement opposed to any government intervention to protect the health of the general population, saw over 3,000 deaths per million people, or a total of over 1 million deaths.

Such a lethal set of beliefs become widely promoted for two reasons. In some cases, those responsible for spreading these theories may well believe them. It is perfectly feasible to be sceptical about the impact on civil liberties of some of the Covid restrictions, even if you accept the need. It is equally possible that some of the politicians who pick up and amplify conspiracy theories do so because they actually believe them to be true. While it is worrying that such individuals have become a normal part of what used to be a conventional centre-right party in the US, at least they have the small defence of believing what they say. More generally politicians such as Nigel Farage and conspiracy-based websites such as *InfoWars* have found in Covid yet another means to fragment our societies and earn money for themselves.

This model of monetising dissent, or more strictly engagement, leads us to the question of the role of the social media companies in spreading conspiracy theories and generally making it far too easy for the populists to undermine democracy.

Social media first emerged as a politically significant force during Obama's first presidential campaign in 2008, when targeted messaging on platforms such as Facebook was first pioneered—at the time, this development was noted, but its future implications were not yet widely understood. Facebook also emerged in 2013 as one of the main enablers of the genocidal attack on the Rohingya minority in Myanmar in 2013—but for the most part, no broader lessons were drawn at the time from those events. Before long, however, both of these historical precedents would establish patterns that are now of huge political consequence in almost every country in the world.

First, social media platforms such as Facebook make it possible to individually target any message and make sure it was only seen by those who would be receptive to it, while making it invisible to everyone else. Thus both open political debate in the *public square* and accountability go straight out the window. And second, once you isolate individuals into information silos (or 'bubbles'), you can increasingly feed them any manner of false claims and conspiracy theories, ensuring their support for just about any kind of political stance or action. The net effect has been to fragment the common understanding of reality that is fundamental to democracy, and make it increasingly difficult for us as citizens to discuss and negotiate our differences in a constructive, or even peaceful, manner.

The social media problem

We should not lose sight of the reason why social media has become so ubiquitous in the first place. It does, after all, come with significant benefits. At both the local and global levels, it makes it easier to link with other people, to run a small business, or to find like-minded communities. Social media apps like Facebook are ideal for creating informal groups to organise anything from family conversations to local book groups. Or if one wants to extract useful information from the immense data-trove that is the internet, one will inevitably need a good search engine to extract that information; a good search engine will give more people more accurate information than anyone will have ever had before in history, and Google is undoubtedly the most effective internet search engine around.

So how do these obvious benefits to people in their daily lives also come with such huge downsides for society? This largely comes down to the business models of the dominant tech giants, and the incentives that these companies work under in our current economic and political context. In the more optimistic readings of the post-1991 world, internet access and widespread computer use were seen as leading to more open societies and making it all but impossible for repressive regimes to survive. Not only did this overlook the substantial development of computing say in the old USSR[34] (in part built on a focus on mathematics in higher education but mostly of use in business and educational roles), but as we know now, internet access is relatively easy for authoritarian regimes to control.[35] In fact, for China, it is now the means of near totalitarian population control.

What we remain less ready to call out is how the business model of mainly US-based technology companies is also inimical to much of the individual freedom and liberal democracy that we mostly still wish to enjoy. And this, of course, is at variance to the image they present of themselves.

The usual criticism of the tech giants focuses on their vast profits and their miniscule tax payments. Facebook in 2020 generated 98% of its revenues from adverts (almost $85bn[36]) and had profits of $32.6bn. Estimates suggest their advertising revenue will be over $114bn for 2021. Google had $182bn of earnings and over $40bn in profits for 2020, again mostly driven by the sale of adverts. Both companies pay remarkably little tax on these earnings. Google pays around 8% in the US and, in 2019, managed to pay just £4m corporation tax on £1.8bn of earnings in the UK.[37] Both companies, perfectly legally, manage their affairs so they are profitable in states or countries with low tax regimes and somehow make very little in countries with higher tax rates. In response to criticisms of the low level of corporation tax paid in the UK, Google, quite rightly, pointed out that they 'pay all of the tax that is due in the UK'.[38]

But this focus on profitability and tax avoidance misses a large part of the problem with the business model of Big Tech, as it is practiced today. This business model distorts many other economic considerations in ethically and politically problematic ways.

For example, there is a question of rewards for production: when it comes to digital 'goods' on the internet there are costs of production, but there is virtually no cost for its distribution—yet distribution is much more easily monetised, because there are a variety of ways of charging for access.[39] As such, this model allows a disproportionate amount of the value produced on the internet to be captured by those who can control access, the 'platforms', at the expense of those who produce it.[40]

This is easy to see from the business practices of Facebook and Google. The value that is produced on their platforms comes from user interaction for Google (supplemented by them accessing content created, and paid for, by others) and user-generated content as well as user interaction for Facebook. In other words, in properly defined terms, the users of these platforms are the labourers who produce the value that these platforms capture, just as much, if not more, than the programmers in their offices. The old adage that 'if a product is free, you are the product' actually misses the point for describing this business model: here you are not the product, you are the worker.[41] And the more of that product you can be encouraged to provide, for free, the more that value can be transmuted into profits on these companies' balance sheets.

This economic model really only came into place after the 2008 financial crash[42] although it had been developed at the end of the dot.com boom. Both firms followed similar routines to earn profits from the data that was being freely presented to them. Shoshana Zuboff[43] suggests that the Al-Qaida attack on the US in September 2001 was equally important as it triggered a shared interest in using the data that existed on line to track and predict actions—in effect it created an alliance between the new technology sector and the much older surveillance sector.

In this model, the key commodity is users' data[44] in the same way that a petrochemical company uses oil or gas. Zuboff describes this commodity as 'Behavioural Surplus'. Nick Srnicek, among others, calls the overall model 'Platform Capitalism'.[45] Both make the point that the companies who engage in this business model make little distinction between the socially valuable aspects of their practices, and the socially harmful ones, and as the case of Facebook shows us, sometimes executives at these companies will blur that distinction deliberately.

As a specific example, the original vision of a digital home was one where the owner had full control of the technology they used, and full ownership of the data that they fed into that technology. The current reality is one where the owner has little choice but to agree to cede all rights to their personal information to a remote, unaccountable corporate behemoth with effective monopoly power, or receive barely any digital services at all.

Google

Google is where the tech giants' current preferred business model was first developed and refined.[46] Google first appeared on the internet scene as a search engine, and in the beginning it was merely one of many options to perform that function.

Given the vast amounts of information that the internet contains, and how difficult the challenge of efficiently finding just the bit of information that one is looking for, the function of a web search engine is absolutely necessary. Google's implementation of such a search engine even now appears at first as essentially benign, akin to the work carried out for a long time by librarians but focussed on the emerging digital world.

However, Google is not some neutral librarian seeking a taxonomy that allows us to readily categorise the digital world. For starters, the task of indexing all the information on the web, as well as quickly and effectively retrieving it billions of times a day in response to every user query is hugely costly. Moreover,

Google is a publicly traded company with shareholders who are legally entitled to profits. Google has to monetise their service in some way or another; and the business model they pioneered is one where your search queries are an instance of data extraction and analysis[47] for Google that they can then sell to advertisers, or feed into the ever-expanding data sets they use as inputs for their artificial intelligence efforts. You searching for something trivial on the web is therefore more valuable to Google than the results that Google yields back on your computer screen. And when you stop to think about it, of course it is! How else would they be able to run a business? The immediate ethical problem, however, is that all of this mostly happens without your conscious comprehension or consent.[48]

But beyond even that immediate ethical problem, Google's business model poses a critical political problem to democracy. Their model of serving you with targeted advertisements and personalised search results means that most of the time if two people run the same search they will be presented with different information. At this stage we have departed from the role of a librarian, we have also departed from the information search model that is used to generate academic studies.

Part of that is a seemingly benign effort to serve you both content and ads 'relevant to you'. And to some extent, such personalisation is obviously sensible: if I search for 'bagels' in Chicago, I have no use for search results which show me bagel shops in London, for example. But as much as targeted advertising might seem sensible for commercial products, targeted advertising and 'personalised' non-advertising content for political news for example, is increasingly obviously a disaster for democracy and the concept of the *public square* that democracy depends on.

To see this, anyone can run the following trivial test: I ran a simple search 'Ukraine' in google.com.

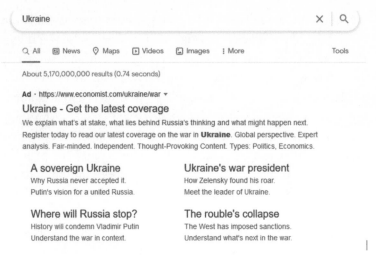

On one computer, at the top of the screen is a link to a website that charges for access, though to be fair, this is a reputable UK-based centre-right publication, focused on politics and economics. You might find such a result politically non-neutral or not impartial, but this is a relevant result, even if the source is not contextualised any further.

Lower down the page, however, we are presented with a set of suggested related questions that purport to provide information and further links:

These are presented here as entirely neutral and are likely to be read by most users as completely factual. But there is no guarantee that either the promoted link, or that the answers in the 'ask' segment, are reliable. What you get from your search is not something like a Wikipedia article that, whatever else you might think about that site, has been carefully vetted and effectively 'peer-reviewed' by a diverse community of human editors who all keep each other to high standards of evidence and editorial impartiality. Instead, what Google gives you are algorithmically generated responses which are 'tailored to you' so that if your previous search history indicates a past preference for populist political messaging, it will try to serve you exactly the political content it knows you like, probably also including conspiracy theory sites. One researcher tested this by asking Google: 'Is Obama planning a coup?' and received recommendations to various conspiracy theories.[49] If you start to run searches on how to cope with bankruptcy or debt, the ads you are presented with become those from dubious lenders more interested in high interest rates for loans than solving your financial problems. In effect, Google is happy to take adverts from loan sharks and make them available to vulnerable users.

Google goes beyond building a profile of your likely preferences based on your past search history. It also uses your search data so it can sell your searches more profitably to potential advertisers.[50] At this stage the relationship becomes one-sided. Google will not tell you what it knows about you; it does not just gather data using your internet searches on its platform but also the contents of your emails (if you use gmail—and you have to use gmail on an Android phone) and, if you use the Chrome browser, all the web pages you visit. So to have an effective product for them to sell, Google basically needs you to work for them, using their technology by generating online activity. This creates the basic product that is at the heart of their business but also the tools for 'continuous experimentation'.[51] Google basically uses the data that you generate for them and then tweaks its algorithms to see if this increases the flow of users to certain sites (including those that it owns itself).

The European Union was the first to take some of these ethical and political concerns seriously, and introduced the notion of the 'right to be forgotten'.[52] This requires considerable care in how personal data is handled and, in some circumstances, requires that sensitive personal information be removed from search engine results. The EU therefore offers citizens a degree of control over their digital data trail. And this was immediately perceived as a serious threat to their core business model: the firm has lobbied hard to ensure the US and other markets do not follow suit, or to persuade them to water down any such initiatives; they have hugely ramped up their lobbying presence in Brussels to make sure that future initiatives by the EU to protect their citizens from this business model are restricted, and so on.

Facebook

When Sheryl Sandberg moved from Google to Facebook in 2008, the financial model was transposed to Facebook and then amplified.[53] Facebook has since then also come to rely on near-continuous user interactions which help it build profiles and sell them to advertisers. Except that Facebook is an even more obviously amoral player, despite the fact that it is still led by its original founder and could, in theory, be expected to be less vulnerable to shareholder pressure to maximise profits at all cost.

There is no better illustration of both the mendacity and the malign power of Facebook than the Cambridge Analytica scandal. Cambridge Analytica was a private company working for political clients (usually either right-wing populists in old democracies, or authoritarian leaders in the developing world) that harvested the full Facebook data of around 87 million people without their consent, including over 70 million US citizens. Their clients were then able to individually target voters with messaging tailor-made to serve the interests of their particular campaigns: thus Republican-leaning voters could be messaged with ads that would get them fired up and more likely to show up to vote in the next election, while Democratic-leaning voters would be messaged with ads which showed their preferred party's ineptitude or hypocrisy, depressing Democratic party turnout, for example.

The kicker? Cambridge Analytica were not hackers, stealing or even abusing Facebook's data, but rather normal clients using the Facebook platform in the exact way in which it was designed for advertisers. Cambridge Analytica extracted the data with the full consent of Facebook using their own technology to set up a seemingly anodyne quiz. Participants agreed (using a very complex consent form) to provide not just their own data, but to allow the company to acquire data on their 'Friends' (who of course were never asked for their consent). And indeed, the resulting data was analysed and used in a variety of political campaigns including Vote Leave in the UK (in favour of Brexit) and the Trump presidential campaign in the US in 2016. Senior figures associated with the company also had close links with individuals close to Putin.

The way in which the criticism of Facebook in the wake of the Cambridge Analytica revelations was handled by the company was also telling. In the Congressional hearings to which CEO Mark Zuckerberg was summoned, the company maintained the old ruse: social media companies are a neutral, and even benign enabler to our chosen actions, and we, as individual users, retain full agency at all times.[54] Responding to queries by some of the more aware members of Congress, Mark Zuckerberg casually dismissed the concerns raised, stressing instead that Facebook merely allows people to connect with each other.[55]

As for the questions surrounding the business model of Facebook? Zuckerberg batted back Senator Orrin Hatch's question with the pithy: 'Senator, we run ads'. And when asked whether Facebook tracked users across platforms, Zuckerberg evaded a clear answer, saying he needed to check—for the record, Facebook tracks everyone, even those who do not have a Facebook account, and they do so across most other websites they might visit.[56] In other words, Zuckerberg was openly scoffing at the notion of democratic accountability for the consequences of his business practices—and unfortunately, Congress has yet to do anything about it.

Court cases related to Cambridge Analytica[57] and individual privacy continue. In places, Facebook is facing legal pressure to actually respond to the complaints and provide the information requested—though the company is aggressively using the legal technique of delay, and the promise to provide clarification later, thus resisting legal accountability even for matters that are clearly laid out on the statute books.[58]

The incredulous and resentful response of the executives of Facebook to the fallout from the Cambridge Analytica scandal shows that, for the company, this was not an unfortunate abuse of their platform: for them, the kinds of things that Cambridge Analytica were doing are the very essence of their business model, and any questions raised of the platform on account of the scandal was a direct affront to their fundamental business model. Opaque targeted advertising is not just a service they intend for Nike, or McDonald's, but a tool they consciously sell to political operatives to manipulate and direct public opinion.[59] It is therefore no coincidence that the Mueller report[60] identified Facebook as the platform of choice for Russian interference in the 2016 presidential election and the Brexit campaign in the UK.

Facebook's active political choices are even more stark in the cases we have seen where the platform was used to organise genocide.[61] Facebook has been cited in a UN report as enabling the 2014 genocidal attacks on the Rohingya in Myanmar.

When, at long last, this issue was finally recognised in the West, Facebook meekly conceded that 'We agree that we can and should do more.'[62] The result of their concession? Scarcely any more moderators of hate and incitement content in languages other than English, and an almost identical situation of how the platform is being used right now in the ongoing crisis in Ethiopia,[63] and the communal violence outbreaks in India and the Philippines, and no pro-active response to any of these emerging humanitarian disasters unless and until these issues bubble up to the forefront of international awareness—especially in the US.

In the past, most of us got news from sources which placed a high value on truth. Some—like the tabloid newspapers in the UK and commercial broadcasters in the US—did so defensively: most stories just had to be true enough to avoid legal consequences. Others sought a more stringent standard. But all played by similar rules: accuracy matters. Certainly the threat of a large libel settlement meant that outright fabrication was rare.[64] Facebook, on the other hand, is all about maximising attention. They sell advertising, and anything which will bring them more eyeballs is useful. As more people started to use them for news, they grew into something they were not built to be: a major supplier of news and comment. A mainstream window on the world. And as they placed a higher value on clicks than truth, they were bound to provide a distorted view. At the moment, since neither Facebook nor Twitter are treated as news publishers, they are also largely exempt from any fear of libel settlements if they allow misinformation to be spread on their platforms.[65]

In the last few years, a struggle has played out within Facebook which illustrates this. We have seen targeted political advertising exclude voter segments from important political information, undermining the democratic process. Studies showed that misinformation and fake news reaches more people and spreads faster than real news on social media.[66] The same goes for hate speech and threats. Facebook prioritises engagement. When it was used to organise the genocidal attack on the Rohingya in Myanmar in 2013, for example, the company registered this as a lot of engagement: a good thing.

By 2019, concerns were percolating inside the company. It commissioned an internal report, since leaked to the New York Times, which said:

> We also have compelling evidence that our core product mechanics, such as virality, recommendations, and optimizing for engagement, are a significant part of why these types of speech flourish on the platform. If integrity' [that's the internal term for the part of the company which could filter content] 'takes a hands-off stance for these problems ... then the net result is that Facebook, taken as a whole, will be actively (if not necessarily consciously) promoting these types of activities.

It is the next sentence of the memo which is the most damning of all:

'The mechanics of our platform are not neutral.'

In 2021, another internal memo concluded that the company missed critical warning signs that people were using the platform to incite the Capitol riot.[67]

The business model works as it is, and Facebook is not about to pro-actively mess with it unless it is forced to by US political authority. After all, Facebook has a fiduciary duty to maximise shareholder value, and employing moderators for every language spoken on Earth is expensive. So in Myanmar, Facebook didn't care if it was being used to organise a genocide, what it was gaining was information on how a technologically limited society engaged with the internet—and that was something they could use elsewhere and sell. So of course it happens again, and again; it is the business model.

What can be done?

We need to be clear: the problems of ready dissemination of conspiracy theories and the social media business model are interrelated. In combination, they are how populists gain public attention and isolate their preferred voters from the wider polity. They are also, as we see in the next chapter, the core tools for Putin's model of information warfare aimed at the West.

Controlling social media

As discussed in early chapters, we have lost confidence when it comes to regulation of capitalism. The axiomatic view that low regulation triggers productivity and social wealth is now well ingrained. Equally, Western democracies tend to be cautious when it comes to regulation of the press and the wider media landscape. State censorship is something that tyrannies do. But all Western states have press and media rules. These variously address issues of ownership and plurality but also an expectation of truth (or at least the avoidance of known, outright lies). But so far, this model of regulation has not been applied to the social media companies, and, at their core, they are news publishers—it is just that most of their content is written by us.

We may reject Barbara Walter's assertion that the current social media ecology is a direct threat to liberal democracy[68] but we have to be clear, they are a major part of the problem. We have a regulatory system that basically accepts the primacy of shareholder rewards as the core indicator of a successful enterprise, and companies that see the main route to this situation as high volumes of activity. They know that people using their platforms for local activities are not going to generate that; they equally know that conspiracy theories, contentious politics and populism do. So the executives of these companies did what officers of publicly traded companies are legally obliged to do in our regulatory environment: they let the algorithms 'optimise' their services to give people exactly the kind of content that would keep them the most 'engaged', so that their company can return maximal profits to their shareholders. Not surprisingly, left to themselves, they have no problem with fomenting contention and division, up to and including genocide.

In looking for alternatives, we have to be clear, the current social media environment offers a lot to many people. Ease of connection, ease of information search and retrieval, the ability to interact and organise with minimal technical skills are valuable. The goal is to retain this and restrain the negative side effects.

Broadly the current social media structure meets expectations in terms of access, but fails badly in terms of individual rights, accountability of those who provide services, and transparency in the trade-offs users are expected to make between access and privacy. At its best, social media allows ready interaction between individuals, for groups or for political organisations, local or national, to run their affairs effectively.

Zuboff[59] in particular is especially adamant that the particular policy choice to put shareholder value over any other corporate interest is to blame for the abuses of Facebook and Google. This mindset, as I have argued before, is anti-democratic in that it removes so much from the field of democratic politics. It also encourages firms to do as they need to optimise a single constraint, rather than address a wide range of issues. Finally it pushes regulators to a mindset where they are unwilling to creatively construct regulations to force firms towards the public good. But let us be clear, Facebook is a good platform to organise genocide not because Mark Zuckerburg et al want to set off genocides. The reason is much more banal: genocide is a non-disrupting side effect of the business model, whereas altering Facebook's platform to allow for the prevention of genocides would be very disruptive to their business model. And shareholders do not want to mess around with the business model any more than Facebook executives do.

One possible solution is to treat platforms such as Facebook as if they were media companies, and regulate them accordingly. That most of their content comes from unpaid labour (or labour paid for elsewhere) does not alter the reality that this is fundamentally what they have become—not least because nowadays they obviously curate content, and do so with well-defined editorial stances. They should therefore be liable to all the constraints of conventional print and broadcast media. Given that they are the ones who monetise the content on their site, and not the users who generate it, it seems absurd that only the users should be held liable if laws around libel or equalities, or foreign agent activity, are breached.

Another solution could be the establishment of publicly owned social media platforms that would operate as public utilities aimed not at maximising engagement and profits, but at helping out citizens at the local level, when they actually need such help. Nick Srnicek,[70] for example, argues not just for better regulation of the incumbent tech giants, but to altogether escape the assumption that the only way to access the advantages of social media and the ability to exchange and share goods and services is to accept the wider model imposed by the current social media companies. His focus is more on firms such as Amazon, Uber and Airbnb which have all distorted benign sharing between ordinary people into the logic of platform capitalism. But the logic applies to virtually all social media and gig-economy platforms.

Silicon Valley start-ups, and their equivalents elsewhere, simply cannot be run exclusively for public benefit. The only way these companies have been able to get off the ground and become established is with heavy investment from private equity capital, which is only interested in super-normal returns at the earliest possible opportunity. As such, even the most benign founders have to alter their platforms to fit the logic of platform capitalism, before their competitors do and eat up their entire market share.

Srnicek's solution is not just better regulation (say of the impact of Airbnb on the wider private letting sector), but for either countries or organisations such as the EU to start to invest and create publicly owned variants. Allied to better regulation of private data, this would actually introduce meaningful competition into these markets, where the private companies would compete on features, and the public platforms would act as guarantors of privacy, data safety, and public benefit. Maybe such a thing would not fly in the US because of its ideological preference for market solutions and the lack of trust in the government to do anything for the common good; but for example, in the UK, a BBC-equivalent social platform with the same standards of public discourse could potentially be both feasible and very attractive to ordinary citizens. And such a model could conceivably be appealing in any country that already has a well-trusted state media ecosystem (Germany, France, the Nordics, Canada, etc.). These platforms would not need to have all the latest bells and whistles, but you really wouldn't need AI-augmented 3D-visualisation to organise a village fete anyway. In effect, the regulatory model, and the constraints on the regulators, become an important part of creating a solution.

Both of these approaches would change our social media landscape dramatically. Big tech lobbyists are frantic in pointing this out, associating disruption with risk in the minds of policymakers and the public alike. But the risky disruption has already happened when we let these business practices take over our democratic *public square*. The disastrous reality that we have come to live in as a consequence of that really could suffer a good amount of disruption itself at this point. We know our societies will not get any healthier if we leave this current situation standing as it is. We therefore have an obligation to our democracy as its citizens to try and reshape this information and media landscape to serve us and our democracy, not just 'shareholder value'.

Fighting conspiracy theories

This in turn leads to the issue of how to challenge conspiracy theories. As with the issue of media regulation, the natural, liberal position is a bias towards as much freedom as possible. But in combination with the social media landscape, conspiracy theories are becoming a fundamental threat to our democracies.

How are we to respond to such potent challenges to our liberal democratic order? For the sake of our democracies, we must fight back vigorously. But more importantly, we must fight back intelligently and effectively.

First, it is necessary to distinguish between those who genuinely believe these conspiracy theories and those who propagate them for their own interests. For the latter, their business models must be attacked and disrupted without hesitation. We must expose the ways in which they profit from what they say, whether that profit is financial or political; we must make public that their reasons for saying what they say have nothing to do with the public good and that they would say the same things whether or not they were true, and we must challenge their channels of communication.

The true believers, on the other hand, must be handled with much more care and empathy. Psychological research has long ago demonstrated that simply telling someone they are wrong is not an effective way to change their minds.[71] It is necessary to understand why it is that they have arrived at the conclusions they have. As was already highlighted earlier, the fundamental instinct that is driving many people towards conspiracy theories in our current world is a sense that the democratic politics of the past few decades has been failing them, and that the political elites who are supposed to represent their interests are all too often busier feathering their own nests—and on both of those accounts, people are sometimes not mistaken.

Yet the conclusions that the conspiracists draw from these obvious facts are both crazy, and also do not serve ordinary people themselves any more than the most corrupt of the political elites. And this can be demonstrated to people if we take enough time and care to explain how things are actually working out in politics, and if we try to be as transparent as possible about everything we do. Not everyone will listen, of course. But some will. And later on, some more will. This process will inevitably be slow and gruelling, but it is very much necessary.

Moreover, this kind of work is already done by many grassroots activists. Unfortunately, all too often, such activists are mistakenly identified as 'left-wing' populists, at least in the United States, and derided as part of the same problem as the far-right populists, instead of part of the solution, by most elements of the liberal establishment including most of the Democratic Party. Whether it is fact-checking organisations like Media Matters, or the environmental groups arguing for a Green New Deal, these political groups operate on the basis of fact, and genuinely seek solutions to the problems of alienation and marginalisation, both political and economic, that have radicalised so many Americans. If we, as liberal democrats, have been somewhat slow at recognising who our political opponents are and what threat they actually pose, we have been even slower to recognise who our friends and allies are, and the ways in which their admittedly different perspectives can help us renew both the liberal and the democratic spirit in our societies. This error must be rectified, and the sooner the better.

This starts to provide the means to explore how various information systems (including radio, print journalism, academic and trade-book publishing, television, YouTube, Facebook, and Instagram) make choices about which messages to promote and how those choices intersect with political messaging and the social engineering of interest groups.

Learning to read the media?

We can't ban conspiracy theories as such, though we can, and should, be prepared to challenge them robustly. We can change the regulatory framework for companies like Facebook or Twitter. At one level, if we apply the same media laws to them as any other news publisher, then they become liable for anything published on their sites (not, as at the moment, only the person who publishes or shares the material). That alone will make them aware of the importance of proper monitoring and control.

But there is another dimension. We all need to learn to read the media, and make informed judgements about the sources and the validity of the argument being presented.

To some extent, the lack of discernment among the public is quite understandable: the communications technologies that are disseminating all this new overwhelming torrent of information have existed for less than a generation, and most people using the internet today have grown up and been educated in a world where the current challenges to our understanding of the world and our political participation in that world were scarcely imaginable. And perhaps as new generations arrive, we will get a citizenry who grew up in this environment, understand it better, and will not be exploited as readily by the populist messaging they are seeing on their social media feeds, or indeed business models currently practiced by the tech giants.

It is therefore evident that in the current information environment created by the internet and social media, citizens of a modern liberal democracy need to have the analytical skills to navigate the masses of information that are thrown at them every time they look at a screen. They need the skills to interpret statistics and understand why they are used, but also how they can be misused by motivated dishonest actors; they need to understand how to research a topic independently of their partisan 'news' sources (e.g., the concept of a balanced review); they need a robust understanding of the differences between opinion, belief and knowledge, and they need to be able to critically evaluate the claims of others. This does not need to be done at the level of a PhD in the philosophy of science, of course, but all these skills need to be taught to children at least as early as secondary school (indeed a major problem in the US and UK is that students first encounter the philosophy of science, and thus of knowledge, when they start doing a PhD). It is more a matter of 'how do we question an assertion?'

Learning how to read and interpret the media is not an issue for post-doctoral students. It now has to be a skill learnt, preferably, at school and part of the mental architecture of every citizen of a democracy. If we have to learn how to interpret conventional written texts then being aware of the issues behind IT systems is equally important. Even without the abuse of the social media companies, many such systems are built on judgements and rules, and those reflect the opinions and understanding of particular people.[72] In effect, the computer system is not neutral, it is programmed by people with their own framing of the desired interaction. The Ukrainian education system starts this process in primary school.[73] At one level this is practically focussed on how to safely use the internet, the right to say no or withdraw from a digital interaction, but it also includes how to interpret online sources. In effect, Putin's Russia has made no attempt to hide its determination to use the internet to disrupt other nations,[74] and Ukraine, very much one of his targets since 2004, has taken this threat seriously. At its core this is not complex; it involves asking common-sense questions. How plausible is this, how reasonable is it that the person presenting this view really understands the issues, why is this being raised now? In effect the questions we should constantly pose to any claim by any political party—including those we agree with on most issues.

Part of this is a willingness to challenge the logic chains used. Many conspiracy theories deliberately start from something that is correct, or at least arguable. But then the leaps to the promoted conclusion make no sense. A simple example might suffice. At the time of writing the first draft of this chapter in early 2022, some supporters of Scottish independence were contrasting the UK government's support for Ukrainian independence (against the threat from Russia) with the UK's opposition to Scottish independence. Testing the leap used here quickly reveals the fallacy. In one case, the UK is upholding a long-standing part of international law and the wider norms adopted between European states. In the other, the UK government is reasserting a policy that, as of 2022, is a purely domestic matter. It is not a matter of whether one choice or the other is right, they simply are not directly comparable.

The second major gap is in terms of statistics. Basic numeracy is essential, but more important is to understand—again—the implications and logic chains. If we hear that something is 10% more likely to cause an illness that sounds terrible. But there are two questions: 10% of what base rate, and how severe is the illness? So if the base rate of catching a given illness is 0.001% then a 10% increase is minimal. Combining base rates with probabilities is essential to understand anything about public health but most people will not think of it, never mind seek to carry it out.

The classic study in this field is of providing people with two pieces of information. All the cars in a given city are either red or green and 80% are red. A car is seen to be involved in an accident and the observer stated it was green. The observer is able 90% of the time to correctly identify red from green. Most readers will assume that the car involved was green (after all they are reporting with 90% accuracy); in fact it was more likely to have been red (and misidentified as green).

Now the mathematics behind this are a complex but the key to understanding this situation is that there are two colour errors. Seeing what was really a green car as being red and seeing what was really a red car as green. Due to these errors our observer is far more likely to believe they saw a green car being involved in the accident than is actually possible (and this is before we consider secondary issues such as green car drivers being less able or less socially aware, or of bias against green car drivers by the observer).

This may sound strange but we either engage, at the level of public information, with how to read sources and look for flaws in logic and some understanding of basic statistical concepts, or we will lose the war against disinformation. There is much that can be done to make conspiracy theories less accessible and less readily promoted, and hopefully to stop populist politicians using it for short term electoral gain. But we live in an information-rich age, and the tools to interpret information must be equally readily accessible.

So yes, there is a need to be clear about public information. It behoves states to use clear language and to explain why a given policy is critical (especially during a global pandemic). But there is an element that falls on individual citizens: we either become aware of the tools to question information (and this is not 'do your own research') or we will constantly be vulnerable to conspiracy theories—especially those that happen to fit our wider world view. These will be critical themes in the penultimate chapter of this book.

A final part is to be aware of the obvious: people can present themselves as pretty much anything on the internet. And while the focus in this chapter is essentially on domestic politics, social media platforms are used by states such as Russia to meddle in the democratic processes of countries in Europe and the US. Between 2015 and 2017, Russian trolls impersonated Black and NRA activists, and used material hacked from the Democratic National Committee. One study found that 50,000-odd Twitter bots set up to share false information during the 2016 US election campaign tweeted about 19% of all the tweets related to the election: 3.8 million tweets. 80% of these supported Trump.[75]

In other words: on Twitter—one of the most significant channels through which Americans sought information to try to exercise their democratic right in 2020—20% of that information was either false, deliberately placed there by a hostile power, or both.

6

RUSSIA

Putin's Russia is a theme that runs across this book with its links to the new populist right and its use of social media as a tool of disinformation and disruption and, in international affairs, as a disruptive force along with its collection of client states. Its increasingly aggressive actions within the former Soviet Union have made it the primary threat to peace in Europe. To understand why it acts as a hostile power and in such a particular way means consideration of how Putin came to power, and of his backers and their goals.

Modern Russia is a product of a complex history. By the late Soviet era, there were tentative, but real, steps towards political pluralism and separating the legal system from direct state control, at the same time as key assets (both productive and raw materials) were kept firmly under state control. However, for export purposes, a series of arms-length companies were set up that created a veneer of non-state enterprises.[1] The period 1991–1999, under Yeltsin's leadership, saw privatisation of most state assets in such a way as to create something closer to a mafia economy rather than conventional free market capitalism.

The winners engaged in a strange form of politics, pluralist and open in many ways as each oligarch funded their own political parties and media outlets. Again not exactly a conventional liberal democracy but there was real pluralism and (sometimes) an enthusiasm to expose the misdeeds of the Yeltsin family or other oligarchs.

Putin's accession to power in late 1999 shifted these dynamics quickly. His pitch to the Russian people was to end the chaos and corruption of the post-Soviet era. To this end, the relative political pluralism rapidly ended as Russia became an early example of a 'managed' democracy, the legal system again became a weapon of state control and not justice, and elements of the economy were drawn back into state control. The latter in particular was an illusion as Putin's backers in the KGB essentially stripped assets from those they felt were out of their control and awarded those assets to more loyal, or more docile, oligarchs.[2] Catherine Belton argues this was a quite deliberate political programme, centred on the cadres of the old KGB to wrest back control.

In the late Soviet era, the KGB had been among the proponents for a semi-market economy and controlled almost all Soviet foreign trade. The ideology underpinning this had nothing to do with Marxism-Leninism (which they blamed for the economic woes from the 1970s onwards) but was one of restoring Russia as a major political, military and cultural power. In effect, the ideology side-stepped the seventy years of the Soviet Union and returned to the ethno-nationalism common in the late Tsarist era.

This mindset has informed Putin's actions in Russia, within the old Soviet Union and internationally.

Domestically, political pluralism had no place and all media outlets were steadily drawn back into state control. A variety of political parties were allowed to exist but any that seriously challenged Putin's rule were closed down and their leaders imprisoned.

Within the borders of the old USSR (or perhaps more accurately the old Tsarist empire) the goal was reintegration, especially of what were seen as the European Slavic republics. The relative regional independence within the Russian federation of the Yeltsin era was quickly ended and various political and economic bodies were set up to try and tie the old Soviet republics together. If Yeltsin had been serious in talking of an integrated economic space running from the Atlantic to the Pacific, Putin's vision was very different. The economies would trade internally and only approved interactions would happen with the outside world.

Finally, the 'West', especially institutions such as the EU or NATO or the USA, were held responsible for Soviet collapse and Russia's loss of status. And if they were responsible, then they would suffer the consequences, especially as they also represented the liberal model deemed ineffectual by the muscular ideology of the new Russia.

The new Russia lacked the capacity to turn its ire into military threat (apart from its nuclear weapons) but had both an interest, and a long-standing focus, on the values of subversion. Ominously for the West and for liberal democracy, Russia has inherited and further developed the propaganda apparatus and the information warfare methods of the old USSR. It relentlessly seeks points of internal division in the countries it deems as strategic enemies (principally the US, the EU and NATO), and spares no effort in trying to amplify them. And the logic is simple: the more time and energy we expend fighting amongst ourselves, the less time and energy we have to look at what Russia is doing in their claimed sphere of influence.

First using its international TV channels, and then social media, the method is not about promoting this or that policy, but rather about creating an environment of constant strife and contestation that hampers the normal democratic process, and over the longer term, altogether discredits the notion of democratic discourse as an effective means of governing a society. It is for these reasons that Russian state media in foreign languages has either created or amplified almost every conspiracy theory they could find, on the grounds that the proliferation of these conspiracy theories would be effective tools to undermine public trust in governance in our democracies. Worryingly it took the impact of Russia's invasion of Ukraine in early 2022 before restrictions were finally placed on Russia Today and Sputnik.

For these reasons, Russia has grown to be the most direct foreign threat to our liberal democracies, in terms of supporting populism, undermining democratic norms, and using social media to peddle conspiracy theories. But even as we look more closely at the nature and potency of these threats from Russia, and how we can tackle them, we should not lose sight of the bigger picture where, over the longer term, China will in fact be the more formidable challenge to the liberal world order. This is because, as we will see in the next chapter, China also does all of these things, but also offers an alternative mode of governance and economics, and a real alternative international structure based on trade, not just culture wars and political and personal affinity between authoritarian populists.

Historical context

In order to understand both the domestic and the international politics of Putin's Russia, one needs to understand the wider context not just of Soviet history, but of Russia both after and just before the Soviet political experiment.

Even as the Tsarist empire spread over huge swathes of Eurasia in the nineteenth century, it was an unstable state, and the nineteenth century was marked by a range of political and ethnic revolts as it conquered Central Asia but also areas within its traditional European heartlands. This led to a search for a unifying belief (beyond the autocratic rule of the Tsar) to create a stable basis for the state but which also justified the retention of autocratic rule. By the end of the nineteenth century, this emerged from various trends as a rather mystical view of Russia as a spiritually and morally superior polity over the 'decadent' West, a 'Third Rome' after the fall of the Byzantine Empire (which had protected Orthodoxy in its moment of crisis), the 'rightful heir' of Europe's Roman and (Orthodox) Christian heritage—in part cultural and in part due to its claimed leadership of the various Orthodox Churches. Domestically, it veered between repression and reform and used anti-Semitism (the Protocols of the Elders of Zion were a Tsarist forgery) as part of trying to suppress the various strands of political and nationalist dissent.

In international affairs however, Russia defined itself mostly as a European power, and successive Tsars did their utmost to make and maintain Russia as a key player among the Western empires, and as a pivotal part of Europe's security architecture. This led to some rapid shifts of alliances as the desire to support fellow autocrats in Prussia and Austria clashed with the problem that those states offered a direct threat to Russian interests in the Balkans and control over Poland. Thus France, notionally secular and ruled by the heirs of Napoleon or as a Republic, became a close ally from the 1860s. Relations with the British Empire, meanwhile, were mostly competitive, due to clashing ambitions in Central Asia, Afghanistan and India. At the same time the Russians took advantage of the relative weakness of China to cement its control over Siberia and, briefly, Manchuria.

The shift from an autocratic monarchy to a Marxist-Leninist state during the Russian Revolution of 1917–18 at one level marked fundamental changes in the political ideology and the practical tendencies of the state, but there were continuities. If the new regime was notionally atheist, it still allowed a special place for the Russian Orthodox Church, and it also retained elements of pan-Slavism.[3] The economic model was modernised, and feudal privileges were rooted out mercilessly, but the means of political control and 'nation-building' of the Tsarist empire aimed at the masses were, if anything continued with even more zeal and efficiency. Russification continued apace, predicated on the old Tsarist tropes about the moral status of the Slavic peoples; the uprooting and shuffling around of ethnic minorities in order to dilute their identities became a commonplace method of integration and control; and the incessant propaganda of the state was increasingly aimed not just at the economic revolution, but at the political and cultural creation of the 'Soviet man'—who implicitly was a Russian speaker. By the 1950s there is a case to be made that its Marxist-Leninist ideology became something to be referenced as a justification for policy choices[4] rather than the driving logic behind practical decisions. Equally its subversion efforts shifted from promoting its ideology to a combination of seeking to disrupt other states and the use of funds to pay for those willing to help. As a state founded on propaganda, the Soviet Union became notorious for dishonesty and for its willingness to assert any argument that suited it.

The late Soviet era saw economic collapse,[5] and the ideological project of nation-building, especially via Russification, became ever more central to maintaining order and the authority of the state. And core institutions of the state, especially the KGB, seem to have started to adapt in this direction surprisingly early on—see for example Catherine Belton's argument in *Putin's People*,[6] which suggests that the KGB had started to plan for the possibility of regime collapse by the early 1980s. This gave them control over the various Soviet–Western economic links, something they lost control over in the Yeltsin years and were determined to regain once Putin was in power.

RUSSIA

The initial post-Soviet era saw the complete collapse of the Soviet economy as the various republics became independent[7] and the emergence of different political trajectories in the new states. The three Baltic states quickly indicated their desire to align to the political, legal and economic structures of the EU and NATO. As noted in the China chapter, the five Central Asia Republics quickly adopted an authoritarian political structure (all but one saw exactly the same leaders remain in power) as they experimented with various degrees of economic liberalism. Of the European republics, Belarus basically saw the old guard rebrand their rule and retain Soviet norms of political and economic behaviour. Ukraine started from a similar position but from 2004[8] started to significantly diverge in terms of political norms, legal structures, economic model and an increasing desire to link to bodies such as the EU.

The Russian Federation became the legal successor to the USSR, taking on its debts, its nuclear arsenal and also its place on the UN Security Council. At that stage it was a great power in name only, unable to even end revolt in Chechnya and in 1998 had to declare itself bankrupt.[9] The post-Soviet privatisation fire sale of the state assets may have been largely done under the cover of the neoliberal exhortations of external bodies such as the IMF,[10] but it was handled in such a way that a small elite group of people were able to take control. What the international advisers missed was that the economic model they were imposing in Russia was not liberalising it and making it into a free market economy, but rather it was just legitimising the capture of the economy by parts of the old Soviet political and security elite.[11]

Many of these had had links to the KGB in the 1980s but also a number turned their backs on their former masters as they sought the political pluralism[12] they believed would enable them to retain their independence; and they started to seek greater wealth by bringing their companies to Western stock markets (especially the far more lax and compliant London over New York[13]). The reality of business in Russia was that it was still corrupt, disputes were often settled by violence, but there was an increasing integration into the corporate norms of the UK at least (where the New Labour government had little interest in asking difficult questions as long as the veneer of money being invested was retained).

Putin's accession fairly rapidly saw major changes. The relatively open political and media space was rapidly circumscribed and the legal system repurposed as an instrument of state control. Some of the oligarchs from the 1990s adapted easily to the new reality of paying Putin and his backers for the privilege of holding their assets, while others were more resistant. In turn that set off a series of corruption trials in Russia (and their assets were then transferred to those acceptable to Putin),[14] usage of Western (especially UK)[15] legal systems to wrest control over assets outside Russia and, increasingly, state-sanctioned murder of those who had fled abroad.

Fairly rapidly, the Russian Federation reverted to being a democracy in form only. Like the old Soviet Union there were a lot of votes; unlike the old Soviet Union their appeared to be political pluralism. But only parties acceptable to Putin had any chance (including some set up to provide an opposition) and anything that offered a threat was quickly outlawed. Superficially the economy had the same structure of rich individuals owning major assets and most external earnings coming from oil and gas. However, no one retained their assets unless they were subservient to Putin's regime and paid regular bribes. The KGB had effectively created the economy they had aimed at since the 1980s, with some relaxation of direct state control but almost all under state direction. There were greater foreign earnings, but all linked to companies that were fully part of the informal network of mafia-style fiefdoms[16] run by clients of the KGB.

This is not to frame the Russian Federation as simply the successor state to the USSR—not least because by the late years of the USSR the state was already wearing its communist ideology lightly.[17] Also, as above, state control of the economy had shifted from ownership and direction to ensuring those who ran key sectors paid their bribes and were loyal to the regime. However, businesses were no longer vehicles for economic growth or prosperity; they were tools by which favours and cash were exchanged. This has had a devastating effect on the non-petrochemical sectors of the Russian economy over the last twenty years. It left Putin and his backers with a problem after 2000. Offering to end the chaos of the Yeltsin years gained them short-term support but they needed to ensure retention of power, influence and wealth in the country. This led to a revival of the sort of ideology that had marked the final years of Tsarism: pan-Slavism, Russia as the saviour of Western civilisation and the role of the Orthodox Church. In effect, the building blocks of most contemporary populist movements as a form of ethno-nationalism veering towards fascism.

It was in the service of this model of political control that Putin's regime also pioneered and implemented most of the political techniques that would later become the model for the various right-wing populist parties we have today in Europe and North America. He captured the legal system to act as an agency of the state, subservient to executive power under the guise of speaking for 'the will of the people',[18] the bounds of political discourse were policed strictly to exclude any genuinely independent actors, even if the guise of political pluralism is maintained by allowing for 'vetted' opposition parties; civil society organisations that are not in lock-step with the goals and methods of the state were labelled as agents of foreign power and constrained or cracked down on relentlessly; universal human rights were derided as the 'unnatural' imposition of 'Western imperialism'; individuals belonging to minorities of sexual orientation, political orientation or religion were persecuted in the name of the majority identity; and so on. The 'ideology' of the state thus became a loose collection of extreme ethno-nationalist themes, majoritarian identity politics and fantastical rewritings of history with few real constants in the detail, with an overriding fixation on the role of the Soviet Union in defeating Nazi Germany in 1945.[19]

Internationally this approach had a range of supporters. Some in the far left, bereft at the fall of the USSR, saw in Putin's regime some form of ideological succession.[20] This led them to support Putin's actions in Georgia, the Crimea and eastern Ukraine in very much the language they had used to defend the old USSR. However, this wishful thinking misses the hard fact that there was no ideological transfer;[21] Putin and his KGB cabal blamed communism for the Soviet Union's[22] economic and political demise. Their ideology actually side-stepped communism and had reverted to the sort of ethno-nationalism common in the late Tsarist era. As such, the bulk of his international support has come from the populist right.

The ideological mindset is well summarised by Alexander Kramerenko, a foreign affairs advisor to Putin. Specifically seeking to defend the 2022 invasion of Ukraine, he framed Russia's apparently exceptional position in terms of:

> the substance of Western culture, which is alien to humanity. In the 19th century, our culture took the baton from the West, which had fallen into permanent crisis. ... Western culture, with its 'Faustian soul'..., has exhausted its spiritual and creative potential. The keepers of European culture: enlightened humanism, Dante, Cervantes, and Shakespeare (it's far from coincidence that we began where they left off), were destined to become Russia, which by that point had completed Peter's modernization (Russia answered Peter's call with the genius of

Pushkin) and provided strategic depth for Orthodox Christianity (after the fall of Constantinople in 1453). ... in Russia blooms a geopolitical tradition of the interaction of its fate with that of Europe, in which Russia is called upon to play a defining role in the world.[23]

This may read as incoherent ramblings to fresh eyes, but this is the ideological rhetoric which the large majority of Russians who watch state TV news have been hearing for at least two decades. These themes about the 'decadence' of the West will also be familiar to those who have followed the political discourse of the populist movements in our own countries.[24] The likes of Steve Bannon, Marine Le Pen, Nigel Farage, Viktor Orbán and Matteo Salvini (among plenty of others)—some of whom are thought to have ties to Russian finance, in the absence of Western backing—have sought the support and endorsements of Putin because they are all singing from the same ideological hymn sheet. This gives Putin a reliable international chorus for his actions and in people like Orbán, supporters quite prepared to undermine the EU from within, even after the invasion of Ukraine in 2022.

It is in this way that the foreign relations element to the problems of populism, conspiracy theories and the role of social media comes into our discussion on what is happening to our democracies. The main fount of this ideology, of these themes, the place where many of these messages were created and where these methods were pioneered, originates with Putin's regime[25] in Russia. And the messages are used as weapons against our democracies both by our own populists and by the Kremlin itself, in the same way that they have been used for two decades against the people of Russia. So how can we fight against this ideological tide?

Goals

In order to counteract this aggression aimed at our political culture and system of governance, we must understand what motivates it. As noted above, despite the wishes of elements of the far left internationally,[26] Putin's Russia is not the USSR reformed and unlike the USSR in the past, or China in the present, it has neither the hard power nor the cultural influence to even attempt to achieve such a role.

In practice, the domestic goal of the regime is to shore up its power, and to divert as much wealth as possible into its own pockets. This wealth in turn may be, and is, frequently used as a tool of influence and power, both for keeping local clients of the oligarchy under control, and also for corrupting, disrupting or even threatening foreign actors that might pose a threat to the regime in one way or another. The most shocking example of the corruption of almost an entire political establishment of a major rival country, for instance, has been in the UK which has been used to launder the proceeds into states that chose not to ask too many questions.[27] Russia's oligarchs became major, almost indispensable, clients of 'the City', the financial sector that is the UK's largest export industry. But this influence has also spread to more visible aspects of public life, such as cultural and sporting institutions, and even political life. The traditional centre-right Conservative Party, for example, was still actively seeking campaign funding in the period before the invasion of Ukraine;[28] Russian support for the eventually successful Brexit campaign was probably pivotal in many ways, and the local populist powerhouse, Nigel Farage, has close if obscured ties to transatlantic Russian interests. But it should be noted that the same model has been attempted, and implemented to various degrees on the American populist right and in the Republican Party, as well as the populist right in France, Italy and Germany—

to say nothing of the partisan political meddling in the nascent democracies of Ukraine (prior to the invasion), Moldova, Georgia or Armenia.

So we have a state that is economically weak, where wealth extraction trumps wealth creation and is effectively dependent on international sales of oil and gas for its income. As we are seeing in Ukraine it is struggling to turn this wealth into real military power and its own domestic ideology has little or no salience outside its borders. So it is not a geopolitical challenger in any conventional use of that phrase, but it has probably become the powerhouse behind the disruption of Western democracies in the last twenty years.

Recreating the Soviet Union?

Those around Putin are clear they wish to restore Russia to its rightful place as a great power. Within the borders of what was the Soviet Union this looks like the reconstitution of the power and influence of the Tsarist empire at its zenith. The advantage of that, in their eyes, compared to the USSR, was that the empire was a unified political entity, not one built off notionally independent Republics. The attraction to them was that no one ignored Russia; it had a place by right at every international discussion and it strongly influenced the emerging Slavic states such as Bulgaria and Serbia. Its place as the head of Orthodoxy even gave it influence in places like Ethiopia.[29] So returning Russia to its proper status means addressing the geographical splintering of the empire that happened in 1991, along the line of ill-conceived republics put in place by the Soviets.

This is the first consequence for the international system of Russian revanchism. When the USSR imploded, the constituent republics found themselves as independent nation states. Nevertheless, most of these states tried to maintain their prior economic and political ties with one another, for example, through various international bodies such as the Confederation of Independent States (CIS) or regional grouping such as those of the Central Asian republics, in part due to leadership continuity and in part due to the nature of the existing trade links. The Russian Federation remained as the dominant economic and political state among them. The exception was the three Baltic States that rapidly opted for Western integration by joining the EU and NATO.

The Russian Federation was the largest single state but was also one that included a substantial mix of ethnic groups, many with their own distinct regions. Under Yeltsin, there was tolerance of a move to greater effective independence as long as they agreed to remain with the Federation. One of the first steps of Putin in power was to reverse this trend. More widely Putin is on record[30] as saying that the biggest flaw in the USSR was that it took the unitary Tsarist state and created a series of false nations, and this mindset drives his behaviour towards the territories of the former USSR—what some Russians came to call the 'near abroad'.[31] In practice, Putin seems to have accepted the relative independence of the Central Asian republics and even tolerates the growing Chinese influence in the region, so long as authoritarian rulers friendly to Russia remain in power. Perhaps the only country in that region that is held on a shorter leash is Kazakhstan, which is oil- and gas-rich and also has a relatively large Russian population. Equally, Putin seems to be accepting greater Turkish influence in Azerbaijan,[32] which in any case serves Moscow's purposes vis-à-vis Armenia and Georgia. However, it is what they see as the really Russian states of Ukraine and Belarus where the focus has been on forcing close unity even if actual reunification is beyond their reach.

In consequence, Putin's position on the former USSR states in Europe that are geographically close to the Russian heartland is much more hard-line: in Belarus and at least some parts of Ukraine he is pushing for unification with Russia, while in the rest of the former USSR lands he has tried to render them utterly dependent on Russia both politically and economically.

The problem for Putin is that, while the leadership of Belarus is a willing accomplice to his schemes (and utterly dependent on Russian power to shore up their own rule), other states, especially Ukraine, Georgia and Armenia, have their own ideas as to their future. From about 2002 onwards, the previous Soviet-era leaders in these states had stepped down and to a greater or lesser extent a degree of domestic democracy took root. With this, many started to look to the EU, and the former Warsaw Pact states in Eastern Europe, as part of their future.

This did not mean cutting ties with Russia or turning their back on a long history of close links and interdependence. It did mean looking at the world afresh. But Putin has a zero-sum mindset: if Georgia was speaking to the EU then his influence was being diminished. In seeking to assert Russian primacy his various assaults on his neighbours from 2008 to 2022 have had the effect of strengthening their interest in a balanced set of alliances. And each such step takes them further away from Putin's dreams of reforging the geographical bounds of the Tsarist Empire.

His first direct act of aggression to stop the spread of independent-minded democracy was aimed at Georgia in 2008, under pretexts that would become all too familiar about protecting ethnic Russians from persecution. The growing democratisation of the country, its relatively successful anti-corruption campaign and, critically, its growing links to the EU,[33] were marginalising the local political clients of the Kremlin in the Caucasus, and to Putin this meant that these developments needed to be stopped. His willing propagandists in the West repeated the Moscow line that the invasion was provoked by expanding US interests (in this the US and EU are often interchangeable despite the substantial real differences),[34] paying little mind, of course, to the wishes of the people of Georgia themselves.

Successive interventions in Ukraine were similarly prompted by increasing democratic support for pro-Western politicians in Kyiv, and increasing popular opposition to the rampant corruption especially among the Kremlin-backed economic and political elite that dominated the country in the first two decades after independence. The annexation of the Crimea in 2014 was a massive escalation compared to the previous modus operandi of the Kremlin in the region, but it was consistent with Moscow's previous actions in response to the growing democratic culture in Ukraine (and which from 2013 started to talk about closer alignment to the EU).

A similar claim of protecting ethnic Russians (now increasingly from 'Nazis' in Putin's propaganda) led to the invasion and quasi-separation of the Donetsk region from the rest of Ukraine after 2014. Again the trigger seems to have been Ukraine's increasing turn to the west in terms of political culture. Clearly all this has come together in the full-scale invasion of Ukraine.

At the start of the war in Ukraine it seemed that Putin was aiming to end Ukraine's democratic reforms and ensure it was closely tied to Russia. But the escalating propaganda about the depth of 'Nazi' influence on Ukrainian society[35] suggests something akin to occupation had become the desired goal, even if militarily it is probably beyond the capacity of the Russian army.

Putin is clearly convinced that he cannot allow the states that were formerly part of the USSR or of the broader Russian sphere of influence to become successful democracies for at least two reasons. First, most ordinary people in these countries do not look to Moscow for governance, or even as a model of how to run their own countries—citizens who want to live in democracies have nothing to learn in terms of either politics or of economics from Russia, and this means that functional democracies are simply not amenable to be part of Moscow's sphere of influence. Such people do not want to be bossed around by a tyrant like Putin. And second, what example would it give to the people of Russia if Ukraine would become democratically and economically thriving like the Baltics, for example? And what would that do to Putin's authority within Russia?

And so, Putin has to be an enemy of democracy in the lands of the former USSR, and indeed anywhere where he wishes to carve out a sphere of influence. Consequently, he also has to be an enemy of the well-functioning and prosperous democracies that keep enticing the people he seeks to control in Eastern Europe, in the Caucasus, in Central Asia, and even in Russia itself. Even if the former unitary state has to remain a set of notionally separate entities, Putin does want to set strict limits for the modes of governance and wider international orientation of the former Soviet republics. Clearly this is easier where he can work with like-minded authoritarian rulers and intervene to shore up their power. As Ukraine, Georgia and the Baltic States indicate, he reverts to open force and direct threats when they start to become too independently minded. This makes the democracies in the West something of a strategic enemy given his zero-sum mindset. The institutions that promote cooperation and democracy such as the EU become a specific target for his actions, and those of his populist proxies.[36]

Disrupting the West

If democracy is necessarily predicated on building consensus through public discussion and negotiation between different interests and different points of view, then the tools of social control developed in Russia during the Soviet era, and further refined during Putin's tenure, are uniquely potent disruptors of our system of governance. Especially when transmitted using social media and amplified by the various populist actors.

From early on, a key aspect to Soviet disruption efforts against the West during the Cold War was to deliberately blur the line between reality and fantasy.[37] The propaganda employed by the Soviets was always designed to be credible, but they never thought that it needed to be true—indeed, eroding trust in the notion of a shared reality was a core aim, precisely because having a shared notion of reality is so essential to a democracy. This feature of Soviet political technology was observed early on. In the 1930s this had the veneer of an ideology but the underlying mindset was to create an environment where nothing could be disbelieved as being false and everything could be challenged. The British diplomat, Fitzroy Maclean, when he observed the Moscow show trials in the mid-1930s,[38] noted that the prosecution case was a mix of the fantastical—with some elements clearly made up—with great weight being placed on small incidents with their role distorted. And set within this, there were attempts to bring in verifiable information, the latter playing the useful role that Soviet apologists could point to it as proving the veracity of the whole charade.

As tools for domestic control, these approaches were not unique to the Soviet Union. Similar patterns could be observed in most pre-war dictatorships.[39] What made the Soviet Union different is that it then started to deploy the very same tools in the foreign affairs arena, especially after the Second World War, as one of the two global centres of power—meaning that the Soviet Union effectively institutionalised the use of such techniques as a normal feature of global politics, both within its sphere of influence and within the West. Soviet subterfuge came to take on three forms: of the recruitment of individuals who would spy for the USSR (either on grounds of ideological affinity or for money), the funding and support of the various foreign Communist Parties, and a wider attempt to undermine the shared core essential to support a liberal democracy.

By the 1980s, most of those recruited to spy did so for financial reasons rather than ideological affinity; the orthodox Communist Parties were mostly either electorally irrelevant, or, like the Italians, increasingly critical of the USSR.[40] There was some direct support for the various left-wing terrorist groups active at that stage[41] but primarily the focus was on the disruption of social norms and shared beliefs. Unfortunately for the USSR (but fortunately for the West) both the means to distribute this and the audience was relatively limited, and attempts to justify the war in Afghanistan were undermined by a degree of official acknowledgement that it was a disaster.[42] The attempt to cover up the Chernobyl nuclear accident probably undermined what little credibility the system had left[43] both domestically and internationally. However, the network for this propaganda, its potential usefulness and the needed funding[44] was all in place and run by the KGB up to the collapse of the USSR. And all the evidence is that this framework survived the fall of the state and was picked up increasingly after Putin came to power.[45]

But Putin's regime did innovate in some unexpected and highly effective ways on the old formulas. They will, for example, also use these tools to promote causes they do not actively care about, and indeed, even causes they would, in principle, oppose. For instance, they put considerable effort into amplifying the cause of Catalonian independence, which culminated in an abortive referendum in 2017, and similarly into the fall-out after the referendum on Scottish independence in 2014.[46] Putin is vehemently opposed to the rights of small nations to secede, but these kinds of political event have proven highly polarising in the countries where they are happening, and it fits the Kremlin's agenda to increase polarisation and therefore democratic dysfunction anywhere in the Western alliance.

The ecosystem of Kremlin TV Networks such as Russia Today and Sputnik[47] have become important. Presenting themselves as offering an alternative to biased sources such as the BBC, it has become a home for many populists sympathetic to the Kremlin's propaganda. Usefully this adds an external dimension to raising doubts about the war crimes of the Russian army in Syria[48] which are then referenced on their main news as evidence that the issue is contested. Whether the atrocity was the use of chemical weapons, bombing aid convoys, or indiscriminate attacks on civilian areas, a recognisable cast of Western politicians and commentators outside of the liberal mainstream would readily appear on Russian state-owned outlets to deny what had happened, blame the 'West'[49] and smear the victims.[50]

Television such as Russia Today does not exist to be watched, it exists to generate short clips that can be used on social media to obscure what has happened and to spread a particular argument.[51] It also happily picks up what it sees as friendly or useful commentary on right-wing news stations such as Fox when that provides external collaboration to its arguments.[52] When even more partisan outlets such as GB News in the UK[53] start to promote the same arguments and claims, then a closed echo chamber is formed. Naturally Fox News forms a key part in this system.[54] One part can raise a controversial viewpoint, another will then pick it up as a controversy, and finally it can be presented as part of the legitimate 'debate', and carefully curated for circulation on social media.

As they moved substantial wealth from Russia, the Russian oligarchy have found a friendly legal and financial infrastructure of those eager to launder and normalise the gains they extracted, to find them grand homes to live in, football clubs to buy, and generally convert money that is often illegally obtained into the currency of the best style of living available in cities like London.[55] And once this veneer of respectability was attained, the natural next step was to fund legitimate right-wing political parties and politicians such as the British Conservatives.[56] Italy has proved similarly attractive, with the route map well developed by Berlusconi's earlier close links to the Gaddafi family regime.[57]

Initially, these efforts were probably less about buying a political agenda, and more about buying political protection for their lifestyle. The result in the longer term, however, was that they created an environment where Russian money had increasingly become relied upon by the Conservative electoral machine, and consequently, the influence of the oligarchs (and especially of the 'Londongrad' business model that could be applied just as well to non-Russian plutocrats) was readily accepted, and there was a correspondingly strong unwillingness to challenge this system of wealth and power.[58] The net effect of this is that some senior British politicians were close enough to the regime for their motives when making decisions to be placed in doubt.[59]

The ways in which this influence turns into disruption have been laid bare most clearly in the growing current of Euroscepticism that the Kremlin has been all too happy to nurture. And the crowning achievement of the Eurosceptic movement has been Brexit. When the UK voted to leave the EU in 2016, the outcome surprised many, including those senior Conservative politicians who had fronted the campaign.[60] But far from the beautiful exercise of the 'will of the people' through participatory democracy that the Brexit referendum was sold as by the proponents of Brexit, the entire campaign itself was extremely divisive and bad tempered, even culminating in the murder of a Labour politician by a pro-Brexit far-right extremist—the first murder of an MP in Britain not killed by members of an Irish Republican group. The campaign was also dominated by social media discourse, and heavily featured baseless claims peddled by both sides: the perfect environment for the Russian disinformation machine to sow distrust and social division—which, incidentally, the British government were warned[61] of in advance, especially in the light of Russian activity after the conclusion of the Scottish independence referendum two years earlier.

There have been persistent questions about the funding behind the 'Vote Leave' organisation, set up for the campaign to leave the EU, and the extent to which this was supplied from Russia. There are a series of links between senior players in this group and organisations such as Gazprom,[62] and those individuals subsequently had considerable influence over how the Conservative government interpreted the narrow divisive vote to leave as a mandate for extreme dislocation of the UK's ties with the EU.[63] Related to this was the decision to use Cambridge Analytica (as noted in the social media chapter) to acquire considerable information on potential leave voters (without their consent) and to use this as the basis of an illegal targeted advertising campaign.[64] Subsequent to the vote there were several enquiries, and fines were issued, around this behaviour but the Conservative government, which contained senior politicians who had been part of the campaign, were not interested in exploring the role of the Russian links.[65]

In many ways the outcome is perfect for the Kremlin. The EU was weakened and the cloud of suspicion about the campaign to leave still pollutes UK politics and ensures it remains fractured and fractious. And a polity marked by deep internal divisions is very vulnerable to further Russian interference and likely to fall into the hands of domestic populists, as happened from 2018.

Still, the main 'adversary' that Putin seeks to disrupt is the United States. And his efforts there have also been quite successful, building on existing fault lines and a media and political structure open to populist arguments. To work, this does not have to be successful, simply to leave a legacy of contentious politics. As with Brexit, the election of Trump in 2016 was partly down to some extremely well-timed interventions from the Russian information warfare machine: notably the DNC hack and the release of the internal emails of the Hilary Clinton campaign which is believed to have depressed critical Democratic turnout, and created an ongoing dynamic in US politics that is fundamentally divisive. In the words of the bipartisan US Senate Intelligence Committee's report:

> Russian President Vladimir Putin ordered the Russian effort to hack computer networks and accounts affiliated with the Democratic Party and leak information damaging to Hillary Clinton ... Moscow's intent was to harm the Clinton Campaign, tarnish an expected Clinton presidential administration, help the Trump Campaign ... and undermine the U.S. democratic process.[66]

In this Putin has been far more successful than his Soviet predecessors. In the main, the US was relatively immune to Soviet subversion (but not Soviet espionage) as the US Communist Party was marginalised and US norms of a somewhat robust democracy left little space for those who wished to sit outside it. When it is possible to nominate a pig to be President then the democratic space is near universal[67] even if it is mediated through two dominant political parties. But the flip side of this is that if people feel a pig is an improvement over the official candidates, there is a degree of dislocation from the political norms of the mainstream.

As I have argued earlier in this book, populism is partly a response to more and more people feeling alienated by the status quo. In the US, these dynamics have been in play for far longer than Putin's efforts to disrupt it as a democracy. Yet President Trump clearly leaned not only on the populist sentiments of a large segment of Americans who have long felt left behind; he also leaned on support from Vladimir Putin, and his campaign actively sought both funding and information from the Russians.[68] And it is equally clear that Putin is one of the main beneficiaries of the fragmentation of US politics and society that Trump further catalysed. And of note is that this division and fragmentation, as well as Putin's role in these dynamics, remain much more pronounced in the US than in Europe. Whereas even the British Conservatives are energetically turning their back on their earlier links to Putin as a result of the invasion of Ukraine, the willingness to repeat the Russian version of events and to spread pro-Russian conspiracy theories remains common among Republican politicians and their media outriders[69].

Foreign interventions

The final strand of Putin's general approach to international relations has been the application of military power outside the former USSR. The most notable instance of this has been his backing for Assad's regime in Syria. In the main, this was a conventional military intervention, although a second dimension of it soon emerged as Moscow realised that the more it brutalised the civilian population of Syria, the larger the numbers of refugees that would flee from the country,[70] which in turn could be weaponised to politically destabilise the EU.[71] And this helped the electoral support of the very far-right populists across Europe that Moscow was already sponsoring.

But the Syrian Civil War also saw Russia's propaganda powers expand, as online disinformation was seen seeping into mainstream political discourse about how the West should respond to the atrocities committed by Assad and his Russian allies against civilians, especially as it related to the use of chemical weapons that had been a long-established taboo in international law. Russia's 'useful idiots' in the West, the populists of both left and right, latched on to every doubt manufactured by the Russian propaganda machine,[72] and this is what ultimately allowed the use of these weapons against civilians, an unambiguous crime against humanity, to go unpunished.[73] That was the first time since the end of the Cold War that Russia's propaganda efforts had had such profound consequences for the international order. Though it would not be the last. The model of warfare developed by the Russians in Chechnya, then exported to Syria, is being applied in 2022 in Ukraine.

More widely, Russian has shown itself willing to intervene in almost any conflict that the US or other Western powers have also shown an interest in. If Washington supported one side in the Libyan Civil War, Russia would send in mercenaries from the notorious Wagner group to support the other side and help derail the peace process in 2019,[74] not out of any particular affinity to one faction or the other but simply to prolong the war. If the West has condemned the military coup in Myanmar, and is (at least rhetorically) supporting the pro-democracy resistance, Moscow jumped to be the first power to supply the junta with weapons and international cover for their human rights abuses. If the French have spent years trying to stem the tide of Islamist insurgencies in sub-Saharan Africa, Russia duly deployed its propaganda machine to disparage and undermine those French efforts to stabilise the region, and then once again moved its own mercenaries into the battlefield to make sure the conflict would continue. And each of these interventions is marked by human rights abuses and support for local authoritarian rulers.

The pattern here is once again one of disruption. Wherever the West, and especially the US, take an interest in the stability of a region and try to support political actors that would like to operate within the rules-based order of the international community, Moscow takes an interest in keeping and amplifying instability and conflict. The rationale appears to be two-fold.

Political actors that want to be part of a rules-based international order seem to the Kremlin to be naturally gravitating towards the Western sphere of influence, and must therefore be opposed. And second, agents of instability who oppose the Western-orientated order need weapons to fight their conflicts, and Moscow is eager to be their main supplier. You will note that Russia's arms-manufacturing sector is the only industrial sector in the country that is still internationally competitive, and it is the only other major export category for Russia outside of primary resource extraction.

In other words, the West wants to build a stable, rules-based international order. And, by the way, to a large extent so does China, though the rules China cares about are essentially economic, and it has no interest in any of the other aspects of international law. But Russia's niche in today's geopolitical struggle is to be the main disruptor of other powers' efforts to create order. In the main, this is aimed at the order promoted by the United States, not least because China's alternative proposed order does not disrupt Putin's model of political power in Russia and his 'near abroad'. But if China eventually prevailed in imposing its own alternative order over the international community, Russia would likely still have to persevere in its niche as promoters of chaos. This is a consequence of weakness. Russia does not have anything positive to offer the world as a model for either politics or for economic development, and this is the only way for Russia to remain globally relevant. Thus, it is only in the form of actors of chaos that it can satisfy its delusional ambitions of 'national greatness'.

And we have seen one global power—Russia—meddle in the elections of another—the United States—explicitly using conspiracy theories as a weapon to sow division and mistrust

A response

Before the invasion of Ukraine in early 2022, the international response to Putin's actions was limited. Clearly his populist allies saw little to challenge and continued to take his funds and promote his arguments. Political parties such as the British Conservatives were awash in Russian funds, closely linked to the Russian expatriate presence in London, while the US Republicans were keen to suppress any investigation into the 2016 elections. Even mainstream countries such as Germany were limited in their response due to the decision to become reliant on Russian gas supplies.

So various attacks, including the use of chemical weapons in the UK, provoked limited responses, with some sanctions aimed at individuals. But no one really wanted to talk about what to do in response to Putin's blatant interference in domestic politics or to acknowledge the many authoritative reports that set his ambitions down clearly.[75]

The invasion of Ukraine in 2022 has been hard to ignore, unlike earlier aggression in Georgia, the Crimea or the Donbas. And this clarity has provoked Germany to a serious reappraisal of its links with Russia, and individuals such as Le Pen to try and rewrite the history of their shared links, while Conservatives such as Boris Johnson have sought to present themselves as stern critics of the Russian regime.[76] Other parts of Putin's network have stayed loyal. Populists such as Nigel Farage reliably push the Russian narrative, Orbán is undermining EU attempts to move towards serious sanctions and the US Republicans, now so absorbed in ethno-nationalist ideologies, remain supportive. Fox News is often favourably cited on Russia Today due to its favourable coverage of Russian arguments.[77]

Despite this, there is now a wider consensus that we have a problem with the actions of Putin's regime. What is lacking is an understanding of how to respond beyond sanctions, asset seizures from pro-regime oligarchs and the slow process of rebalancing Europe's energy sources to eliminate dependence on Russian gas. Putin's wider gamble around his invasion of Ukraine is that the 'West' lacks the moral fibre to really follow through with these actions. In the opening months of the invasion NATO has supported Ukraine with the transfer of military capacity and this has gone a long way to effectively halting Russia's attack. The emerging challenge is whether this can be sustained into the winter (and likely energy shortages), to the point where Ukraine is supported to recover from the devastation. And this matters: to Putin the West is effete and weak and in the end will only follow its short-term interests.

So the first part of responding to Putin's aggressions is to name them as such, challenge them and, yes, adjust our economies to isolate his regime. This needs to be moderated by common sense; there is no route to externally imposed regime change but the more his approach is shown to fail the more likely it is he will be removed. His backers, and the oligarchs, like their lives in the West; they like the access their money gave them and the loss of that hurts. This may see little but a change in the figurehead, but even that would help. With hindsight, many observers missed how profound the change was when Yeltsin gave way to Putin; replacing Putin opens the scope for a similar reset.

The other part to a response is to essentially turn Putin's model of information warfare on him. If he seeks to create division, let us do the same. There are plenty of fault lines in the Russian Federation and plenty of people doing very badly under his rule. So far this has been a one-way bet for Putin; we need to be prepared to respond in kind. This is uncomfortable but we have a very uncomfortable regime to deal with.

I will return to the wider issues in terms of resetting international relations in a later chapter.

7

CHINA

In 1991, China might have stood outside the new international order but it did not yet offer a relevant alternative model of global governance. Nevertheless, it had started to create its own development model before the fall of the USSR and this steadily took on an international dimension after 1991. Initially this saw an attempt to tie the former Soviet republics in Central Asia economically to China rather than Russia, but on a wider scale it was essentially the export of Chinese capital to new locations (primarily Africa and Central Asia) allied to having no interest in promoting a wider human rights agenda. All that China appeared to wish from its new allies was domestic stability. As in the states that emerged from the Soviet Union, this led to the creation of what can be called 'managed democracies' where the veneer of a democratic system (elections, multiple parties) existed but with little real impact. Pragmatically, the Chinese don't seem to really care: if a classic one-party regime wishes to accept its aid, that is acceptable; if one that still has a degree of democracy looks for its aid, then, again, that seems to be acceptable.

This leads to a complex picture. In many ways the West has gained from the Chinese model. Its difference to the US–UK approach means it has weathered several economic crises, such as 2008, in a way that has helped global recovery. Equally it is not just the Global South that has sought Chinese capital to fund domestic infrastructure; the UK (especially in the 2010–16 period) and Italy have done so substantively. Where China presents a real threat is as an alternative. Crudely it seeks to portray its domestic economic model as having the advantage of not being a democracy; its wider success is then used to argue that there is no link between economic growth and political liberalism. In terms of its international investment (the Belt and Road Initiative) it then offers a clear deal: accept Chinese investment, deliver domestic stability, and there will be no difficult demands around corruption or for political pluralism. Not surprisingly many authoritarian regimes find this an attractive package.

There are several large buts to this reading. If there is a direction of travel when a state is under Chinese influence it is from what could be called managed democracies back to autocracy, in contrast to the hopes prevalent in the early 1990s when such systems were seen as a temporary situation as a state moved from authoritarian to full democratic rule. These managed democracies appear in the early 2020s to be stable, with no evidence that their elites have any intention of risking the vagaries of full democracy. Equally, states are finding that life within the Belt and Road Initiative can be uncomfortable. China may make few demands in terms of reform of governance but it expects full payment for its investment—both in terms of cash and loyalty.

In terms of supporting populism, undermining democratic norms and using social media to peddle conspiracy theories, Putin's Russia is probably the most direct threat. However, China has adopted some aspects of the Russian playbook of disruption, and is getting increasingly competent at wielding similar information warfare techniques as the Kremlin. Even so, China is not intent on being an agent of chaos in the same way that Moscow is, which in turn means that its deployment of these tools is much more circumspect: it does not wish to undermine faith in all governance, not least because it want to promote its own political and economic model as overall beneficial to humanity. However, what China will do is to turn the full force of its ire on a state it deems to be too independent, something that Australia in particular has faced in recent years.[1]

In that respect, and allied with its far more successful economy, Beijing is a real competitor to the international hegemony of the United States, and of Western-style liberal democracy, mainly because it is seriously trying to offer a structured alternative.

Context

China at the start of the twentieth century was falling apart. Various Western powers had de facto control over the major eastern ports, Russia occupied Manchuria (and would soon lose it in turn to Japan) and the country had endured probably the bloodiest civil war in history in the Taipei Rebellion. Possibly the only real success of the Qing Dynasty was to reassert Chinese control over what is now Xinjiang[2] (and more widely into Central Asia). The dynasty was overthrown in 1911 and the new Republic effectively fell apart into a series of enclaves. By the 1930s, some of these, such as Xinjiang, were nearly fully independent (and the local leftist administration much closer to the USSR), the Chinese communists had carved out their own region in the north-west, and in 1937 Japan invaded. In a war of utter brutality, by 1941 Japan had taken almost all of the eastern coastal provinces.

The collapse of Japanese rule in 1945 set off a new civil war between the Communists and the Nationalists. Initially the Nationalists seemed likely to succeed but the Communists were bolstered when the Soviets withdrew from Manchuria and basically set them up as the local administration. In 1949, the People's Republic of China was announced, under Chairman Mao Zedong, and the Nationalists withdrew to Taiwan while some isolated forces retreated across the border into Burma.[3] Mao's rule was initially marked by substantial repression of individuals, social classes and ethnic groups seen to be unreliable,[4] with this particularly targeting the Muslim populations of central and western China. The 'Great Leap Forward' in the 1950s was an economic disaster while domestically the 1960s were dominated by the chaos of the Cultural Revolution.

By the 1980s, Deng Xiaoping sought to bring a degree of political calm and also restructure China's domestic economy.[5] At its core was a more pragmatic attitude to economic organisation and the acquisition of personal wealth. In its initial stages, China became a cheap mass producer of the most basic goods but over time the economy developed and China started to outsource some of its production to cheaper locations. Interpreting these changes provoked a range of views. To some this was China turning its back on Marxism-Leninism (as reinterpreted by Mao) and embracing capitalism[6] as an economic system while rejecting political pluralism. Others saw a combination of a potentially huge domestic market and finding a balance between state direction (especially of large capital projects) and an innovative economy as marking the economic paradigm of the future.[7] On the other hand, some saw in this mix a fundamental flaw that China would become stuck between a full capitalist economy and the degree of political control the Party wished to retain.[8]

The economy certainly modernised but social problems worsened as the Maoist 'iron rice bowl' social contract fell apart. It also adapted and developed its technological base through a series of experiments[9] but it remained fundamentally reliant on technology theft to fuel its advances.[10]

However, what Deng was not prepared to compromise on was the retention of the single party state. The massacre of the pro-democracy protesters in Tiananmen Square in 1989 made this plain to all. China in effect turned its back on the nascent Soviet experiment in political pluralism and instead took the view that a liberalised market could coexist with an authoritarian state. For some time it steadily allowed more individual freedoms but not in the sphere of political action.

By 2015 there is a case for saying this approach was paying off for China. China increasingly designs the technology which shapes our world. It leads the world in surveillance, facial recognition technology, 5G, and synthetic biology. It has twice as many supercomputers as the US. The US National Security Commission[11] has said openly that the US is at great risk of falling behind China. There is a good chance that the next generation of great tech companies which will create and build the technology that our children and grandchildren use will be designed to reflect the values of the Chinese Communist Party in terms of ethics and privacy rules. That the data collected from the 'internet of things' will flow back to China.

China had become a part of the global economic system, was a member of key international bodies (some more successfully than others[12]) and its tensions with the US and its neighbours were manageable. The Belt and Road Initiative was giving it influence across Asia and Africa and into Europe where states such as Greece, Italy and the UK were seeking Chinese investment where domestic funding was lacking.[13] Its growing, increasingly totalitarian, domestic surveillance systems[14] (which it was also exporting to other regimes looking to suppress domestic dissent) were largely ignored,[15] as was the clear evidence of genocide in Xinjiang.[16]

China is also developing its own model of influencing perceptions. The United Front, the Communist Party's influence project, creates educational and exchange programmes abroad and tries to shape the conversation among Chinese exile communities. Its economic expansion makes countries more reliant on it for consumption, raw materials, technology, and bond purchases. In turn, they have more to lose from challenging its policies diplomatically.

When they do, China often retaliates. In 2010, the Nobel Prize Committee gave the Peace Prize to Liu Xiaobo, a Chinese dissident. China responded by banning Norwegian salmon imports. In 2021, Lithuania let Taiwan open a representative office in Vilnius. China recalled its ambassador, stopped Lithuanian goods from entering its territory, and warned European companies such as Continental not to use Lithuanian components.[17] It has tried similar trade coercion against Canada, Japan, Lithuania, Mongolia, Australia, the Philippines, South Korea and Taiwan.

By 2022, this has led to a shift in wider attitudes. Mishandling the Covid-19 crisis has raised serious doubts about how reliable the Chinese Communists are when what they see as their interests are challenged, and with their desire to hide information that casts them in a poor light. International attention has now fallen on the persecution of the Uyghurs and with this substantial pressure on Western companies to ensure slave labour is not part of their production chain. The ripping up of the 'one country, two systems' arrangement of Hong Kong calls into doubt their reliability in terms of existing treaties and the increasingly heavy-handed threats to Taiwan make conflict (intentional or accidental) much more likely.

This in turn has led to a consensus in Washington, perhaps the only one now between Democrats and Republicans, that China may remain a key partner but that relations for some time will be contested. There is a risk that this rebalancing may go too far. Up to 2016, the British Conservatives were courting China, seeking investment in key infrastructure such as nuclear power plants and the 5G network. As of 2022, both leading candidates for the Conservative leadership were happily describing China as a major threat. It is a threat, but it remains a state we have to engage with.

This links to the need to pay attention to how democracy remains a key point of difference between the global vision offered by the West and that offered by China. China has a governing model, and one it wishes to export, although it has long stopped using the Maoist language of communist revolution. It is a model of a particular form of economic development, authoritarian rule and allowing local elites to enrich and entrench themselves. The Chinese argue this can be adopted, or not, but it closely follows the pattern of Chinese economic and political influence.[18] Equally, at the level of rhetoric, China is clear that it sees Western-style liberalism and democracy as inefficient[19] and decadent.[20]

On the other hand, China remains a vital partner. It is now fully embedded in the global economy and several times since 2000 has played an important role in stabilising the wider system. Any attempt to deal with the climate emergency needs Chinese support and, in some ways, China is making serious strides in this direction.

Analogies are tricky in international relations but it is feasible to draw one from modern China to Wilhelmine Germany in the 1890s. Both saw themselves as the emergent power,[21] both felt they had an economic and social policy that would aid all humanity.[22] This meant having to push the current dominant powers out of the way (read Britain or the US respectively). Both in many ways wanted to be part of the international order (and treated as important voices) but both chafed against institutions that had been designed when they were not that relevant. Both would cooperate with other states as well as on more general issues.

The problem was that Germany's self-identified role and desired status could only lead to sustained tensions with the British, French and Russians. There is no reason to argue that the First World War had become inevitable in the 1890s, but the tensions that later allowed a minor crisis to expand out of control were formed at that stage. This doesn't make open conflict with China inevitable[23] but it does mean it is something we need to take into account—mostly to work out how to engage with China in a way that does not pander to its own imperial ambitions.

The Chinese economy is set to overtake that of the US by 2030. If China becomes a global hegemon, it will be a bleak day for democrats. Some say this is inevitable, so why worry? Others say the threat is muted because autocracies, China included, are constrained by the same multilateral global system, with its venerable institutions and norms, as the democracies. In this optimistic reading, China is simply a different player but bound by the same rules as everyone else.

Why does China matter?

As shown above, China can be one of many things. It might be proof that capitalism is readily divorced from political liberalism, it might offer the mix of central direction and individual enterprises that creates a new economic paradigm, it might have an economy that is permanently hampered by the political role of the Chinese Communist Party. Equally it might be aiming for global domination, to reshape the wider world into its image or it might have its own sets of interests and attitudes but largely be simply seeking to operate in a rules-based international order.

The problem so far is the West's response has been incoherent.[24] This is, in part, because different elements of the wider liberal world interact with China in different ways. The EU has, not surprisingly, emphasised trade and international economics. The US and Australia, more geographically linked to the regions where China is flexing its muscles, have tended to mix caution with a desire for close trading relations. As a particular instance, the UK has been all over the place. The Conservative–Liberal Democrat coalition from 2010–15 was happy to pander to Chinese demands in return for Chinese investment in critical aspects of the domestic infrastructure. By mid-2022 the Conservatives had flipped to seeing China as a purely hostile entity, one they will seek to challenge politically and economically, with a dollop of military sabre-rattling added on. There are reasons for this shift, not least the Chinese abrogation of the agreements made about Hong Kong, but it does suggest a lack of clear thinking.

At its core, the issue of China is different to the threat posed by Putin's Russia. China is heavily integrated into the international economy, it is populous and is fast becoming rich. In many ways it seeks to play a part in the emerging global responses to issues like climate change. When it is acting as a hostile entity, it tends to do so as a conventional state. It will use social media to pump out its conspiracy theories,[25] it will attack a nation's infrastructure,[26] and, as is the case with Taiwan, it clearly is making military preparations for a war—even if it is not actively seeking that war.[27] However, fundamentally, China challenges the assumptions of Western liberalism because it claims it has a successful model for economic development that removes any need for political plurality. In a way we know this already: supposed free market capitalism has often coexisted with dictatorship. Depending on how the West manages its relations with China over the coming decades, the differences may allow much-needed diversity into the international economy while China broadly plays a conventional role. Or the differences maybe the template for an authoritarian future, one funded and protected by China.

Economic success without political liberalism

As discussed earlier, the Chinese have a very definite view of the merits of their form of governance. To some extent this can be seen as drawing heavily on Chinese history in that the Party has taken the role of the large Imperial Civil Service that effectively administered China even as emperors and dynasties came and went. This was centralised, at its best able to draw vast resources to a given project, and to a limited extent meritocratic. At its worst it was a closed, hidebound, self-serving system but it created the basis of a unified China (and in the periods of fragmentation, the capacity to pull it back together).

Unlike many authoritarian states where the main goal is to secure wealth for the elite, China claims it offers a model that will lead to better outcomes for all, especially compared to what it sees as the declining United States and liberal international order.[28] At the 2021 centennial party conference, Xi described this as a 'new model for human advancement'.[29]

The basic building blocks of the Chinese economy have been large-scale state-directed infrastructure investments, a network of mixed state–private firms, substantial inward investment and a banking sector that is quasi-independent. Up to the 2008-2009 financial crisis the main method of creating demand for Chinese products was production for export. This allowed for substantial income inequality to emerge following the reforms in the early 1980s[30] along with the maintenance of a large, increasingly unproductive, heavy industry sector. The slowing of the global economy saw substantial use of domestic infrastructure projects but also more attention paid to domestic demand. The approach to exports also shifted from one of foreign firms manufacturing in China to what were deemed 'advantage industries' such as cloud computing, synthetic biology, telecommunications, high-speed railways, and renewable energy.[31]

In the early 2020s, Xi has indicated some important changes, in particular a focus on reducing inequality and emphasising the degree of state planning in the economy. This has seen greater implicit control of major enterprises and a decision to emphasise the importance of certain sectors as China seeks to rebalance its exports.

Thus the desire to develop sectors such as cloud computing and synthetic biology involves substantial state subsidies and a willingness to ignore the international standards developed by the US or the EU. So in terms of cloud computing there is no emphasis on standards for the collection, protection or governance of data. This may have short-term benefits but also lies behind decisions of countries such as the UK to remove Chinese involvement in the development of the national 5G network.

Again, related to this, there is a strong shift to no longer looking for inward investment to create manufacturing assets but instead to generate capital. Thus US investment is being used for high-tech innovations that slot well into the hybrid civil–military economy being developed.[32] There is a technical issue here in that the traditional US finance approach relies on an assessment of the specific entity seeking capital. Given the nature of China's economy this leaves firms open to reputational damage, such as the use of slave labour in production, or of indirectly funding Chinese military innovations.

When we make decisions about which technology companies to support, commercially and in terms of national infrastructure, let's not just ask about capabilities and cost-effectiveness and carbon footprint and labour standards. Let's also ask whether the company helps extend the reach and power of an autocratic government like that of China. In the UK, these questions about Huawei were asked too late. When domestic companies make decisions about which international markets to enter, let's not just ask about the commercial opportunities. Let's also ask about whether doing so will involve compromising our commitment to freedom and data privacy. In the case of Google, for example, asking those questions earlier would have avoided the embarrassment of helping the Chinese government censor the internet.[33]

More broadly, China aims for what it says is a mid-income economy. Clearly minimising domestic dissent is vital and near full employment and increasing incomes are important tools to this aim. However, despite Xi's announcements it is hard to see the Chinese economy moving to a focus on domestic consumption given the importance of the state in setting the focus and of the military as a recipient of new developments. However, and this needs to be stressed, it does not aim for an economic model that is 'good enough' but one that fills the appointed role of replacing the failed approach of liberal capitalism. That puts its decision making to test.

So far China would claim it has shown it is possible to move from a low-income society to a mid-income one using an economic model significantly at variance to the monoculture that has characterised Western policymaking since 1990. However, this may not last, and if it doesn't, that will have serious implications. First, China faces substantial demographic problems emerging from its 'one child' birth control policies. Essentially, it has to find some way to provide for an increasing proportion of non-productive citizens. Almost 20% of the population in 2022 is over 60[34] and the birth rate is well under that needed for population replacement.

Also, its financial services sector faces major problems due to speculative investments in the property sector (ironically the same issue as almost wrecked the Western economies in 2008). This has been a particular feature of heavily indebted real-estate giant Evergrande[35] which threatens to undermine the Chinese financial sector. Given its status in the Chinese housing sector, a failure threatens household income, those firms that supply the property sector banks and the many local government bodies that have invested in it.[36]

Finally, while the leadership stresses a hi-tech economic future, it has not ended its reliance on acquiring technological gains from the United States and other advanced economies.[37] More generally, it is reasonable to characterise Xi's approach as turning its back on the model of economic liberalisation started in the 1980s. This may have serious implications as he places primacy on the perceived needs of the state over economic development.

The relative success of China's domestic economy is not just the means to fund its expanding military capacity; it sits at the core of what China thinks is its appeal to the wider world. If it is widely seen to be stalling, or to have applicability in very limited situations, China will not just lose the basis of their burgeoning hard power but also the key to its soft power. So far, taking the examples of Covid, we know China reacts badly when it believes its wider self-image is being damaged. There are already substantial doubts about the veracity of its economic statistics,[38] something that will worsen if the real performance of the Chinese economy does falter.

In effect, a system of governance that is closed to outside views, intolerant of dissent and sees itself as the future for humanity is not one that is stable. It may often work, especially when it is a matter of organising resources or directing its domestic economy, but it can go very wrong when faced with external constraints. Covid was one such example, and international relations both in the region and globally are another. And relative economic liberalism along with totalitarian social control are key parts of the package being offered by the Chinese.

A model of social control

The Chinese embraced digital technologies for government early on and eagerly, although from the beginning, their interest appeared to be more motivated by surveillance rather than offering improved services to citizens.[39] From 2015 onwards, they have increasingly been used to build a degree of totalitarian control over citizens that was previously beyond the capacity of any regime.[40] More generally, this represents a significant difference in how a state can use the internet to control its population[41] compared to the normal practice elsewhere. However, not surprisingly, other authoritarian regimes, or those with restive populations, have shown considerable interest in adopting Chinese technology for this purpose. And this Chinese technology continues to rely on US and Western technology to build it.[42]

WeChat has a key role in Chinese surveillance. It exists on every mobile phone and acts as a combination of Facebook, WhatsApp and online banking (in fact it replaces debit cards and often cash transactions). And every interaction, post, response (and, of course, location) is logged by the Chinese government. Not only can this information see you arrested but it determines your citizen credit score. Engage in Party-approved actions (including reading the works of Xi) and you gain points; if you lose points then you find yourself banned from certain locations. And China's network of facial recognition cameras is more than adequate enough to track you, even if you have left your mobile phone at home.

The result is not just a complete surveillance system. It is that, even more than Facebook, the Chinese amass predictive data to judge your likely responses. It is a closed system: if you try to access information from non-approved sources, even if it is not stopped by the usual state-controlled firewalls, it will be spotted and you will lose citizenship points. And like Facebook, it is convenient; almost all your interactions are catered for on a well-designed, easy to use, app.

Citizenship points have become the key to social status in China. Acquired by being a good citizen (as defined by the CCP), continually updated by electronic surveillance, they open doors to better jobs, higher education or living in the most desired locations. The reverse is also true: fail to gain points and you become marginalised, lose enough and you are liable to arrest and re-education to encourage you to change your ways.

Xinjiang is where all this has come to the fore. From 1991 onwards there was a degree of low-level communal violence[43] and from 2008 this escalated with a series of violent attacks by Uyghur extremists both aimed at officials and Chinese people simply using the train system. Digital surveillance has become a key tool as the Chinese seek to destroy the Uyghur community's culture and independence.[44] There is a strong cultural element as Xi, in 2014, announced a 'struggle against terrorism, infiltration, and separatism' as he claimed that extremism was now endemic in Uyghur society and thus the Chinese state could 'show absolutely no mercy ... even after these people are released, their education and transformation must continue'.[45]

Xinjiang matters in several ways. First the CCP is using the region to test out full-scale population surveillance and basically to reorganise human relations to suit its ideological framing. Second, forced and slave labour is now endemic in the local economy. That means any Western company that sources goods from China runs the reputational risk of having slave labour as part of its production chain. Finally, China, for all its advances in IT, still remains reliant on imports of Western technology.

This approach to social control is exported to China's client states and sits alongside its economic model (and is a hidden cost to taking its development funding). China is serious in divorcing economic success from personal liberties.

An alternative development model

As noted above, there is a close relationship between the Chinese approach to domestic economic development and their approach to international issues. Initially this was strongly focussed on the attraction of foreign investment to create a manufacturing base that was then used to produce exports. From 1991, this has shifted; China is now an exporter of capital, a major investor in other countries and has mostly outsourced its low-technology manufacturing.

In the form of the Belt and Road Initiative (BRI) all these factors are at play. In South-East Asia, China is seeking both clients and to protect what it sees as its vital trade routes (which in regions such as Singapore are vital to global trade). The pattern of export of capital, and in some cases export of low-technology manufacture and massive infrastructure investment, is consistent. Again there is a link to domestic economics as the massive domestic investment of ¥4tn in 2008 to create railways, bridges and airports saturated the Chinese market. The Belt and Road framework provides an alternative market for China's vast state-owned companies beyond the borders of China. Equally, an often overlooked aspect is that the domestic part of the BRI is designed to increase economic activity in the poorer central regions.[46]

While the BRI is often seen as a feature of Chinese involvement in Africa,[47] the Pacific region and Asia, it has more far-reaching aspects. Debt-strapped EU nations such as Greece and Italy have turned to China for capital. The British Conservative–Liberal Government of 2010–2015 went so far as to look for substantial Chinese capital[48] (as it engaged in the economics of austerity[49]), not only for infrastructure but also to build nuclear power stations,[50] and involved Huawei in the 5G network.[51] Growing concern about Chinese actions saw some of these policies reversed by 2019 but there was a serious risk that a notionally major West European power would effectively have handed over its infrastructure to Chinese control.

More generally, the BRI is sometimes seen as a means to trap the recipient states into debt rather than just a tool to export Chinese influence. While the debt is no doubt useful, evidence suggests that economic factors are the primary driver of BRI projects,[52] The main reason for this is the somewhat fragmented and opportunistic manner in which the BRI is being developed. The degree to which the host nation will accept Chinese influence is variable and the funding comes in part from China's non-state banking system. Equally, while the BRI is sometimes presented as a homogenous model, in reality it is fragmented due to the varying degrees of power of China and the host nation. Sri Lanka and Malaysia are sometimes cited as 'victims' of China's 'debt-trap diplomacy' but the projects in question were originally started by the host governments with financing from Western institutions. Poor governance by the local elites created both the debt and the turn to China for extra resources.[53]

However, again this is where the unique nature of the Chinese state and economy is important. Some of the consequences of the BRI are unexpected, possibly even unwelcome,[54] but the Chinese can exploit them. If a state is looking for minimal investment then the deal is one of minimal Chinese influence (but always some; up to 2015 the UK government was consistently supportive of China even as the freedoms of Hong Kong were eroded). If there is a combination of funding and poorly conceived infrastructure projects, then the Chinese (like Western banks and bodies such as the IMF before them) will use the resulting dependence to assert more influence. But in the end, China is looking for the BRI to yield economic results, so it cannot afford too many projects that result in nothing but a debt-laden client state (where the population are unhappy even if the elite remain content).[55] In effect, there is tension between China using its economic power to lever desired political change and the need for the Chinese economy (including its external investments) to remain fiscally profitable.

In 2022 China is second only to the US in terms of the usage of direct aid and development funding; it provides the bulk of its funding directly via Chinese financial institutions and implemented by Chinese state-owned enterprises (SOEs). The balance is carried out by investing in existing finance institutions and creating new structures such as the New Development Bank (NDB) and the Asian Infrastructure Investment Bank (AIIB).[56]

Beijing therefore remains an attractive source of inwards investment, and especially so for developing nations that would not be evaluated very favourably under Western measures of financial propriety and credit-worthiness. But the whole world is becoming increasingly aware of the pitfalls of the politicised nature of Chinese credit. So in principle, many aspects of the Belt and Road sound positive, but the way Beijing approaches the implementation are likely to continue to dampen the appeal of their model for many of their potential partners.

In practice, their model offers a comfortable approach for corrupt authoritarian elites anywhere. Take Chinese funding, sidestep all concerns about governance or corruption, as long as you deliver stability. And one lesson of the last decade is that authoritarian regimes seem far more able to face down domestic dissent[57] than was expected in the period after 1991.

Interaction with the global community

China does not just interact with its client states under the BRI programme. It also seeks to engage with existing international bodies and with the US and other democratic states. In each, the mix is of aggressive self-interest and seeking to cooperate as a conventional state.

Multilateral institutions

As with many emergent powers, China has both sought to engage with the existing multinational architecture and to see it as serving the interests of the older, established, powers. The entire BRI is an attempt to sidestep bodies such as the IMF and World Bank and is effectively a set of disconnected bilateral interactions with the recipients. In turn, China looks for, and expects, their support at international bodies such as the UN. Equally, this starts to give China leverage not just in setting standards and norms in its own economic sphere but in competition to those promoted by the US and EU.

Some existing bodies, such as the World Bank, have reacted to China's growing power by increasingly its relative voting powers.[58] On the other hand, bodies such as the WTO have tended to ignore Chinese proposals of reforms in part as they contrast to the hard-negotiated norms already agreed. One possible reason for the mismatch is that in the context of the World Bank China has the means both to be cooperative and also to act in a way that forces organisational change (even when its development funding is delivered in contradiction to the World Bank's own norms). In the context of the WTO, China has less leverage in that the organisation can function with its existing rules despite Chinese actions. More generally, UN-related bodies, such as the WHO, have been more willing to adapt to China's concerns reflecting both its role on the Security Council and its ability to gain key votes from states in receipt of its funding.[59]

At a political level, China's main leverage is its membership of the UN Security Council. Here it has used its status to protect itself and its allies from criticism and has had a pragmatic alliance with Russia in the twenty-first century. In combination the two have managed to reduce the effectiveness of the UN.

The head of the World Health Organization in 2022 was Beijing's candidate. Its first report on Covid-19 reiterated the

Chinese government's talking points. The World Bank still designates China a developing country and gives it billions of dollars in funding, including for projects related to the Belt and Road Initiative. It has recently started to require Taiwanese nationals to get Chinese passports if they want to accept World Bank jobs. A 2022 UN report on the persecution of the Uyghurs could as well have been an official Chinese press release[60] and we rely on the UN as the cornerstone of the increasingly frayed concept of universal human rights.

China now uses Interpol to target dissidents—especially Uyghurs. Russia plays the same game, even as it also uses the UK legal system to persecute those who fall out with the Putin regime. The International Telecommunication Union helped Huawei emerge as the leading global provider for 5G equipment. At the UN, in 2022, Chinese nationals under Beijing's direction run four out of fifteen specialised agencies; and the International Civil Aviation Organization has introduced new aviation standards which benefit the nascent Chinese aviation industry.

On the other hand, China plays a largely positive role in some international organisations. Generally it has been supportive of the need to adapt to the climate emergency and has invested substantially in sustainable energy both domestically and internationally. It has also acted to help the world economy emerge from various financial crises, especially after 2008. Here, having an economy with a different model to that of the narrow neoliberalism discussed in earlier chapters can play a positive role in that it is more exposed to some stresses but more able to deal with others. In effect, in some situations its weaknesses can be strengths.

The US and other democratic states

At one level China is clearly a rival to the US. It has a mode of domestic governance, an economic model and international interactions that are profoundly different. Equally, it believes its own model is superior. At this level, there are clear grounds for contention, difficult interactions and also substantial agreement. After all, the EU offers a different governance model that often is at odds with US preferences. The EU modes of regulation,[61] especially around the tech sector have led to several disputes.[62] To some extent the EU even has a different model of international economics. So the differences are real but not in themselves a source of fundamental tensions.

One argument in the earlier chapters of this book is that Western liberalism (especially in terms of economics) has dangerously narrowed the range of acceptable approaches. This means that any weaknesses (such as using debt to compensate for low wages) tend to be magnified in a shock leading to greater turbulence. Basically, one could make a case that the very different Chinese model played an important role in stabilising the world economy after 2008, in the same way that the EU's approach to regulation has altered the approach adopted in Washington towards the tech sector.

There is, of course, a 'but' in this argument. China's leadership does not just think it has a better model for itself, one worthy of consideration by others (more or less the view of the more social democratic states in the EU). It is clear that its model is the route by which humanity will have a better future and the decadence and flaws of Western liberalism and the existing power structures hold this back. China often claims the importance of the independence of states to do as they wish domestically. At the UN Security Council it will often vote with Russia to protect this or that autocracy on the grounds of 'state-rights' and to stop Western actions. However, for itself it sees no such constraint. It has a geography of places that should be part of mainland China and were lost in periods of historical weakness. Top of this list is Taiwan and the wider South China Sea,[63] with disputes with the

Philippines and Vietnam over control of the waters. Historically the US has supported the status quo of Taiwan retaining its autonomy without openly challenging China's claims. More recently, in part in response to Chinese pressure, it has moved to a more open relationship with Taiwan. The resulting possibility of a Chinese military invasion is probably the most dangerous potential flashpoint for armed conflict between the US and China and will need care (on both sides) to manage.

More widely, the US continues to try and restrict technology transfer to China, and the trade barriers erected by the Trump administration could limit Chinese growth to 5% in 2022. Here tone matters. Yes, the US should stop the Chinese gaining technology it will use to challenge the US (and spy on its own people) and there is a case to review some of the attitudes that underpinned Sino-US economic interaction before 2015. But if the framing is just one of punishing the Chinese then it is likely that economic disputes will mesh with the existing territorial ones. In effect, the less that China has to lose in terms of wider relations, the more likely it is that it will act in what it sees as narrow self-interest.

In this respect the steadily improving Chinese armed forces create options (for the Chinese) that have not been available before. Mao may have threatened Taiwan but an invasion would have been very low technology, dependent on just how many soldiers China was prepared to lose as it invaded. The modern Chinese state has heavily invested in the sort of navy that could give it control over the waters and a modern air force that constantly tests Taiwan's defences. Equally, the modernisation, expansion, and diversification of China's nuclear forces means it also has that threat—not necessary to use, especially as a first strike, but to deter any US response to aid Taiwan. As we have seen in Ukraine in 2022, where Putin is using the simple existence of his nuclear arsenal to try and limit NATO's response to his aggression, China's enduring refusal to engage in arms control makes it harder to agree limits and could well trigger a hostile US into a global arms race.[64]

China's response to Australia is instructive. Australia openly criticised China's handling of Covid and in April 2020, the Chinese launched a major cyberattack on the country.[65] This carried on into the summer, disrupting government agencies, universities and businesses. There was little that was subtle about this and it was clear the decision to target Australia was deliberate—it was a means to warn other Asia-Pacific powers of what could happen if they challenged Beijing. Since then, there have been several instances of Chinese submarines and planes challenging Australian naval assets. The warning is clear: cross us and we can respond, almost with complete impunity.

Towards a response

In effect, while challenging China is sensible, being aware of its goals is essential, and simply framing it just as a threat can be very misleading.

China is a major competitor and likely to remain one for the foreseeable future. However, its goals and mode of interaction are very different to that of Putin's Russia. In effect it wants something and is building new things, so it is a vibrant, productive power. Moscow nowadays can only destroy things. This means it is both possible and desirable to work with China, while not giving it all it demands.

In some disputes, perhaps the best we can hope for is the status quo, not least because, since China considers both Taiwan and the South China Sea to be not issues of international relations but issues of domestic exercise of sovereignty, it is unlikely that there can be meaningful and stable compromise between the West and Beijing on those issues. The best we can hope for is the kind of arrested stasis that we have been having in the last few decades. And that should continue to be carefully managed, as it has been in the past.

But given that China is not fundamentally a spoiler, that it wants a well-ordered world (even if its vision differs from that of the West), and given that we do share existential threats from climate change, the migration crises that will entail, the disruption of food supplies, the collapse of fragile states, etc., there is plenty of scope for constructive engagement.

We have practical experience of negotiating with a hostile power in the various nuclear weapons treaties made with the USSR and that model of negotiations and implementation could prove very productive. We are not yet in a place of outright rivalry and hostility with China as we were with the USSR during the Cold War. So if we could negotiate those kinds of mutual arms controls with the USSR, we can negotiate many more things, more productively, with Beijing. And we should be engaging with them on all those matters where both sides can win, because we can trust them to also want those wins—in a way we could not trust Putin, for example.

So we cannot hope for détente and a stable agreement on all issues, and some very important issues will probably remain forever tense. But that should not stop us from working together on the things where we do agree, not least because we absolutely have to on at least some of those things (e.g. on climate).

8

FUNDAMENTALIST ISLAM AND
THE NEW FAR RIGHT

While notionally these two disparate movements are fundamentally opposed, they actually share much in common. Neither has any tolerance for democracy and both offer an all-encompassing world view to their adherents. This creates a constituency where they feel excluded and often self-exclude from wider society. More practically, while most of their adherents are non-violent, both contain an extremely violent element. Equally, both in effect create an eco-system where someone can move from being interested in the underlying ideas to full-scale radicalism, sometimes at surprising speed. This is particularly dangerous as both sit to the fringe of larger movements—Salafist interpretations of Islam and right-wing populism respectively. This means there is a constant risk of individuals or small groups self-radicalising at worrying speed.[1]

In both these wider communities few would engage in violence, but they are more often tolerant of those who do and unconcerned about the fate of those attacked. Equally, both have a structure of basically legal figures who act as ideologues for the

211

wider community—and, of course, both rely on the excesses of the other side for much of their support and propaganda. Thus every Islamist outrage is used on sites such as Breitbart to argue for the expulsion of all Muslims from Europe or North America. And this threat of isolation and persecution fits neatly with the Salafist demands for Muslims to distance themselves from their wider communities and that all Muslims, apart from those in theocratic pure regimes, are constantly under threat.

This places the issue of how to deal with violent extremism as closely linked to the wider issue of how to engage with anti-democratic political stances. In one sense this should be clear: violence in the end is an issue for the criminal justice system while dissent is an acceptable part of the wider scope of democratic structures. The difficulty is the extent to which the two coexist in an ideological space, and that a combination of the internet, and closed-information echo chambers, seems to have made it far easier for individuals to shift from political dissent to terrorism than it has been in the past.

Ideological frameworks

This section concentrates on two ideological frameworks that present a serious challenge internally to liberal democracies. At its core, what degree of dissent can a liberal regime tolerate and not face the threat of it being destroyed? Equally, there is the enduring problem of at what point does someone holding ideas we find repellent become a serious problem, clearly not at the level of personal beliefs but when this passes over into action? And as I note later in this chapter, this can happen very quickly.

Pragmatically I have ignored the radical left. Mainly as, with the exception of maybe France, this has no current electoral grip in any major democracy and is lacking the international sponsorship so important to the new radical right. In effect, if one changes the underlying ideological building blocks, the same issues apply to the far left as to the far right (and they both share the same taste for conspiracy theories). If it was a real problem then the response should be much the same, as most residual movements of the radical left have much in common with the populist right, with the important caveat that they have not spawned an openly terrorist fringe.

Radical Islam

The threat of radical Islam is not the same as that of the modern populists, or indeed the traditional fascists, at the level of political goals. However, there are close similarities, not least in the importance of past glories (often made up) and a lack of a practical programme. Turkey is possibly the country where a form of Islamism has become contiguous with populism, but it is worth stressing that Erdoğan's tradition, for all its flaws, does not promote terrorism as a political tool. The focus in this chapter is on the more extreme, violent wings of both Islamism and populism and the different threat they pose, particularly to liberal democratic states.

Like all established religious, social and political systems, Islam has seen the development of more or less austere interpretations and varying degrees of textual literalism. It has also, not surprisingly, seen various movements dedicated to reforming the faith and returning it to a claimed early purity. Within the Sunni tradition there are now at least five major schools of jurisprudence with different views on how to interpret the Koran and other key texts in the light of changing demands. What is important is that for all their differences, this process of interpretation is seen as a skilled intellectual challenge undertaken by those who have engaged in substantial scholarship. However, Islam has always had a backward-looking, extreme element in its broad make-up and at various times this has fused with state power (or resistance to external rule) to produce a regime that is intolerant not just of non-Muslims but also Muslims who do not follow their interpretation.[2]

The variant that is the core of current Islamic extremism is the fusion between the Wahhabist school of Islamic jurisprudence and oil-rich Saudi Arabia. As a school of Islam, the former stresses how Islam became corrupted as it expanded in the eighth century, and that if the religion is to be safe in its homelands and to expand again it must return to this earlier purity.[3] Given this reading, the sect started to declare other Muslims to be not just wrong but apostates and from this, lacking all rights and indeed deserving of death.[4] When the Saudi state was poor, fighting for its independence from the Ottoman Empire, this had little wider impact (but it did lie at the core of the violence of that conflict and the death and destruction inflicted by Wahhabist raids into Syria). Over time it was co-opted as the state religion of the increasingly rich Saudi state and shed some of its violence (of deed rather than of language) as it morphed into modern-day Salafism.[5] In this form it is widely exported by the Saudi state when it sets up new mosques and provides staff and funding.[6]

However, the form that sits behind the current Islamist movements is not just an extreme interpretation of an already hard-line strand in Islamic thought; it has produced a unique variant. Ideologically it represents a fusion of the views of the Muslim Brotherhood (many of whom fled Egypt to Saudi in the 1950s)—with their mindset of seeing the rulers of Muslim countries as apostates who need to be overthrown—with an increasingly do-it-yourself approach to religious interpretation.[7] As Al-Qaida emerged from the fusion of Islamist traditions present in Afghanistan, at a doctrinal level it retained the approach that a religious decree (a fatwa) could only be issued by a suitably qualified individual. However, to the basic approach that all other Muslims were apostates, and a belief that in having beaten the Soviet Union their approach worked, was added the adoption of the Mardin fatwa as a core to their ideology.

This may sound obscure but is important to understand how radical Islam spread and how the current ad hoc nature of its terrorism in the West emerged. The Mardin fatwa stems from the thirteenth century when the notionally Muslim Mongols conquered (and massacred) much of modern day Iraq. The Mongols were deemed to not be really Muslims and thus their lands lay outside the borders of Islam—justifying violence against them. The Wahhabists later dusted this down to excuse their excesses against the populations under Ottoman rule.[8] At its core, if rulers are deemed insufficiently Muslim, then violent resistance is perfectly acceptable. And the do-it-yourself aspect is that any individual Muslim can make such a designation. No need to engage with the complex and lengthy Islamic jurisprudence around war (both when it is justified and how it should be conducted), just declare your state non-Muslim (in the sense that Muslims are not safe there) and you can carry out acts of violence.

In effect we have a state-sponsored school of Islam—Salafism—that states that all other Muslim traditions are wrong: often to the point of apostasy (of ceasing to be Muslims), always in fundamental error as they have turned from the purity of early Islamic doctrine; that Muslims in non-Muslim countries are always at risk and if they live there should try as far as possible to avoid engagement with non-believers. But, at least in the official Saudi-sponsored version, this does not justify acts of violence. However, the framing of being the single correct interpretation, constantly under threat and needing to isolate makes self-radicalisation very easy—as we will see below. And there, the jihadi interpretation of the Mardin fatwa comes into play: declare your state the 'abode of war' and all restraints are removed.[9]

The threat posed by Islamist extremists had been clear since the early 1990s. Al-Qaida emerged from the war in Afghanistan as a fusion of various disparate rebel Islamist groups who fought the Soviet occupation, some of which had in fact been armed and trained by the United States during that conflict. But the motivating ideology of the group was Saudi-style Salafist beliefs,[10] which compelled them to violently oppose any kind of international power that was not 'Muslim'.[11] The group initially carried out a number of violent attacks against US targets, and against states they felt were insufficiently Islamic in their governance, and participated in various regional conflicts throughout the Islamic world. The main fear the West had about the group was that they might somehow be able to access nuclear or chemical weapons,[12] especially as the arsenals of the former Soviet Union were poorly secured and the technology was spreading to new regimes.[13]

Traditionally, groups influenced by Muslim Brotherhood ideology had focussed primarily on overthrowing the government of their own country—especially those governments seen as 'socialist', like Nasser's in Egypt, and the Ba'athist governments of Syria and Iraq. Al-Qaida, however, evolved the ideology to argue that the barrier to the re-establishment of a new Islamic Caliphate was not this or that local government, but rather, the global hegemon: the US. In this framing, the US supported Israel (regularly described as a 'Crusader State') and local autocratic rulers specifically to stifle the emergence of a 'true Islamic' state that would elevate Muslims to their rightful place in the world. So if the Islamic world was to be remade to meet its 'full potential', the United States would have to be defeated.

Of course, the gap between these lofty goals and the practical power of Al-Qaida means its revolt is best understood as akin to an eighteenth-century peasant uprising, rather than a serious challenger with an alternative programme of global power. The group had no realistic strategic goals, just a unified narrative to integrate their tactical attempts to overthrow this or that regime.[14] But its messianic message proved appealing to many Muslims who found themselves excluded from the new economic and political order.[15] Al-Qaida presented them with a world view that explained their marginalisation, and offered a clear path to 'salvation'.

The far right

In dealing with the far right, it is again useful to disentangle the actual violent strands from those that share aspects of a wider ideology. As noted earlier in this book, the ethno-nationalism, virulent Islamophobia and anti-Semitism of the far right are readily echoed by the wider populist right and increasingly by mainstream centre-right politicians (who really should know better). But as with the relationship between Salafism and violent jihad, the differences matter, not least in framing a response.

Fascism has its origins in the various right-wing ideologies that emerged in the nineteenth century rejecting the intellectual strands based on rationalism and modernism.[16] It took on different forms in different places, so in France it emerged from those opposed to the Third Republic, often with ties to the reactionary elements of the Catholic Church and fundamentally anti-Semitic.[17] In other European countries, there were similar themes but they also often reflected national obsessions. As noted earlier, the German right (and large elements of the state) embraced an extreme form of Social Darwinism with its belief in a hierarchy of ethnic groups (with Germans bound to lead the world) and, intermittently, anti-Semitism. In Russia it took the form of pan-Slavism, ideas that Russia's unique background would enable it to save the world, as a protector of true Christianity (the 'Third Rome'). In the US themes of racism and isolationism were common in the nascent far right. If there was a unifying theme, in a world where it was widely accepted that states would act in their own national interest, then the right embraced an extreme form, often built on implausible national origin myths.[18]

The various outcomes of the First World War gave a new basis to the views of the far right. Some of the states that lost almost immediately embraced the view that they had been 'stabbed in the back' by unreliable elements in their own states. Others, such as Italy, felt their sacrifices had not been properly rewarded.[19] Conventional capitalism was seen to be a failure, especially by the end of the 1920s, and the internationalism notionally espoused by the Soviet regime made communism an unacceptable alternative. The result was a mishmash of ideas that came together in fascism. Each national variant reflected its particular history but some themes reoccurred.[20] There was a careful curation of national myths, reaching back to a previous period of glory, and this was capable of being recreated, if the national polity was remade. Lines were carefully drawn on ethnic, religious or political grounds as to who should be inside this new polity and who did not fit (and indeed usually were seen as traitors and a mortal threat to national renewal). Democracy was effete and only a single party could properly speak for the 'people'. And nation states were only to be respected if they acted with violence and force on the international stage.

The results varied. Mussolini's Italy could never become the industrial or military power fascism required. The mismatch between rhetoric and wishful thinking and reality led to a series of failed military adventures.[21] Nazi Germany crumbled into complete military defeat in 1945 and, in a European context, fascism lost its intellectual force, and became authoritarian rule in the Iberian peninsula (and briefly returned in Greece). Small groups retained the faith, but like Marxist-Leninist movements in the Western democracies, were effectively isolated. Tainted by association and in a world where the trend was towards international cooperation to solve problems, their ultra-nationalism seemed a thing of the past. The residual far right in Western Europe and North America tended to reflect local dynamics. Italy had the legacy party of Mussolini's that tended to win around 8% of the vote, with this heavily concentrated in a few districts. The UK saw minuscule, openly fascist, groups survive. In the US there was a degree of crossover between the far right and racist organisations such as the Ku Klux Klan, especially as racial integration progressed in the 1960s. Of importance, while European fascism often aims at state capture, in the US many such groups emphasise the malign role of the state—giving them an ideological form and range of options that are unique.

Economic decline in the 1970s opened the door to some of these groups but any success was episodic and, critically, they were marginalised by the conventional right leaving them little purchase on the wider electoral system. However, from the 1990s a semi-coherent ideology started to emerge, shared on nascent forms of websites such as Breitbart and that overlapped with the new generation of populist politicians. As with the original form of fascism, in reality this is an incoherent mix of random prejudices and conspiracy theories but is none the less dangerous for that. Common themes are the 'great replacement' where the ethnic white population will be replaced (usually by Muslims but this does vary)[22] and of 'cultural Marxism' where nameless elites have captured social institutions such as the media and universities to destroy the idea of the ethnically pure nation state. Beyond this, there is a repeat of the emphasis on the importance of economic nationalism, and of the state acting forcefully in its own interests. And, most often, a willingness to use violence to achieve their goals since they are doing so to protect Western civilisation. Of real concern is that this is no longer the view of a handful of fringe groups, but the basic ideas and concepts are readily repeated by conventional right-wing politicians[23] and accepted by significant parts of an electorate already disengaged from conventional politics.[24]

Specifically in the US, this new far right has been marked by regular violence and terrorism. One report suggests there were almost 900 attacks or serious plots between 1994 and 2020[25] with the far right dominating in terms of frequency and religious/ Islamist groups in terms of the death toll (mainly due to the near 3,000 deaths on 9/11[26]). In the period 2018–20, nearly 90% of all recorded terrorist incidents came from the far right. In Europe far-right terrorism has so far been more episodic, marked by individual attacks on specific communities delineated by their left-wing politics, sexuality, gender or religion. However, it has also merged with belief systems such as those of 'Incels' with this becoming the reason for outbreaks of gender-based attacks.

Self-radicalisation

At one stage the journey from feeling alienated or angry at the state of the world to actual terrorism was slow and complex (at least in Western Europe and North America).[27] In the 1970s Europe had several sustained terrorist campaigns, from the radical left in Italy[28] to nationalist groups in Northern Ireland and the Basque Country and others that briefly flared into life including leftist and nationalist terrorism in France, and right-wing terrorism in Italy. In the main the groups that lasted some time tended to be very careful over who they recruited, often from the same extended families or local communities, in part due to a fear of infiltration by informers. Those who wished to become involved had to spend time running errands, going between safe houses and generally on the fringe of the core groups (which themselves were small: the Provisional IRA at the height of its campaign probably only had 150–200 active members).

In the US at the time the main terrorist groups were poorly organised but variously reflecting the far left (the Weather Underground splitting from the SDS), black militancy (the Black Panthers) and the far right in the form of various 'militias' and the white supremacist movements. These probably did not police their own boundaries as carefully as some of the longer-running European groups but still it took real effort to engage with them, be accepted and start to commit acts of terror.

Psychological studies of terrorists suggest there are no real consistent background factors.[29] In some groups, education level is a signifier but in others, while a degree of narcissism is common it is not, in itself, a predictor.[30] Some terrorists are also psychopaths but again many psychopaths, even if active, do not claim a political motive (handy though that can be). There is, however, a psychological framing that is common and indeed essential. All the research suggests that we can accept decisions or outcomes we really do not agree with, if the process was seen to be fair. So, to be trivial, if our favourite sports team loses we can accept this; we may not like it, it may even upset us, but in the end it can be explained by vagaries of skill, luck, the rules and perhaps human judgement. In terms of politics, this is what most people do when their preferred political party loses an election; we don't expect them to like the result, they don't even have to congratulate the winner, and they are perfectly entitled to immediately set to work to win the next election instead. But they accept the process.

This returns us to the theme raised earlier: the accepted fairness of a democratic process is a critical step, and if this is lost then there is a real risk of a turn to extremism and possibly violence. If individuals reject the process, and both Salafist radicals and the various forms of the modern far right do this, then acceptance is lacking if the results are not what they wanted. Not all will turn to violence but this creates a psychological framing where doing so becomes more likely.

At this stage, all the material earlier in this book about social media, conspiracy theories and populism become too relevant. Especially in the US, with relatively easy access to weapons, it is all too easy to both self-radicalise and access the means to carry out an attack. The racist attack in Buffalo in May 2022 perfectly fitted this framework. And the killer, of course, wrote their 'manifesto' which was the usual mix of white supremacist, globalist conspiracy theories and fears of white 'replacement'. That, in turn, is picked up and added to a depressingly growing body of such literature and leaches across into the discourse of the non-violent populist right.[31] So the Norwegian far-right mass murderer, Anders Breivik cited a predictable range of Islamophobic and right-wing populist columnists and authors. In turn his claims of a 'white replacement', that Europe is heading for a civil war aided by the actions of 'traitors', seep into the discourse even of elected Conservative politicians.

Political violence

Despite this, it is worth bearing in mind that political violence is still rare in the Western world. With its culture of ready access to guns, the US is probably the most violent but even here, if the death toll of 9/11 is set to one side then less than 500 people have been killed between 1994 and 2019.[32] Now of course that is horrific, not least because almost every attack also leaves people badly injured and each of those fatalities scars the lives of their family, friends and social groups. To put this into context, in 2017 there were around 26,500 global deaths from terrorism, and of these 124 occurred in North America[33] and less than 100 across Western Europe. So at one level, terrorism really is no threat to the state, but it is a threat to communities in our societies and to the extent that we can sustain some key freedoms.

In the US, the far-right terrorist threat is not from particularly organised groups. Since the targets are a state (run by elites) and ethnic groups, then pretty much any social event, place or institution is a potential target. So the Federal Building targeted in Oklahoma in 1995 did contain some functions associated with the US criminal justice system but most had no such role. In effect, if you have decided the US government is a tyranny, then anybody who works for it is a legitimate target. If you believe that white people are facing a genocide and being replaced, any member of another ethnic group is a legitimate target.

While much of our current era is defined by the response to violent jihadists, the reality is they have failed to mount regular devastating attacks in Western Europe or North America since 2001. There have been murderous instances, use of tactics such as stealing trucks to kill as many as possible but in the main they have dropped away as a large-scale threat. Some of this may reflect good police and security work, and the fragmentation of ISIS and Al-Qaida certainly limits the degree of coordination, but it may also reflect a drop in tacit support for extreme Salafist stances among the wider Muslim community.

A political response?

Despite this, terrorism is a major worry and is clearly a threat to some communities and has the scope to disrupt social cohesion. However, there is no terrorist group active in the early 2020s that is a threat to the continuity of any Western state, the economy or the wider social fabric. This is not to argue for neglect, but dealing with it should remain fundamentally a criminal justice process. The ability to disrupt plots, arrest those involved and dismantle any supporting networks is the key. Some of that is going to fall on domestic intelligence agencies, some on the mainstream criminal justice system. If all we were dealing with was relatively isolated discrete groups we could see terrorism as a horrible, but manageable problem. However, it is too optimistic just to pretend that nothing has changed. That all we face today is the ongoing low level of political violence just with different actors espousing different goals. There are two reasons for this.

One is that their ideology has gone into the mainstream. The Saudis do not promote violent jihad (indeed often they are the targets) but the wider ideology of Salafism, taught in the mosques they fund, by the Imams they send, does create an environment in which those who do promote violence can exist. Equally most right-wing populist politicians and parties are very careful not to actively promote violence (although Donald Trump as President sometimes found it hard to condemn far-right violence) but their language, claims and mode of discourse all readily interact with the views promoted by the far right.

Second, social media simply makes it far too easy for such groups to set out their views, attract the interested and influence people. Each 'manifesto' by a far-right terrorist is full of the same arguments cut and pasted from readily accessible sources. Not only has social media become a repository of such material, but the model of generating engagement through conflict and controversy is a major source of self-radicalisation.

9

SKETCHING A RESPONSE

As ever, it is one thing to analyse why acceptance of the basic tenets of liberal democracy are fraying and it is another to resolve the problem. One, far too optimistic, reading is that we are reaching the high point of domestic populism. In states with proportional representation, they are tending to gain around 10–20% of the vote but make no more sustained progress (and like the AFD in Germany fall back substantively if they fail to sustain their progress). In Australia, the increasingly populist Liberal Party has been replaced by a Labor Party offering a technocratic agenda. In France, Le Pen again failed badly in the presidential elections (but has continued to do well in regional elections). In the UK, Keir Starmer has replaced the populist Jeremy Corbyn even if the Conservative Party shows no signs of returning to being a traditional centre-right party. In the US, Biden defeated Trump in 2020, a result greeted with relief internationally not least as it saw the US start to re-engage with key international problems such as the climate emergency. Internationally, it is clear that Putin's attempt to forcibly destroy Ukraine has failed in its immediate goals.

Starting at home

Are we winning?

However, this promise of gains across a particular electoral cycle needs to be treated with extreme caution. None of Albanese (Australia), Macron (France), Biden or Starmer have gone beyond presenting themselves as a step back to the old, comfortable (for them) status quo. Either due to their own attitudes, or constraints from their own parties, none even start to consider why populism took a hold in the first case, never mind the sort of changes now needed if we are to avoid the return of genuinely mass poverty in rich societies or take the steps needed to ensure climate change does not destroy the stable basis on which our societies are based.

So domestically we need progressive politicians and political movements to make a step. Reworking the 1990s New Labour/Clinton Democrat model of a third way, carefully triangulated against an (often mythical) left-wing threat is not enough. In many ways, as a framing it lies at the root of the wider problem but it goes nowhere near to dealing with two uncomfortable issues. First, some of the critique of conventional liberal democracy, especially in how it became framed after 1991, is valid and if not addressed will continue to undermine the core acceptance of the system. Second, Trump gained more votes than most winning presidential candidates in previous electoral contests. Le Pen gained over 40% of the votes in the French election, Starmer is ahead in the UK opinion polls due to the short-term unpopularity of the Conservatives and Albanese gained under 33% of the first preference votes in the Australian election. We cannot simply declare the problem of populism is over on this basis.

If we do not respond, both in the US and more generally, with full acknowledgement of these uncomfortable dynamics, future electoral contests will increasingly become one form or other of populism and a predictable centrist political party. France has walked this tightrope for a number of presidential contests as the National Front (now the National Rally) challenges a not very inspiring centre-right or centre-left establishment politician. Sooner or later they will win, as it is too uncomfortable to rely on people to constantly support the 'least-worst' candidate. Given the lack of challenge from senior Republicans to Trump's lies about electoral fraud, it appears as if the US is going to face the dilemma of France for many electoral cycles.

Some of the response should be technocratic and specific to individual countries. In the US, the extent of electoral gerrymandering in terms of districts and electoral representation, of suppressing the votes of the poor and excluded and the workings of the electoral college are all topics that need to be addressed. In the UK, the unelected House of Lords and the wider voting system both act as barriers to change. There is some evidence that states with multiparty electoral systems seem to be less vulnerable to populism, perhaps as this format allows dissenting voices to be heard, to gain representation and to be challenged for what they are. If so, this would suggest that states such as the US and UK need to move in that direction nationally, but so far there is little sign that the Democrats or Labour Party have grasped this.

Acknowledging our current failures

So far the focus in this book has been on the problems we face if we wish to sustain the basic political project of living in liberal democracies. And one thing worth noting is that few of those who dissent or disengage from the way that has been presented wish to live in authoritarian states. They may be less concerned about the rights of others than ideal but they are not indicating any desire to live in a non-democratic state for themselves.[1] But the risk is that current trends will indeed see less rights for us all. The evidence of states where modern populism takes power ranging from India to Hungary to Russia is that the new elite hoard power, reduce the scope for democratic debate and engage in systemic corruption. Even for those who form the notional electoral coalition they depend on, there is little left in terms of individual political, social or economic freedom.

So a key part of understanding the problem is the rise of populist ideas, parties and leaders. As noted earlier, these are not some new unified political project, but each reflects specific national experiences, the previous form of the centre-right in their polity and the electoral system they exist within. However, they share much in common: populism is a mindset. Its leaders style themselves as representing the will of the people against elites. They are more interested in popularity and power than policy and programmes. They base their appeal on feelings of resentment, abandonment and discontent. Once in power they erode democratic rules and norms, demonise opponents, and attack independent sources of power. They have little respect for informed policymaking, leading to a willingness to govern by propaganda and to embrace conspiracy theories to mask their lack of a real programme of government.

The extent to which this marks a retreat by the political right from democracy matters. Perhaps the defining feature of the slow democratisation of political systems in Europe and North America in the nineteenth and early twentieth century was the acceptance by the traditional right of this new form of governance.[2] The acceptance of democracy across right-wing traditions as varied as European Christian Democracy, British Conservatism and American Republicanism also marked a clear divergence from their more reactionary elements. The latter still spoke in terms of a unitary state, with a defined culture and religion, that could only be protected by autocratic rule. Some of this tradition fused with fascism in the 1920s, but by the post-war era was seen as a matter of historical interest as it became politically irrelevant.

If our economic model not only cannot guarantee increased living standards for many, but also tips more and more into outright poverty (and of course more again to the condition where this is a real fear) then what happens to support for democratic norms? We are facing real food shortages and higher energy costs in the very short term, to an extent that could easily push a significant proportion of the population of the Western democracies into the sort of mass poverty last seen in the 1930s. And so far, we are seeing no real response from the technocratic politicians who are our current alternative to populism.

In some ways one can regard populism as the latest incarnation of the political philosophies that essentially reject democracy, and, of course, conspiracy theories are as old as human interaction. At times both have been less widespread but clearly we do not have to look far to find places or periods of human history where authoritarianism and conspiracy theory were the norms. What is clear now is that the two are entwined, with populists readily spreading conspiracy theories as a substitute for political analysis and policy formulation. However, what has amplified both as a threat to democratic norms is the current form of social media. As noted earlier, the economic model this is based on is designed to trigger engagement and, essentially, anger and misinformation are very effective sources of revenue.

It is tempting to downplay the threat belief in conspiracies poses to democracies. However, they can become the basis for mass-murder and by their existence they pollute the idea that politics can be contentious but has to remain grounded in real information. Today, for example, right-wing politicians flirt with claims about a stolen election and themes from QAnon at the expense of the health of their democracy. They repeat the arguments of the 'great replacement', and some such as Orbán openly embrace these narratives. Second, populist authoritarians tend to use conspiracy theories to maintain power. Populist parties, after all, are normally weak at practical governance. To cover for this, they often reach for public narratives which blame secretive elites, treasonous opponents or foreign interventions.

So the problem we face is complex. We have an economic and, to some extent, a political system that really does not meet the needs and expectations of a significant part of the electorate. This dissent, disengagement, unease, has been ably manipulated by the current (mostly right-wing) generation of populists. As a group, they have little regard for the truth or honesty and this has made them into both users and creators of conspiracy theories. Theories designed to stoke fears of 'others', to distort or prevent democratic debate and readily spread by social media platforms that have no real interest in the veracity of the information they publish as long as it grabs attention.

Reforming politics?

One theme in this book is that if the domestic threat to democracy comes mostly from the populist right, the door has been opened by failures of the liberal centre to actually operate democratically and to enable people to see the benefit of democracy. This may sound harsh but it is true. The post-1991 retreat from the ideas of political economy to an almost theocratic belief in the 'market' has not only left many people much worse off, it has created a view where politics and politicians have nothing useful to say about these very real problems. It is easy to mock the NRA's 'thoughts and prayers' response to the latest massacre, but in many ways that was the response of liberal politicians to those who suffered as a result of the 2008 financial crash. It was terrible that people lost their homes, it was regrettable, but it was the reified market that had caused it (and to many, would correct it).

We are not going to return to some (rather mythical) golden age where politicians were honest and mutually respecting and policy was constructed on the basis of rigorous analysis. That world never really existed although its ideals did shape (and constrain) practical actions. Equally we need to be aware of the flaw that many notionally liberal centrist parties fell into in the period 1991–2010. They became very intolerant of those who did not share their analysis and world view to the extent that some of liberalism's critics have used the phrase of the 'intolerant centre' in response. What matters is recreating a set of norms that influence the conduct of public politics and tend to smooth the rougher edges. There we can return to politics as a debate (not always genteel) about how to solve agreed problems without seeing our opponents as traitors.

We need to accept that populism is not going away easily. So we need democratic politicians to stand up for democratic processes and the precise steps will vary by country.

In the US, a policy list should include:

Abolish the filibuster, as the populists won't be constrained by it anyway. Plus the populists have too much incentive to use the filibuster to prove that 'the other (liberal) party cannot get anything done and we need to overthrow/revolutionise the system altogether, so let's have a strongman do everything by executive authority'.

Abolish the electoral college to make sure that you do not end up with a minority-rule semi-dictatorship that only needs 40% of the electorate. As much as we may hate Orbán or Erdoğan, at least they have majority support.

Impose from the federal level state-level electoral regulations (as was done after the Civil Rights Era to prevent Southern states from disenfranchising black people), for example, force proportional representation in elections for federal representatives to actually guarantee against gerrymandering.

In the UK, the regular risk is of majority government relying not just on a minority of the vote but a very unrepresentative minority. That, in turn, sets the stage for clientelism[3] where pandering to that narrow portion of the electorate becomes more important than wider policymaking. At one stage, the argument in the UK was that the two main parties represented broad coalitions and, in combination, the votes of the great majority of the population. Neither now apply, the Conservatives have purged their traditional centre-right, and very few Labour politicians these days come from the traditional left based in trades unions or local government. It is not the capture of the Conservatives by populists that is the real problem; it is that in that form they can claim the vote of those who want a non-populist centre-right government.

So in this case, electoral reform to something that allows a multiparty system is needed. Scotland already holds its elections using a system that both retains the link between elected representatives and geographical communities and largely ensures that the spread of representation is a close match to the spread of votes (the exception is that it does tend to exclude parties with under 5% of the vote unless this is very localised). The second element has to be long-overdue reform of the House of Lords to make it an elected democratic chamber that fulfils the role of similar bodies in many other democratic systems.

The EU faces particular problems. It is largely a democratic institution but it has never really resolved the tensions between the various components. The parliament is mostly elected on a proportional basis and does a good job of converting votes cast into representation (with the various national parties then forming supra-national blocks based on ideological affinity). The problem is that the Commission mainly focusses on the member states, and to some extent broad policy will reflect the centre-right/left split in the national parliaments. The technical difficulty is in how parliament and the Commission interact as it is not the conventional relationship between executive and elected body. More generally, the EU is struggling to deal with both populist parties and populist governments. This is something I will return to later in this chapter.

The point of the proposed reforms in the US and the UK is to create a platform to challenge populism. In a multiparty system, if the Conservatives or the Republicans embrace populism it is easier for a new party to pick up the now disenfranchised traditional centre-right. If people want more radical policies than are acceptable to the leaderships of the Democrats or Labour Party, they can vote for that without fear of handing the election to someone else.

The Netherlands is an example of a state where everyone knows the outcome of an election will be a coalition. So the voting pattern both establishes which party can expect to lead that new government and also sets its wider alignment. If I vote for the Greens I am hoping for both a wider centre-left government and one that is more radical on climate change than the mainstream Labour Party would offer on its own. If I vote for D66 I probably expect a centre-right government but one that takes civil liberties seriously. In effect, people's views can be captured, the wider political norms shaped, even if the end result is a broad coalition.

Only after we have addressed the preconditions of the liberals' actual failings in democratic governance can we then persuasively turn around to the electorate and tell them: 'Look, this is a better system of governance, and the reason why it is better is precisely because of this list of values that we as liberals advocate for, and which the populists are disparaging. Both our values and our model of governance will serve you, your family and your community better than the seductive hate-mongering and scape-goating of the populists.' So it is only after you've started showing that you can govern well as a liberal democrat that you can tell people that the populists are wrong when they claim that the government is only serving elites and not serving them.

In short: if we want to argue that the populists are wrong about liberal democracy, we actually have to make it the reality that they are wrong. Because as of the early 2020s, they are not wrong—especially not in America's current political dysfunction. The US political system is broken (in part as they broke it), it fails many (in part as less than 50% actually vote), and it reflects a narrow range of ideas (in part due to the importance of large amounts of funding).

There is an antidote: reform the liberal institutions to conform more closely to democratic ideals of representation (notably the gerrymandering), remove arbitrary barriers to making and delivering on policy (the filibuster), and embrace the analysis of the populists (right and left) where their analysis of things going wrong is actually factually correct, and offer actual (liberal) solutions to the real problems that people face, from economic insecurity, to crime, to the opioid epidemic, to the extent that being ill and poor in America is a death sentence. If we make liberal democracy work for people, they will like and support it. If we fail to do that, they will abandon it. Simple as that. And really, no erudite argument alters that simple equation. One precondition for a democracy is that it is the form of government people want.

Dealing with contentious issues

How to conduct contentious politics in this era is an important question. Once it could be seen as a matter linked to electoral politics as parties promoted a much-needed change and, if they won votes, converted it into practical politics. The problem when this is part of the wider electoral process is being sure just what people voted for. They may have indeed elected party X that contained proposal Y in its wider platform but it is quite feasible that proposal Y was treated with some scepticism, or disinterest, when making a choice of who to vote for.

Plenty of states built the idea of plebiscites into their constitution and then created a series of safeguards[4] so that specific issues could be addressed outside the wider electoral process. These safeguards included the type of information to be made available, thresholds, verification of both the question and the subsequent claims, and also preventing a referendum on a question outside the power of the relevant political system to deliver (so a small local council in Switzerland cannot, for example, vote to end the possession of nuclear weapons by China).

Ireland added the idea of a citizens' convention when it wished to reform abortion rights.[5] This acknowledged it was a field with genuinely held beliefs on both sides. The convention was drawn at random from the Irish population, met over a two-year period, heard evidence from all sides and professionals, and ran itself according to the principles of 'openness of proceedings; fairness in how differing viewpoints were treated and of the quality of briefing material; equality of voice among members; efficiency; respect; and collegiality'. In the end 56% of the convention voted for change, and agreed the wording of the question and the legal bounds to the campaign. Some 64% of the electorate then voted to liberalise abortion.

In contrast, before the UK's vote to leave the EU, the then Prime Minister, David Cameron, insisted the referendum was not binding but advisory. This removed almost all constraints on how the campaign was conducted, and no one was responsible for articulating just how the UK was to leave the EU. The result, as discussed elsewhere, was a vote still mired in controversy, heavily influenced by cash from opaque sources (which included Putin's Russia) and with an approach to social media so abusive that even Facebook had to acknowledge the problem.

In effect, contentious issues, where someone with genuinely held beliefs will lose, cannot be avoided because we fear populism. But, as with Ireland, they can be handled and in a way that gains acceptance from most of those on the losing side. In part this is an acknowledgement that for some issues traditional political approaches may not be the best solution.[6]

The Covid pandemic has made this a real issue for many governments: how to engage with their population on a complex issue, where much was unclear and where conspiracy theories abound. There are various approaches being explored and it is important that we see this as an opportunity to challenge lies in a much wider sphere than public health. In the same vein, some senior members of the Scottish National Party (with its policy of breaking away from the UK) are seriously and carefully discussing how such a debate could be held given the likelihood of Russian interference and conspiracy theories. They, as yet, have no answers, but it is an example of where practical politicians are doing more than just accepting the current norms.

And running beneath much of this, the best antidote to populism is for our politicians to rediscover the language of universal rights. Universal rights are, by definition, a birthright due to everyone. That makes them a useful way to talk about the security and respect we owe to people we disagree with. Talking about them can help us rebuild a set of norms which smooth out the rougher edges of politics and guard against a descent into authoritarian tactics. It is all too easy to pander to the populists by marginalising this or that group, but they cannot be pandered to. If they win, then democracy loses.

Or should the focus be international?

To set out why the loss of structured multilateral interaction matters it is useful to briefly sketch out the implications of four major policy areas. In effect, none of these can be adequately addressed by the realist state model.

Climate emergency

The designation of what has previously been described as climate change as an emergency is a quite deliberate attempt to force governments across the world to accept the shared risk and make suitable adaptations in domestic policy.[7]

To place the situation into context, the UN Environment Programme summarised the climatic events of 2019 as:[8]

- The global average temperature was 1.1°C above the pre-industrial period and 2019 was the second hottest year on record;
- Average temperatures for the period 2015–2019 are the hottest on record;
- 30% of the world's population faced extreme heat for at least 20 days;
- Given international commitments as of 2022, the amount of greenhouse gas emissions is set to rise, as opposed to falling as is needed simply to slow the process.

If global warming is to be held below 1.5°C then these emissions need to fall by 7.6% per year from 2022 to 2030. Some solutions are technological in that it is possible to engage in manufacture, agriculture and transport activities that contribute to global warming, with substantial reductions in actual methane production. Conservation and restoration of nature is another way to mitigate the worst effects and make the process of adaptation much easier. However, all this falls away if states remain dependent on fossil fuels.

While some right-wing groups and industrial lobbying bodies continue to promote outright denial of the problem,[9] and use their regular tropes of mistrust of expertise (as this reflects the attitudes of elites)[10] in the main, in the face of overwhelming evidence, the common stance has shifted to trying to debate the need to adapt, or the cost of adaptation, rather than claim there is nothing changing in the climate.[11] To this must be added that many states at one level accept the problem but there are always pressing immediate needs. Russia's weaponisation of gas deliveries since its invasion of Ukraine has not so much triggered a focus on faster movement away from fossil fuels but instead towards exploitation of domestic sources,[12] adding to global production.

In effect between the residual impact of outright denial of climate change (and the close correlation between this and populist movements), curated arguments about the cost of change (that ignore the clear costs of not changing) and simple short-sighted state interests, there is a huge risk of no effective response being made to the climate emergency. In effect a set of promises made in Glasgow in late 2021 are already in danger of being ignored.

But the crisis knows no national borders. The worst effects may be found in relatively arid regions such as North Africa and the Middle East,[13] the under-populated Polar regions or small island states. But the US is experiencing heat waves that threaten human habitation of large areas, Arctic climate change is affecting the weather across the northern US, the east coast faces more frequent and severe hurricanes and the disruption of ocean currents affects fishing on both coasts.

More to the point, climate change has the capacity to spark conflicts over water resources[14] adding to the range of possible international conflicts and civil wars. Most clearly, it is adding to the global refugee crisis.[15]

None of this is solvable by an 'America First' or 'Fortress Europe' approach, and if the climate emergency is not met at a global level then it will overwhelm even the richest, most distanced, societies. But the populists, and their backers, are determined to wreck the multinational frameworks we need even as they promote denialism as part of their domestic policies.

Nuclear proliferation

If this book had been written in 1982 then a clear focus would have been on how to mitigate the risks of nuclear war between the US and the USSR.[16] By 1992, the focus could have fallen on how to manage the nuclear arsenal of the former Soviet Union[17] and stop more states acquiring nuclear weapons.[18] By 2002 the twin concerns were to control the further spread of nuclear weapons to more states[19] and to prevent any chance that Al-Qaida could access any form of nuclear technology.[20] At the same time, given relatively good relations between the US and Russia, it was feasible to talk about going beyond arms control towards nuclear disarmament.[21]

To some extent, since then the issue has dropped away. There is an unwilling acceptance that states such as North Korea, Israel, India and Pakistan do possess nuclear weapons,[22] and there remains a tattered international approach to trying to stop Iran gaining them and vestigial concerns about nuclear terrorism,[23] but it broadly appears to be a limited issue.

However, it is not, and again the fracturing of the old international system will make it worse. The various nuclear treaties between the US and the USSR/Russia are coming to the end of their lives, at a time when both are increasingly suspicious of the other. During the Cold War the concept of the Doomsday Clock was widely understood: the closer it was placed to midnight, the greater the risk of nuclear war. As things stand, we are back on the brink. Putin openly discusses using his weaponry (without, so far, doing anything that suggests real intent),[24] and China is developing the sort of capacity that may allow it to limit US response if it invades Taiwan.[25] The loose, never well-articulated, goal of elimination or serious reduction in nuclear weapons has ended.

Again this is a field where there is a need for structured international bodies. Controlling nuclear weapons matters to all, so involving a wider group of states can help offset bilateral tensions (the basis for the Iran deals has been that Iran trusts the EU more than it trusts the US as an external voice). And yet, not only do populists like Trump and Putin talk about their usage; their collective actions undermine the main tools we have to manage the risks and perhaps revive earlier moves towards reduction.

International terrorism

Again, if this book had been written in 2002, how to deal with Al-Qaida would have been probably the number one international issue.[26] By 2012, the concern was the implications of the split between Al-Qaida and the seemingly unstoppable (and even more brutal) ISIS as it cemented its rule in Iraq and Syria.[27] Since then, we have seen the threat of specifically Islamist terrorism in the West change to one of relatively low technology (knives, stolen trucks, homemade bombs) attacks mostly carried out by those who self-radicalise.[28] Attacks on state institutions in the US or Western Europe seem to be beyond the capacity of those groups now, leaving them dependent on increasingly sporadic attacks on citizens by those who already live in the countries.[29]

However, this is only part of the story. Both ISIS and Al-Qaida are very much alive. Their focus is on inserting themselves into a range of disputes between Muslim minority populations and repressive states across Africa, the Middle East and the Philippines. The return of the Taliban in Afghanistan possibly offers them the scope to again find a safe space to hatch their long-term plans. Equally the economic and social factors that propelled the rise of Islamist terrorism in the period 1990–2000 have not eased globally, in fact they are far worse.[30]

Refugees

In a way, the emerging problem of massed, forced, human migration pulls all these strands together. People are fleeing the impacts of climate change,[31] wars (in part fuelled by Islamist movements) and economic and social collapse. Neither the US nor the EU is exactly handling the resulting human misery with competence or humanity. Issues such as trafficking,[32] irregular migration,[33] asylum and the right to seek refuge[34] are being deliberately conflated for political ends[35]—and not just by the populists.

The evidence from Germany is that a liberal asylum policy rapidly pays off,[36] and the evidence from the wars in the former Yugoslavia is that many who seek asylum return home when they can.[37] In addition, we now know that the creation of waves of refugees is a quite deliberate part of Russian policy, first in Syria[38] and then in Ukraine. Finally, most refugees stay as close to their original home as they can and this means the great majority are hosted by the poorest countries in the world.

Instead, even within multilateral groups such as the EU, the tendency is to adopt the easy solution. Leave the states closest to the conflict to absorb the refugees as best they can, or seek to create barriers that breach the fundamental rights enshrined in the UN Charter.[39]

So there are going to be two responses. One based on existing international law accepts that people have the right to seek refuge, and does its best to ensure their safety, their integration into their host society and, if possible, their return to their own country. The other in some ways blames them for needing refuge, fragments responsibility so most falls on countries immediately bordering the crisis and offers little but inhumanity for them if they do arrive. And this is against a world where climate change, among other issues, is destroying livelihoods even where it does not spark actual conflict.

Russia and China

As noted in the earlier chapters, these two share a contempt for pluralist democracies, seeing them as ineffective and fundamentally flawed. Picking up on those chapters there was a strong view that we need to find different approaches to them regardless of this. In effect, Putin's Russia is a spoiler and disrupter, rarely bringing a positive agenda to any issue. China veers between this—and sometimes a model of great power rivalry—and often one of real cooperation. In addition, there are real tensions between them and areas where they may well fall out.

Having said all that, in the early twenty-first century the two nations are backing each other up. Both are working to make the world less democratic. Russia supports populist governments around the world and undermines democracies by finding points of division within democracies and amplifying them. Using international TV programmes and social media, it has worked hard to meddle in elections, undermine public trust in the process, and spread misinformation in the West and beyond.

In practical terms, early in 2022, at the opening of the Winter Olympics, Xi Jinping welcomed China's highest-profile guest to the Games: Vladimir Putin. They talked about 'unprecedented' close relations between the two countries.[40] They declared opposition to NATO expansion, stated that Taiwan was part of China, and criticised what they called 'interference in the internal affairs' of other states. They talked about an independent financial infrastructure to reduce their reliance on Western banks and vulnerability to Western economic pressure, with a clear framing of how they see the world developing as: 'a trend has emerged towards redistribution of power in the world'—namely toward them, and away from the United States and its democratic partners and allies.

This was followed by a formal declaration of their shared goals.[41] At its core they declared that their model of cooperation steps beyond their links during the Cold War[42] and that there are no 'forbidden' areas of cooperation.[43]

Returning to the Winter Games, they were politically boycotted by most democracies, so most of the world leaders at the ceremony were autocrats: the leaders of five former Soviet States, Egypt, Saudi Arabia, Qatar, and the United Arab Emirates. In effect, a summit of states that are even more repressive than the managed democracies being constructed by the wider group of populists.

If Russia is still fundamentally a spoiler in international affairs, China has a different trajectory. China is dismantling democracy in Hong Kong, and offering diplomatic and economic support to autocracies. And by providing a successful economic model combining a managed market system with authoritarianism, it is not just incentivising emerging powers away from democracy, it is also providing an example of the benefits of that path. Meanwhile China lends and exports capital to Africa, Central Asia, and beyond. Its Belt and Road Initiative offers infrastructure deals to countries around the world, which often enables local leaders to take kickbacks and get positive media coverage, which it often subsidises.[44] However, in some respects they are very different. If China is proving difficult in international discussions about the balance of who bears the cost of adapting to a low carbon future, domestically it is taking steps to reduce its dependency on fossil fuels. The Russian economy, on the other hand, is essentially kept afloat by the sale of oil and gas.

Multilateral autocratisation

The emergence of China, and its norms, allied to Russian subversion of any state (or institution) it sees as a problem is creating a wider problem in that China is contributing to the risk of our being dominated by autocracy and authoritarianism. The constraints on autocrats are weakening and for emerging leaders and states, autocratic tactics and strategies are becoming an increasingly viable option.

This is happening for two key reasons.

The first is simply that autocrats help each other. In June 2021, the last dictatorship in Europe, Belarus, hijacked a Ryanair flight to imprison an activist. As a result, Belarus is today not allowed to land planes in Europe, many of its goods are banned in the US, and it is routinely criticised by international civil society. But its dictator, Lukashenko, can look elsewhere for support. His country is the site of one of China's largest development projects. Its relationship with Iran is flourishing. It gets support at the UN from Cuba. Autocrats help each other.

The picture is similar for Venezuela. Many people within Nicolás Maduro's circle have been added to lists of sanctions. The US bans most trade with the country. Sanctions from Canada, the EU, and many South American countries remain in place. But Maduro enjoys loans and investment from Russia and China. Turkey supports Venezuela's trade in gold, and Cuba provides security advisers and technology. Autocrats help each other.

Look at Turkey. Under Erdoğan, independent media and courts have suffered, and dissidents have been arrested and jailed. But there has also been a move towards echoing Chinese propaganda. Anne Applebaum relates how on the 100th anniversary of the Chinese Communist Party, Erdoğan's party flagship newspaper published a long article, sponsored by China, under the headline 'The Chinese Communist Party's 100 Years of Glorious History and the Secrets to Its Success'.[45] This shift in direction has come at the expense of Turkey's migrant Uyghur population, who have been surveilled, detained, and in some cases, even sent to countries likely to deport them to China. Autocrats help each other.

This cooperation is the first reason that constraints on autocrats are weakening. At one stage, it was becoming clear that if you committed war crimes you had a real chance of being caught (perhaps many years later) and taken to the Hague for trial.[46] This constraint is weakening; yes, those on various lists have to be careful about which countries they visit, but there is a fairly broad list of destinations where no such threat exists.

The second is that China, in particular, is trying to shape the multilateral system to serve its interests. It puts special effort into controlling international institutions which give it authority over global rules and norms as it seeks to mould these to fit its view of the future.

In short, our multilateral system isn't set up to curb a rising autocratic power. It was created out of a consensus of the non-Soviet powers at the end of the last war. It was indeed rather self-serving but a system was built that we benefit from. If China was simply calling out past problems and demanding a wider set of voices be heard, then it would have a case. But it is stopping those bodies functioning in the wider interest.

The WTO wasn't able to curb China's unfair trade practices. The WHO couldn't call out China on false Covid data, and the UN law of the sea hasn't stopped China expanding in the South China Sea. So when people look at the rise of China and other autocracies and say we don't need to worry because these countries are constrained by the same multilateral global system as every other country, my response is: the system is warping under autocratic pressure. This is the second reason that constraints on autocrats are weakening.

And that matters for emerging countries and emerging leaders. Month by month, year by year, the balance of risk and reward for aspiring autocrats is tipping towards autocracy. A local elite has a choice. Shore up their power, and don't worry about looting and human rights abuses in the Chinese system or low-level nagging from the World Bank and other agencies in the US system.

Linking internal and external issues

If this book has a core theme it is that the idea of a liberal democracy is under attack, in part by malign states and in part by internal political, economic and social factors. To go forward, we need to see the issue as one of both international and domestic politics. At one level, Putin's Russia is more of a threat than the old Soviet Union: quite clearly at an ideological level it intends to undermine the pillars of liberal democracy.[47] This includes amplifying any issue of contentious politics, it particularly means targeting institutions such as the EU and NATO and fundamentally it means weakening the US.[48] So when a former President continues to peddle lies about the electoral integrity of the US, he is acting (willingly or not) for a hostile foreign power;[49] when Fox News readily repeats Putin's arguments over the war in Ukraine, they are acting (willingly or not) for a hostile foreign power.[50]

The UK establishment, with close links to the Conservative Party, were not just earning money off a new set of rich clients when they enabled the arrival of Russian finance in London.[51] They enabled the corruption of British politics by a power hostile to the concept of liberal democracy. When Italian populists have taken money from Putin they do so well aware it comes at a cost.[52] That cost is their part in the undermining of Italian democracy in particular and the EU more generally.

This is uncomfortable to say; in the end a liberal democracy functions on an acceptance of limits to power, of outcomes we do not personally want and that our opponents are acting (genuinely) for what they believe is the best for the wider polity. This may imply the problem is just about Russia, or Putin, but it isn't. Even without Russian interference, the problems of the current model of social media, of the spread of conspiracy theories and the impact of populist politicians on a polity where many have already decided the status quo offers little, would remain. We can't just blame Putin for Facebook/Meta's economic model and the implications, it is not just down to Putin that so many believe in QAnon,[53] and checking Putin's actions will still leave us with some real problems.

Do we have a response?

Before concluding this book it is useful to stop and bring in the viewpoint of a set of actors who have largely been silent. We have said much about the logic of populists, about the policy failures that followed from 1991, about the self-serving economic model of the social media companies, about how Russia and China pose an international threat and how the risk of terrorism is steadily increasing. Some of the chapters discuss particular solutions to aspects of this problem but what we have not considered is whether the states or institutions being targeted have produced a coherent analysis of the threat and the start of a structured response.

The honest answer is no. The US has an emerging military and diplomatic strategy that works from the premise of a multipolar world with Russia and China as the main threats. Despite all the warnings, it does not really have one to deal with domestic subversion, especially the reality of US Republicans happy to sign up to Putin's agendas.[54] The UK is even worse—it has a defence strategy at odds with its global capacity and again, despite the warnings, says nothing about how to tackle Russian or Chinese interference.[55] The EU might be expected to focus on issues of trade and the legality of actions within its block, but again it has left EU–Russia and EU–China relations primarily to member states and it skitters around the issue of how to handle illegal actions of populist regimes like Hungary.

This section looks at the state-level responses of the US, the UK and the EU in more detail. This gives us some idea as to how the domestic and international threat is being treated and some idea of the gap between the current discussion and what is needed.

The current US response

Early in the Trump era, there was a view in the US foreign policy establishment that things could be reset (even that some of his actions might trigger useful responses such as more military spending in other NATO states) but that basically his presidency was an aberration and the traditional broad agreement would be recreated.[56] This optimistic view missed two key issues. First many allies are now cautious that the Trump presidency was not a one-off, that the US electoral system could return him, or one of his allies, to power. Equally as the UK has found, once a state loses the trust of others, it is very hard to regain. The Biden administration is basically trying to revert to a more conventional US stance in most international forums and returning the US to key international agreements on climate change but so far this is mostly relatively conventional in its approach.

At a level of military strategy, the Trump era actually made less impact. The US's formal strategy (constructed when he was in power) is now based around an assumption of great power competition, in particular with China and Russia[57] using a '1+1+3' framework. China is the 'most consequential strategic competitor', followed by 'acute threats' from Russia, and then 'persistent threats, including North Korea, Iran, and violent extremist organizations'.[58] In effect, Trump personally may have found much in common with Putin and Xi but practically the US has been planning on the basis of sustained tensions with both. Since they have declared their cooperation 'has no limits',[59] then at least theoretically this has to involve planning for hostilities with both at the same time.

However, while the US now talks about 'strategic competition' it is unclear just what this means. The 2022 update uses the formulation 'campaigning'[60] with this largely framed as confrontation at levels below actual armed conflict. This is an important shift but so far the US has not responded to attacks on its democratic systems, to wider disinformation campaigns or to the Chinese land grabs in the South China Sea. Possibly the deliberate release of intelligence on Russia's intentions in the build up to the invasion of Ukraine may hint at a more pro-active stance in such matters. Clearly that did little to deter Russia but it made it much harder for Putin to use his tried-and-tested propaganda techniques, amplified by his populist allies, to create confusion as to his intentions. What still seems to be missing is a willingness to actually use its own capacities to directly challenge Russian (or Chinese) attacks (accepting that the US, of course, still wishes to hold its intelligence services to higher standards than those of Putin or Xi). Finally, the emerging National Defence Strategy goes further in showing how the US can engage in 'great power' competition using all the government resources to 'operate forces, synchronize broader Department efforts, and align Department activities with other instruments of national power'.[61]

This is welcome but still leaves the US lacking a grand strategy (and also still leaves open the chance that the next US President will revert to Trump's approach and undermine all these efforts). The US approach can be best described as one that emerges from the various strands of the bureaucracy, interest groups, long held analyses and the specific response in a given situation. In many ways this is sensible, the US has alliances, links, past engagements and needs to navigate those as it adapts. Obama tried to move the US away from its Saudi alliance and so far this has seen little practical change. Trump may personally have been pro-Putin but this did not stop the US challenging Russian actions in Syria and elsewhere. In effect, the institutions of the US state functioned in the Trump era, but were lacking coherent support from the President. However, the prospect of a renewed Trump presidency in turn scars the policy framework of the early 2020s as, at a practical level, actions are taken with an eye towards a return to domestic instability.

The threat posed by both Russia and China to US domestic politics has been clearly spelled out in a series of Congressional reports over the last few years.[62] But so far it has not provoked a structured response. It clearly doesn't help that in regard to Russian interference the Republican Party has no desire to explore what happened, but that shouldn't end the issue. The evidence is clear, set out in formal reports, often gathered under judicial or quasi-judicial enquiries. The easiest way for Putin to undermine the West and for China to dominate the US is to undermine the US democratic process from within.

When the Soviet Union was channelling funds to relatively marginalised (and clearly delineated) Communist Parties the issue of foreign cash flows into domestic political parties could be ignored. It can't now, and this links back to the discussion above. A major reform of US political funding is long overdue.

The UK's response

Any attempt by the UK to come to a coherent response is hampered by a combination of financial austerity since 2010 and the complicity of that generation of Conservative politicians in the Brexit vote of 2016. The latter not only weakened the ability of the UK to collaborate with its traditional allies; it also, as in the US, meant they have had no interest in understanding the extent of Russian interference, and funding, in UK elections.[63] After Russia's invasion of Ukraine, the ruling Conservative Party has flipped from close ties to Putin's regime to presenting itself as the primary backer of Ukraine. This may, or may not, be the case but in many ways the damage is done. What matters is to come up with a clear strategy for the conduct of future elections that removes the scope for Russian interference. Instead the Conservatives are busily undermining the previously neutral electoral commission—perhaps the ideal body to explore how to ensure fair elections in the modern digital environment.

There are some serious discussions about how to conduct contentious politics in the current environment: how to stop social media distorting and poisoning debate, how to limit the scope of the Russians (or the Chinese, or the Iranians) to try and convert contentious debate into the sort of thing that fractures societies. Perhaps oddly, this seems to be the preserve of the nationalist SNP. They want a new referendum on Scottish independence, they want an independent Scotland to fit readily into a rules-based international order, and they are very aware that how they achieve independence will ease, or hamper, that process.[64] It would be reassuring if the British government was putting the same degree of care into protecting the wider UK democratic process.

The EU's response

The EU as a collective entity has two dimensions to consider. First, how it trades and interacts with Russia and China, and second, how it handles the increasingly undemocratic portion of its membership—notably Poland and Hungary.

At its core, in terms of international interactions the EU is a trading body. Specific to its interactions with Russia, while it has imposed sanctions on individuals after the invasions of Crimea and the Donbas in 2014[65] it did nothing to prevent Germany, in particular, in deepening its energy relationship with Russia. As in other situations, its internal commitment to democratic governance falls apart when looking for trade relations outside its border. Initially its response to Putin's invasion of Ukraine was really more of the same, sanctions on named individuals.[66] However, this rapidly became much more far reaching with bans on broadcasters such as Russia Today and on specific Russian companies, restrictions on Russian banks, and an export ban on certain industries. As the war has continued the EU has put in place a structured programme to reduce the reliance of some member states on Russian energy imports, steadily overcoming resistance from Germany (on the grounds of relative dependence) and Hungary (due to Orbán's pro-Putin attitudes). In addition, for the first time the EU has offered financing to allow Ukraine to purchase military equipment and revived discussions with Ukraine about accession.

In 2019, the EU formally set out its view that China was a partner, a competitor and a systemic rival. Since then, there have been practical difficulties triggered by China's response to individual member states, its response to limited EU concerns over human rights and its support for Russian actions in Ukraine. However, the economic links are substantial and the EU continues to argue that China has a crucial role in certain global challenges (in particular climate change) and needs to be treated as a serious actor in the wider East Asian region.

On the basis of this, one could argue that slowly the EU has reached pragmatic responses at the economic and diplomatic level to both Russia and China. For the former, the intention is to limit links until the regime changes approach in terms of its external aggressions. For the latter, the response is less clear, but given China's multiple roles, that may be both pragmatic and sensible.

However, the EU is struggling to handle the domestic fallout of Russian subversion. At one level it is, as it has to be, a reflection of the political centre of gravity of its member states and their internal political dynamics. Given that in many states, right-wing populists have substantial electoral support and in some are likely to form the government (in Italy in particular), this makes some sense. One significant change has been a retreat from the imposed austerity economics of the 2008–2015 period which has been designed to give member states more leeway to absorb pressures from domestic populist movements.[67] To some extent, the EU collectively could argue it has a limited role in the domestic politics of its member states and thus it is not its job to challenge this or that populist party. However, this hands-off approach has become problematic when populists take over states, most notably Hungary and Poland, and run them in a manner inimical to the core values of the EU.[68]

Fidesz has always made clear its opposition to the legal norms of the EU even as Orbán has taken EU subsidies and used them to reward his electoral coalition. The EU has a basic attitude of seeking to be as encompassing as possible but in the case of Hungary and Poland this relative tolerance has produced two member states whose internal governance is now utterly at variance to the EU's political norms. In many ways this is a dynamic the EU is ill-equipped to handle and so far the response has been a series of legal challenges (often then ignored by both Poland and Hungary) but no real discussion as to the point where either or both states might face suspension or expulsion. In terms of the 2022 crisis in Ukraine, Poland is supporting the EU's wider policies (not least because it too fears Putin's aggression) but increasingly Hungary is backing Putin and undermining the EU's approach.

The real challenge for the EU is that at some stage it ends up prioritising its relative spread within continental Europe and its single market structures over its commitment to political liberalism. The more it indulges Hungary, seeking consensus, the more it risks undermining the political norms that underpin the entire structure. At the least, clear sanctions on Hungary are needed or Orbán will continue to take EU funding while undermining the EU. And offering a clear model to all the other populist elements within the wider European polity.

Going forward

If we accept the analysis presented in this book, then what practical steps can the major players in the West take to sustain the wider liberal international order?[69] I think one thing has to be said. If the US re-elects Trump, or one of his close allies, in 2024 then most of this discussion is irrelevant. We can expect the US to revert to undermining its allies, (at best) ignoring the climate crisis and seeing authoritarian regimes as having a natural affinity. So unless significant efforts are made to reduce the appeal of populism domestically in the United States, little can be done internationally.

Looking at the stances of the US, the UK and the EU as of 2022, it is clear that to some extent they have military and diplomatic postures that do reflect the emergence of China and Russia as major new actors on the international scene. Equally, these stances do differentiate between the two, as the EU says China is both competitor and partner, whereas Russia has ceased to be anything but a threat (which is not to say the EU then has to stop talking with them).

At one stage any discussion of defending an international rules-based system would have seen the UK as a key aspect. The depressing truth of the trajectory of the Conservative Party since 2016 is that this is no longer the case. It may be that a change of leadership from Boris Johnson will mean that the party is more settled in the future, but it is telling that neither of the two main contenders to replace him made it a priority to seek good relations with the EU. So to some extent, that leaves us with the stances of the US and the EU as the main actors.

The US strategy in the early 2020s notes the importance of alliances but does not really articulate what this could mean. The practical application is in terms of military operations looking to integrate forces from other nations into US operations, and, to a lesser extent, burden-sharing in regions where fellow states are the natural alternative. Missing from this framing is the more political aspect, both in terms of the security of domestic electoral processes and of the complex trade off between working with like minded states as opposed to more generally. In this respect there are clearly states and/or multinational bodies that have a profound commitment to a rules based international order but it is not feasible just to work with such like minded bodies.

So far, the EU has been problematic for the US to engage with, especially in foreign affairs. While there is a substantial crossover with NATO, even states which have been close allies in NATO discussions (such as Germany) can be far more independent minded in matters of trade policy. Equally the EU, itself, has long struggled to find a way to gain a coherent voice in international affairs partly as it tends to see issues as matters of trade, partly as there are often substantial internal differences and partly as it has tended to leave some issues to the member state (usually the former colonial power) most closely involved (such as France in sub-Saharan Africa). To this can be added disputes stemming from different approaches to regulation, especially of the tech sector, creating significant tensions at times. Historically the UK has played a useful role in mediating (and also helping the EU and the US to understand each other's positions) but this work-around no longer exists.

So that is the negative side, and it suggests serious reservations. On the other hand the EU is a bloc of comparable population and wealth to the US. It takes the rule of law seriously, it takes working on a multilateral basis seriously and its entire basis rests on a broadly liberal,[70] social, economic and political structure. If the US is serious about protecting and enhancing the liberal international order then the EU needs to be the prime partner. There are plenty of other states that can (and would) contribute but like the US, the EU is powerful enough[71] to influence the global rules of trade and the wider norms. If this means working with the EU to marginalise or expel its populist members (now primarily Hungary and Poland) then here the US can usefully offer a NATO perspective. The Polish regime as of the early 2020s may be prepared to push the EU to the limit in risking suspension, but it will not risk its NATO membership. Even Orbán in Hungary may have to adapt if the threat is not just loss of EU membership but of wider isolation.

In the worst case of the US reverting to populism, then the EU becomes the primary proponent of a rules-based international order. This suggests a simple priority for the Biden administration. Work with the EU to enhance this, support the EU to create the sort of structures and capacity that will be needed if the US slips back. The global problems we all face are too profound for a state-centred international order to deal with and, basically, US politics is too volatile to be sure we will not have a populist Republican President in 2024 or 2028 (in effect we cannot expect a complex global system to live hand to mouth across US electoral cycles).

Beyond this, it is clear that we are now in a multipolar world and that great power tensions are here to stay. It is feasible that Putin's regime may collapse but then the most likely outcome is that another of the closed elite circle will take power—probably less openly aggressive but equally steeped in the now dominant post-Soviet ideology of the Russian elite. Chinese domestic problems may bring down Xi, but again this would see replacement from within the current elite. Some things would change, but China would still be a major competitor with a powerful military.

So there is a need to plan to manage these tensions. Periods when a new power emerges are often challenging and we have plenty of examples, such as Europe 1880–1910, of how crises can compound to the point where war occurs more or less by accident. This means looking to work with both Russia and China where this is feasible. This is far easier in terms of China given its broadly realist international model (and that it is not involved in a near-genocidal war with a neighbour) and we need to build on this; not to stop challenging China, but to acknowledge that in areas such as climate change we can make no progress without China and that, broadly, it is trying to adapt its own economy.

Part of this involves addressing the problem of what to do with the current landscape of international bodies. Most of these stem from the post-war era and few would be constructed today in their current form. Many are failing to deal with the demands on them, lack of funding and political direction and the emerging pressure from China. In terms of organisations such as the UN, the WTO, WHO, World Bank et al., I suggest a very simple question. If they didn't exist, would the problems set out earlier in this chapter become easier to deal with? If the answer is no, and in most cases this will be the answer, then the solution is to work with them (even if in a limited way, expecting little positive from them), seek to reform, use them as places to discuss and defuse tensions. If the answer is yes, then start creating alternatives; if, as an example, this ends up creating a new World Bank as an alternative to Chinese finance and development models then so be it.

Even stripping out the international dimension, there is a deep-seated problem. There is no evidence that the new wave of populist politicians are particularly worried about the impact of their actions[72] and there is no evidence that those who own platforms such as Google, Facebook or Twitter are really worried about what they enable. Being summoned to the US Senate for hearings is clearly not what they want, but it is not (so far) any deterrent.

Bringing all these strands together is like a puzzle, and when you piece them together they reveal a picture which is much more consequential and uncomfortable than each piece alone. Countries dominated by authoritarian systems are driving the erosion of global democratic norms and multilateral institutions. Populist ideas and leaders are gaining support around the world, eroding support within democracies for their norms. These trends are enabled by dangerous beliefs: democratic complacency which downplays the threat, disenchantment which saps the motivation to defend democracy, and conspiracy theories which corrode democracy from the inside. All this is amplified by social media. Taken together, I believe that these pieces reveal a risk that our century will be dominated by authoritarianism.

So do we just give up? Accept that public political discourse is now polluted by conspiracy theories where anyone can 'do their research' and be an expert, where politicians quite deliberately lie as there are no consequences and where the electorate fragments into silos marked by complete incomprehension about others?

Certainly some politicians would like us to do that as they focus on their core supporters and ensure those people are angry enough to really come out and vote when it matters.

The alternative means to start by acknowledging the depth of the challenge. That means doing more than assenting to this argument when we hear it in the context of debates about democracy and autocracy. It means recognising that democracy and democratic norms need our support in other contexts. It also means that non-populist parties need to seriously address the very real day-to-day concerns of their electorates—or, for perfectly predictable reasons, that electorate will start to look elsewhere.

NOTES

1. INTRODUCTION

1. 'Realist' in the meaning of the so-called Realist school of international relations theory. How *realistic* some of its assumptions actually are is another discussion altogether.
2. United Nations, 1948
3. Price & Zacher, 2004
4. COP26, 2021
5. Davey, 2022; McBride & Siripurapu, 2022
6. Buranyi, 2020
7. Clearly this is not the case, for good or ill US domestic political choices have global importance in the same way that Chinese policy choices matter for far more than just the citizens of the PRC.
8. For example, Lissner and Rapp-Hooper's book *An Open World* makes an argument along these lines.

2. LIBERAL AND MANAGED DEMOCRACIES

1. Parker, 1985
2. Ingrao, 2019
3. Scurr, 2006
4. James, 1980
5. Collier & Levitsky, 1997

6. Goertz, 2006
7. Munck, 2009
8. It is useful to note there is also a need to mediate between these issues. So there is need to balance the right to hold particular religious beliefs personally about, say, abortion or sexuality with the right not to be discriminated against on the basis of one's sexuality. Again this points to a critical difference between majoritarian attitudes and those compatible with a liberal democratic polity.
9. Hirschmann, 1970
10. Tusalem, 2007
11. Department of Legal Cooperation, 2011
12. Clayman, 2017
13. Ibrahim, 2017
14. United Nations, 1948
15. Most recently during the Civil Rights era and the Republicans' 'Southern Strategy'.
16. Sassoon, 1997
17. Rodrik, 2015
18. Dalton, 1974
19. Becattini, Pyke, & Sengenberger, 1990; Brusco, 1982
20. Lundberg, 1985
21. Cochrane, Clarke, & Gewirtz, 2001
22. Hayek, 1944
23. Dorling, 2015
24. Rostow, 1959
25. M. Friedman, 2007
26. Rodrik, 2006
27. T. L. Friedman, 1999
28. Zuboff, 2019
29. MacMillan, 2002
30. Notably, the settlement between Greece and Turkey, with Turkey forcibly regaining Anatolia, and Greece expelling the Turkish population from cities such as Salonika.
31. United Nations, 1948
32. United Nations, 1951

33. United Nations, 1947

34. Mansfield & Pevehouse, 2000

35. World Trade Organization, 2007

36. Karns & Mingst, 2004

37. Brown, 1986; Hirschmann, 1970

38. Stets & Burke, 2000; Tajfel & Turner, 1986

39. Tarrow, 1998; Tilly, 2003

40. Hennessy, 1992

41. Douglas et al., 2019; Douglas, Sutton, & Cichocka, 2017

42. Rutenberg, Corasaniti, & Feuer, 2020

43. Müller, 2016

44. Shafir & LeBoeuf, 2008

45. Weiss & Shanteau, 2004

46. Hochschild, 2018

47. Herman, 2014

48. Applebaum, 2021

49. Applebaum, 2021

3.   TRIUMPH AND HUBRIS

1. Kotkin, 2001

 2. Alexievich, 2013

 3. Belton, 2020

 4. Kotkin, 2001

 5. Steele, 1994

 6. Belton, 2020

 7. J. Anderson, 1997

 8. Fukuyama, 1992

 9. T. L. Friedman, 1999

10. Simms, 2001

11. Plant, 2008

12. Piven & Cloward, 1979; Tarrow, 1998

13. Cohn, 1970

14. Meijer, 2009

15. Ibrahim, 2017

16. Rees, Kessner, Klemperer, & Matutes, 1999
17. Vaughn, 1998
18. For a broad defence of this outcome see: Dani Rodrik, *Economics Rules* (Oxford: Oxford University Press, 2015).
19. Mazzucato, 2018
20. M. Friedman, 2007
21. Pennings, 2017
22. Barba & Pivetti, 2009
23. Deacon, 2000
24. Gould, 2020
25. Gould, 2020
26. Hochschild, 2018
27. OECD, 2021b
28. Boglioni & Zambelli, 2017
29. Aguilar, 1993
30. Elson, 2019
31. Caliendo & Parro, 2014
32. Chatzky, McBride, & Sergie, 2020
33. Chatzky, et al., 2020
34. Elson, 2019
35. Petri & Banga, 2020
36. A. S. Posen, 2021
37. Grubel, 2002
38. Falkenstein, 2009
39. ABC, 2017
40. Moak, 2017
41. J. Williamson, 2005
42. Hanna, Bishop, Nadel, Scheffler, & Durlacher, 2011
43. Wohlforth, 1999
44. B. R. Posen & Ross, 1996
45. Cirincione, Jon B. Wolfsthal, & Rajkumar, 2005
46. Plant, 2008
47. Watson, 2002
48. Bliscoe, 2011
49. Slaughter, 2004

50. Draper, 2020
51. Ibrahim, 2017
52. Bliscoe, 2011
53. Draper, 2020
54. Draper, 2020
55. As in many one-party states, joining the ruling party was a pragmatic means to access or retain employment; it was not always indicative of any particular zeal towards the regime.
56. Ibrahim, 2014
57. Silberman & Robb, 2005
58. Blanchard, 2016
59. Winter, 2015
60. Applebaum, 2016
61. Corbyn, 2013
62. Zingales, 2008
63. Bradford & Linn, 2010
64. Federal Reserve System, 2021
65. OECD, 2021a
66. Kwarteng, Patel, Raab, Skidmore, & Truss, 2012
67. Johnson, 2011
68. Barba & Pivetti, 2009; Treck, 2012
69. Bochel & Powell, 2016
70. Christensen, 2011; International Consortium of Investigative Journalists, 2019
71. Boushey & Weller, 2006
72. Pennings, 2017

4.   WESTERN POPULISM

1. Samuel, 2008
2. Cobban, 1965
3. Hayes, 2021
4. Ingrao, 2019
5. Stourzh, 1992
6. B. Anderson, 1983

7. Biddiss, 1994

8. Ibrahim, 2016

9. There are exceptions, such as the treatment of the Turkish Gästarbeiter who are denied German citizenship even if they are second generation and born in Germany.

10. Hobsbawm, 1992

11. MacMillan, 2002

12. Müller, 2016

13. A. Mueller, 2019

14. Ginsborg, 2001

15. Ganser, 2005

16. Sassoon, 1997

17. Lane, 2004

18. Ginsborg, 2001; Willan, 2002

19. The British populist politician, Nigel Farage, carefully studied the structure and approach of the Five Star Movement when founding his latest electoral vehicle so as to avoid all the inconveniences of a party with real members and some form of internal democracy.

20. Felice & Vecchi, 2015

21. Brook, 2007; Philo & Beattie, 1999

22. Winder, 2005

23. Shipman, 2016

24. Shipman, 2016

25. Zuboff, 2019

26. Shipman, 2016

27. Bochel & Powell, 2016; R. M. Page, 2007

28. Here the distinction matters, Scotland and Wales had both voted for the Labour Party with large majorities

29. Bolton & Pitts, 2018

30. Ibrahim, 2019

31. Ibrahim, 2019

32. Arbuthnot & Calvert, 2022

33. Hochschild, 2018

34. Haidt, 2012

35. Hochschild, 2018

36. Haidt, 2012
37. A. Mueller, 2019; Müller, 2016

5.   CONSPIRACY THEORIES AND SOCIAL MEDIA

1. B. Anderson, 1983; Finlayson, 2004
2. A. Mueller, 2019
3. Douglas, et al., 2017
4. Hochschild, 2018
5. Hayes, 2021
6. This may be more complex than it appears. Traditional centre-right voters in both the UK and the US are rejecting the Conservatives and Republicans respectively because of their populist narratives. The electoral equation is whether sticking to a populist approach retains more votes (perhaps often from those who previously didn't vote) than it loses. And of course, those who feel repelled in turn need to find somewhere else to go—which returns us to the problems of a two-party electoral system discussed earlier.
7. Hochschild, 2018
8. Cohn, 1970
9. BBC News, 2016
10. Langmuir, 1993
11. Department of Justice, 2022
12. Ben-Yehuda, 1980
13. Draper, 2020
14. Douglas, et al., 2019; Douglas, et al., 2017
15. Hochschild, 2018
16. Haidt, 2012
17. Ibrahim, 2017
18. Fister, 2021
19. Argentino & Amarasingam, 2020
20. Russonello, 2021
21. Argentino & Amarasingam, 2020
22. Russonello, 2021
23. Buranyi, 2020

24. Arbuthnot & Calvert, 2022
25. X. Wang, Zuo, Chan, Chiu, & Hong, 2021
26. BBC, 2021
27. Arbuthnot & Calvert, 2022
28. Jensen et al., 2021
29. Yang, Luo, & Jia, 2021
30. Jensen, et al., 2021
31. Ullah, Khan, Tahir, Ahmed, & Harapan, 2021
32. Steck & Kaczynski, 2021
33. Arbuthnot & Calvert, 2022
34. Graham, 1984
35. Moynihan & Patel, 2021
36. Statista, 2022
37. Sweet, 2020
38. Sweet, 2020
39. Coyle, 2017
40. Mazzucato, 2018
41. Zuboff, 2019
42. Zuboff, 2019
43. Zuboff, 2019
44. Srnicek, 2017
45. Srnicek, 2017
46. Zuboff, 2019
47. Zuboff, 2019
48. S. Levy, 2011
49. Podnar, 2017
50. Zuboff, 2019
51. S. Levy, 2011
52. Wolford, 2016
53. Zuboff, 2019
54. Zuboff, 2019
55. Congress, 2018
56. Zuboff, 2019
57. United States District Court, 2022
58. Kint, 2022

59. Zuboff, 2019
60. Muelle, 2019
61. Stevenson, 2018
62. Stevenson, 2018
63. Mackintosh, 2021
64. A favourite trick of newspapers to avoid this problem was to wait till one of them had made a claim and then report the 'debate' on that claim. The other, where they couldn't name a given individual was to publish a photograph of them on the same page but apparently connected to a different story. Again, the point is not to claim that pre-social media the press culture was beyond reproach, but that there were real constraints and they could only be avoided either by taking a risk or clever tricks.
65. The contrast here to the 'below the line' comment sections of many newspapers is valid. While they take the risk that their readers may indeed add something libellous, since the newspapers are responsible they take care with moderation and/or which topics they allow comment on. A post on Twitter can be libellous, or in contempt of court, and individuals have suffered the penalty for this. The platform is, as of 2022, exempt.
66. Meyer, 2018
67. Mac, Silverman, & Lytvynenko, 2021
68. Walter, 2022
69. Zuboff, 2019
70. Srnicek, 2017
71. Bannister & Fransella, 1986
72. Zerilli et al., 2021
73. Fediy, Protsai, & Gibalova, 2021
74. United States Senate, 2018
75. Marineau, 2020

6.   RUSSIA

1. Kotkin, 2001
2. Belton, 2020

3. It also had problems with those elements in Marx and Engels' writings that were German-centric, especially in the context of the 1848–50 revolutionary wave in Europe where the Slavs were cast as a backward threat to the progressive revolutions in places like Germany and Hungary.

4. Typically journal articles by Soviet academics would have to open with suitable quotes from Lenin; once this was out of the way, there was a notable lack of ideology apart from in the social sciences.

5. Kotkin, 2001

6. Belton, 2020

7. Steele, 1994

8. Dickinson, 2020

9. Belton, 2020

10. Kotkin, 2001

11. Belton, 2020

12. Admittedly in practice this meant each funded their own political parties and media but it created a competitive environment.

13. Heathershaw, Cooley, & Mayne, 2021

14. Belton, 2020

15. House of Commons, 2022a

16. Glenny, 2008; McIlvenna-Davis, 2019

17. Steele, 1994

18. Foy, 2021

19. Kramarenko, 2022

20. Ibrahim, 2019

21. Heller, 2017; Wesslau, 2016

22. And this framing is important: to Putin, the boundaries of the Tsarist empire, and thus of the USSR were the natural borders of a unitary state—not the mosaic of supposedly independent republics that formed the basis of the USSR, and its geographical splits in 1991.

23. Kramarenko, 2022

24. Wesslau, 2016

25. Kirchick, 2017

26. Milne, 2015

27. Heathershaw, et al., 2021

28. House of Commons, 2022a
29. Russian military advisers were present when the Ethiopians defeated an Italian invasion at Adwa in 1896 and Russian weaponry had been supplied to provide some modern weapons, giving the Ethiopians a capacity denied to most other African regimes attacked by Western powers in this period.
30. Belton, 2020
31. Steele, 1994
32. Danforth, 2020
33. Pop, 2009
34. Milne, 2008
35. Kramarenko, 2022
36. Kirchick, 2017
37. Belton, 2020
38. Maclean, 1949
39. An example of this type of Soviet propaganda can be found in Murphy, 1941. This is a near perfect example of how the Soviets were trying to justify the 1939 Nazi–Soviet pact even on the verge of the Nazi invasion of the USSR—when, of course, this inconvenient history was rewritten.
40. Urban, 1986
41. Belton, 2020
42. Alexievich, 2013
43. Alexievich, 1997
44. This is where the various foreign enterprises of the late Soviet era play a role and why the KGB dominated them—some of the money was diverted to fund KGB operations and never had to be accounted for to the Soviet state or, even, the Soviet Communist Party.
45. Belton, 2020
46. House of Commons, 2022a
47. Ibrahim, 2019
48. Applebaum, 2016; Engel, 2016
49. Ibrahim, 2019
50. Blumenthal, 2016; Sputnik, 2015
51. Ioffe, 2010

52. Thompson, 2022
53. Stillito, 2021
54. Thompson, 2022
55. Heathershaw, et al., 2021; House of Commons, 2022a
56. House of Commons, 2022a
57. Bawden & Hooper, 2011
58. House of Commons, 2022a
59. Sweeney, 2022
60. Shipman, 2016
61. House of Commons, 2022a
62. Geoghegan & Corderoy, 2018
63. Shipman, 2017
64. Zuboff, 2019
65. House of Commons, 2022a
66. Muelle, 2019
67. McGreevy, 2020
68. Muelle, 2019
69. Thompson, 2022
70. BBC, 2016
71. Migration Policy Centre, 2019
72. Blumenthal, 2016; Corbyn, 2013; Lucas, 2016; Sputnik, 2015
73. Applebaum, 2016
74. Borshchevskaya, 2020; Megerisi, 2020
75. House of Commons, 2022a; Muelle, 2019; United States Senate, 2018
76. As recently as 2021 he was putting a lot of effort into ensuring a report on Russian political activity in the UK was not published and has suppressed every investigation into the funding behind the 'Vote Leave' Brexit campaign. See Sweeney, 2022
77. Thompson, 2022

7. CHINA

1. Tarabay, 2021
2. Fuller, 2016

3. Callahan, 2005

4. Fuller, 2016

5. Denmark, 2018

6. Arrighi, 2007

7. Jacques, 2009

8. Bardhan, 2010

9. Gebhardt, 2013

10. Bartholomew & Cleveland, 2021

11. Bartholemew & Cleveland, 2021

12. J. Wang & Simpson, 2021

13. OECD, 2018

14. Moynihan & Patel, 2021

15. Byler, 2019; Moynihan & Patel, 2021

16. Diamond, 2021

17. Kuo, 2022

18. Bartholomew & Cleveland, 2021

19. One reason China covered up Covid was simply that it put China's entire system of governance in a poor light. An analogy can be drawn to the impact on Soviet domestic politics after the Chernobyl disaster.

20. Gat, 2007

21. Gat, 2001

22. While Social Darwinism was common among the ruling elites of Europe at the time, it profoundly influenced German military and political thinking.

23. Rudd, 2021

24. Gracie, 2015; Press Association, 2016

25. BBC, 2021

26. Tarabay, 2021

27. Rudd, 2021

28. Bartholomew & Cleveland, 2021

29. Bartholomew & Cleveland, 2021

30. Denmark, 2018

31. L. Jones & Hameiri, 2020

32. Bartholomew & Cleveland, 2021

33. D'Onfro, 2018

34. Feng, 2018
35. Rudd, 2021
36. Bartholomew & Cleveland, 2021
37. Bartholomew & Cleveland, 2021
38. P. J. Williamson, Hoenderop & Hoenderop, 2018; Yu, 2014
39. Seifert & Chung, 2005
40. Byler, 2019
41. Lissner & Rapp-Hooper, 2020
42. Peterson, 2020
43. Hastings, 2011
44. Lissner & Rapp-Hooper, 2020
45. Ramzy & Buckley, 2019
46. Jie & Wallace, 2021
47. Alessi & Xu, 2015
48. Gracie, 2015
49. Rajan, 2010
50. Press Association, 2016
51. Morris, 2013
52. L. Jones & Hameiri, 2020
53. J. Wang & Simpson, 2021
54. L. Jones & Hameiri, 2020
55. Alessi & Xu, 2015
56. L. Jones & Hameiri, 2020
57. Applebaum, 2021
58. J. Wang & Simpson, 2021
59. J. Wang & Simpson, 2021
60. Davidson, 2022; M. Page, 2022
61. European Parliament, 2015
62. Wolford, 2016
63. Of course the Chinese do not frame these disputes as 'international', they are problems that should be seen only as domestic Chinese matters.
64. Bartholomew & Cleveland, 2021
65. Tarabay, 2021

8.   FUNDAMENTALIST ISLAM AND THE NEW FAR RIGHT

1.   Liang & Cross, 2020
2.   Ibrahim, 2017
3.   Commins, 2009
4.   Allen, 2007
5.   Ibrahim, 2017
6.   Mohammed, 2016
7.   Ibrahim, 2017
8.   Ibrahim, 2017
9.   Allen, 2007
10. Ibrahim, 2017
11. And they also had a very particular and narrow view of what it meant to be Muslim. So particular, in fact, that the Saudi royal family did not qualify—and Saudi Arabia also saw a number of terror attacks as a consequence.
12. Allison, 2010
13. Kroenig, 2009
14. Cohn, 1970
15. Cronin, 2002
16. Passmore, 2010
17. Hobsbawm, 1987
18. B. Anderson, 1983; Connor, 1984; Hobsbawm, 1992
19. MacMillan, 2002
20. Stanley, 2018
21. Knox, 1982
22. Karen M Douglas, et al., 2019
23. Argentino & Amarasingam, 2020; Steck & Kaczynski, 2021
24. Hochschild, 2018
25. S. G. Jones & Doxsee, 2020
26. Ritchie, Hasell, Appel, & Roser, 2019
27. Lichbach, 1998
28. della Porta, 2010; Ginsborg, 1990
29. Horgan, 2008; Ibrahim, 2017
30. The key here is that many in terrorist groups may have a narcissistic personality but very few with that precondition go on to terrorism.

Equally German research suggested that many members of that country's Red Army Faction either came from a single-parent family or were alienated from their father. But, again, the overwhelming majority of those from single-parent backgrounds do not engage in any form of radical politics.

31. von Brömssen, 2013
32. S. G. Jones & Doxsee, 2020
33. Ritchie, et al., 2019

9.   SKETCHING A RESPONSE

1.   Hochschild, 2018
2.   Fawcett, 2020
3.   Hidalgo & Nichter, 2015
4.   Serdült, 2014
5.   Palese, 2018
6.   Qvortrup, 2018
7.   McHugh, Lemos, & Morrison, 2021
8.   UNEP, 2022
9.   Carroll, Daub, & Gunster, 2022
10. Krange, Kaltenborn, & Hultman, 2021
11. Leigh, 2021
12. Frost, 2022
13. CMCC Foundation, 2021; El-Geressi, 2020
14. Freitas, 2013
15. UNHCR, 2021
16. Brodie, 1976; J. Mueller, 1988
17. Mearsheimer, 1993
18. The Economist, 2021
19. Sagan & Waltz, 2002
20. Allison, 2010
21. Daalder & Lodal, 2008; Ferguson, 2010
22. Cordesman, 2013
23. The Economist, 2021

24. More generally, there is substantial research into the sort of low-level nuclear weapons that might be used in an otherwise conventional conflict—this is not just a matter of Russia making threats—the technology already exists where the nuclear threshold is close to that of conventional weapons.

25. Bartholomew & Cleveland, 2021; Rudd, 2021

26. Watson, 2002

27. Ibrahim, 2014

28. Ibrahim, 2014

29. Ali, 2016

30. Abadie, 2005; Levitt, 2002

31. UNHCR, 2021

32. Migration Data, 2019

33. EUROPOL, 2016

34. Gibney, 2008; Gower, 2011; C. Levy, 2005

35. Foreign Affairs Committee, 2019

36. Bershidsky, 2019

37. Taylor, 2012

38. Migration Policy Centre, 2019

39. UNHCR, 2011

40. Deng, Simmons, Gershkovich, & Mauldin, 2022

41. Kempe, 2022

42. Which as we have seen were more often than not very tense with China turning to the US as a counterbalance in the early 1970s

43. Kempe, 2022

44. Applebaum, 2021

45. Applebaum, 2021

46. International Court of Justice, 2015

47. Belton, 2020

48. Muelle, 2019; United States Senate, 2018

49. Rutenberg, et al., 2020

50. Thompson, 2022

51. Belton, 2020

52. Wesslau, 2016

53. Russonello, 2021

54. Muelle, 2019; United States Senate, 2018

55. House of Commons, 2022a

56. Lissner & Rapp-Hooper, 2020

57. The Joint Staff, 2018

58. Pavel, 2022

59. Kempe, 2022

60. Pavel, 2022

61. Pavel, 2022

62. Bartholemew & Cleveland, 2021; Muelle, 2019; United States Senate, 2018

63. House of Commons, 2022a

64. Mackay, 2021; McDonald, 2022

65. Kruk, 2019

66. House of Commons, 2022b

67. Ongaro, Di Mascio, & Natalini, 2022

68. Theuns, 2020

69. Every nation that sees itself as part of, and benefitting from, the liberal order has a role to play but some quite simply have greater weight—for good or ill.

70. Here, as elsewhere in the book, the term 'liberal' is used in its broadest sense. The member states of the EU are ruled by a variety of political parties running from Social Democrats, Greens, Liberals, Christian Democrats and various nationalist parties. Apart from the populists, there is a broadly shared core set of beliefs that together can be described as 'liberal'.

71. Globally it is the third largest economy, it contains two of the G7 powers, one of the world's nuclear states and is the largest multinational trading bloc in both manufacturing and services.

72. Clearly there are members of both the US Republican and British Conservative Parties who are deeply worried about this turn in right-wing politics. But in both countries, their party is now dominated by populists and has a membership increasingly different on demographic grounds to the country they wish to rule.

BIBLIOGRAPHY

Abadie, Alberto. (2005). Poverty, Political Freedom, And The Roots Of Terrorism. *American Economic Review, 95*(4), 50–56.

ABC. (2017, 25 January). ABC News anchor David Muir interviews President Trump. Retrieved 15 March 2018, from http://abcnews. go.com/Politics/transcript-abc-news-anchor-david-muir-interviews-president/story?id=45047602

Aguilar, Linda M. (1993). NAFTA: a review of the issues. Chicago: Federal Reserve Bank of Chicago.

Alessi, Christopher, & Xu, Beina. (2015, 27 April). China in Africa. Retrieved 2 June 2015, from http://www.cfr.org/china/china-africa/ p9557

Alexievich, Svetlana. (1997). *Chernobyl Prayer*. London: Penguin.

Alexievich, Svetlana. (2013). *Boys in Zinc* (Andrew Bromfield, Trans.). London: Penguin.

Ali, Luqman. (2016, 31 January). Why is ISIL able to find recruits in the West? Retrieved 2 July 2016, from http://www.thenational.ae/ opinion/comment/why-is-isil-able-to-find-recruits-in-the-west

Allen, Charles. (2007). *God's Terrorists: The Wahhabi Cult and the Hidden Roots of Modern Jihad*. Philadephia, PA: Da Capo Press.

Allison, Graham. (2010). Nuclear Disorder: Surveying Atomic Threats. *Foreign Affairs, 89*(1), 74-85.

Anderson, Benedict. (1983). *Imagined Communities: Reflections on the Origin and Spread of Nationalism*. London: Verso.

BIBLIOGRAPHY

Anderson, John. (1997). *The International Politics of Central Asia.* Manchester: Manchester University Press.

Applebaum, Anne. (2016, 29 August). The disastrous nonintervention in Syria. Retrieved 31 August 2016, from https://www.washingtonpost.com/opinions/global-opinions/what-exactly-nonintervention-has-produced-in-syria/2016/08/29/45826402-6e08-11e6-9705-23e51a2f424d_story.html?postshare=3011472525819354&tid=ss_tw&utm_term=.7d4c9b61f4b2

Applebaum, Anne. (2021). Tbe Bad Guys are Winning (p. 28). Washington, DC: The Atlantic.

Arbuthnot, George, & Calvert, Jonathan. (2022). *Failures of State:* (2nd ed.). London: HarperCollins.

Argentino, Marc-André, & Amarasingam, Amarnath. (2020). Q-Pilled: Conspiracy Theories, Trump, and Election Violence in the United States: International Centre for Counter-Terrorism.

Arrighi, Giovanni. (2007). *Adam Smith in Beijing: Lineages of the Twenty-First Century.* New York: Verso.

Bannister, D., & Fransella, F. (1986). *Inquiring Man: The Psychology of Personal Constructs* (3rd ed.). London: Croom Helm.

Barba, A., & Pivetti, M. (2009). Rising household debt: Its causes and macroeconomic implications – A long-period analysis. *Cambridge Journal of Economics, 33*, pp. 113–137.

Bardhan, Pranab. (2010). *Awakening Giants, Feet of Clay: Assessing the Economic rise of China and India.* New York: Princetown University Press.

Bartholomew, Carolyn, & Cleveland, Robin. (2021). 2021 Report to Congress of the US-China Economic and Security Review Commission (pp. 551). Washington, DC: US Congress.

Bawden, Tom, & Hooper, John. (2011, 22 February). Gaddafis' hidden billions: Dubai banks, plush London pads and Italian water. Retrieved 15 April 2018, from https://www.theguardian.com/world/2011/feb/22/gaddafi-libya-oil-wealth-portfolio

BBC. (2016, 2 March). Migrant crisis: Russia and Syria 'weaponising' migration. Retrieved 28 July 2022, from https://www.bbc.co.uk/news/world-europe-35706238

BIBLIOGRAPHY

BBC. (2021, 23 August). Wuhan lab leak theory: How Fort Detrick became a centre for Chinese conspiracies Retrieved 1 February 2022, from https://www.bbc.co.uk/news/world-us-canada-58273322

BBC News. (2016, 20 May). David Icke on 9/11 and lizards in Buckingham Palace theories. Retrieved 27 January 2022, from https://www.bbc.co.uk/news/av/uk-politics-36339298

Becattini, Giacomo, Pyke, Frank, & Sengenberger, Werner. (1990). *Industrial districts and inter-firm co-operation in Italy*: International Institute for Labour Studies.

Belton, Catherine. (2020). *Putin's People*. London: William Collins.

Ben-Yehuda, Nachman. (1980). The European Witch Craze of the 14th to 17th Centuries: A Sociologist's Perspective. *American Journal of Sociology, 86*(1), 1–31.

Bershidsky, Leonid. (2019, 6 September). Germany's Refugees Are Starting to Pay Off. Retrieved 15 November 2019, from https://www.bloomberg.com/opinion/articles/2019-09-06/germany-s-refugees-are-starting-to-pay-off

Biddiss, Michael. (1994). Nationalism and the Moulding of Modern Europe. *History, 79*(257), 412–432.

Blanchard, Christopher. (2016). Libya: Transition and US Policy (p. 29). Washington, DC: Congressional Research Service.

Bliscoe, Amy. (2011). The Cost of Iraq, Afghanistan, and Other Global War on Terror Operations Since 9/11 (p. 59). Washington, DC: Congressional Research Service.

Blumenthal, Max. (2016, 2 October). How the White Helmets Became International Heroes While Pushing U.S. Military Intervention and Regime Change in Syria. Retrieved 23 May 2019, from https://www.alternet.org/2016/10/how-white-helmets-became-international-heroes-while-pushing-us-military/

Bochel, H., & Powell, M. (Eds.). (2016). *The coalition government and social policy: Restructuring the welfare state*. Bristol: Policy Press.

Boglioni, Michele, & Zambelli, Stefano. (2017). European Economic Integraion and Comparative Advantages. *Journal of Economic Surveys, 31*(4), 1011–1034.

Bolton, Matt, & Pitts, Frederick Harry. (2018). *Corbynism: A Critical Approach*. Bingley: Emerald Publishing.

BIBLIOGRAPHY

Borshchevskaya, Anna. (2020, 24 January). Russia's Growing Interests in Libya *PolicyWatch*. Retrieved 27 March 2020, from https://www.washingtoninstitute.org/policy-analysis/view/russias-growing-interests-in-libya

Boushey, H., & Weller, C. E. (2006). Inequality and Household Economic Hardship in the United States of America (Vol. Working Papers (18)). New York: United Nations, Department of Economics and Social Affairs.

Bradford, Colin I., & Linn, Johannes F. (2010, 5 April). The April 2009 London G-20 Summit in Retrospect. Retrieved 4 December, 2021, from https://www.brookings.edu/opinions/the-april-2009-london-g-20-summit-in-retrospect/

Brodie, Bernard. (1976). On the Objectives of Arms Control. *International Security, 1*(1), pp. 17–36.

Brook, Stephen. (2007, 23 January). Mail and Express deny asylum bias. Retrieved 5 December 2011, from http://www.guardian.co.uk/media/2007/jan/23/pressandpublishing.immigrationasylumandrefugees

Brown, Roger. (1986). *Social Psychology* (2nd ed.). New York: Free Press.

Brusco, Sebastiano. (1982). The Emilian model: productive decentralisation and social integration. *Cambridge Journal of Economics, 6*(2), pp. 167–184.

Buranyi, Stephen. (2020, 10 April). The WHO v coronavirus: why it can't handle the pandemic. Retrieved 14 April 2020, from https://www.theguardian.com/news/2020/apr/10/world-health-organization-who-v-coronavirus-why-it-cant-handle-pandemic

Byler, Simon. (2019, 11 April). China's hi-tech war on its Muslim minority. Retrieved 20 April 2019, from https://www.theguardian.com/news/2019/apr/11/china-hi-tech-war-on-muslim-minority-xinjiang-uighurs-surveillance-face-recognition

Caliendo, Lorenzo, & Parro, Fernando. (2014). Estimates of the Trade and Welfare Effects of NAFTA. *The Review of Economic Studies, 82*(1), pp. 1–44.

Callahan, Mary P. (2005). *Making Enemies: War and State Building in Burma*. Ithaca, NY: Cornell University Press.

Carroll, William K, Daub, Shannon, & Gunster, Shane. (2022). Regime of Obstruction: Fossil capitalism and the many facets of climate denial in Canada *Handbook of Anti-Environmentalism* (pp. 216–233). Cheltenham: Edward Elgar Publishing.

Chatzky, Andrew, McBride, James, & Sergie, Mohammed Aly. (2020). NAFTA and the USMCA: Weighing the Impact of North American Trade. New York: Council on Foreign Relations.

Christensen, John. (2011). The looting continues: Tax havens and corruption. *Critical Perspectives on International Business, 7*, pp. 177–196.

Cirincione, Joseph, Wolfsthal, Jon B., & Rajkumar, Miriam. (2005). *Deadly Arsenals: Nuclear Biological, and Chemical Threats* (2nd ed.). Washington, DC: Carnegie Endowment for International Peace.

Clayman, Steven E. (2017). The Micropolitics of Legitimacy: Political Positioning and Journalistic Scrutiny at the Boundary of the Mainstream. *Social Psychology Quarterly, 80*(1), pp. 41–64.

CMCC Foundation. (2021, 27 April). Middle East and North Africa: Heatwaves of up to 56 degrees Celsius without climate action. Retrieved 1 June 2021, from https://phys.org/news/2021-04-middle-east-north-africa-heatwaves.html

Cobban, Alfred. (1965). *A History of Modern France, 1871–1962* (Vol. 3). London: Pelican.

Cochrane, Allen, Clarke, John, & Gewirtz, Sharon (Eds.). (2001). *Comparing Welfare States* (2nd ed.). Buckingham: Open University.

Cohn, Norman. (1970). *The Pursuit of the Millenium* (3rd ed.). London: Paladin.

Collier, David, & Levitsky, Steven. (1997). Democracy with Adjectives: Conceptual Innovation in Comparative Research. *World Politics, 49*(3), pp. 430–451.

Commins, David. (2009). *The Wahhabi Mission and Saudi Arabia*. New York: IB Taurus.

Congress. (2018). Facebook, Social Media Privacy and the Use and Abuse of Data (p. 385). Washington, DC.

Connor, Walker. (1984). *Ethnonationalism*. Princeton, NJ: Princeton University Press.

COP26. (2021). COP26 Goals. Retrieved 20 June 2022, from https://ukcop26.org/cop26-goals/

BIBLIOGRAPHY

Corbyn, Jeremy. (2013, 11 August). Interview: Use of Chemical Weapons in Syria. Retrieved 7 May 2019, from https://www.youtube.com/watch?v=wmFudc6MT9g

Cordesman, Anthony H. (2013). Red Lines, Deadlines, and Thinking the Unthinkable: India, Pakistan, Iran, North Korea, and China (p. 17). Washington, DC: Center for Strategic and International Studies.

Coyle, Diane. (2017). Do-it-yourself digital: the production boundary and the productivity puzzle (p. 26). Manchester: Economic Statistics: Centre of Excellence.

Cronin, Audrey Kurth. (2002). Behind the Curve: Globalization and International Terrorism. *International Security, 27*(3), pp. 30–58.

D'Onfro, Jillian. (2018, 15 October). Google CEO on censored search app in China: We could serve 'well over 99 percent of queries'. Retrieved 5 June 2022, from https://www.cnbc.com/2018/10/16/google-ceo-sundar-pichai-discusses-censored-search-app-in-china.html

Daalder, Ivo, & Lodal, Jan. (2008). The Logic of Zero: Toward a World Without Nuclear Weapons. *Foreign Affairs, 87*(6), pp. 83–95.

Dalton, George. (1974). *Economic Systems and Society: Capitalism, Communism and the Third World*. London: Penguin.

Danforth, Nicholas. (2020, 11 December). Perspectives: What did Turkey gain from the Armenia-Azerbaijan war? Retrieved 14 February 2021, from https://eurasianet.org/perspectives-what-did-turkey-gain-from-the-armenia-azerbaijan-war

Davey, William J. (2022). WTO Dispute Settlement: Crown Jewel or Costume Jewelry? *World Trade Review*, 1–10.

Davidson, Helen. (2022, 9 June). Fury at UN human rights chief over 'whitewash' of Uyghur repression. Retrieved 21 June 2022, from https://www.theguardian.com/world/2022/jun/09/fury-at-un-human-rights-chief-over-whitewash-of-uyghur-repression

Deacon, Alan. (2000). Learning from the US? The influence of American ideas upon 'new labour' thinking on welfare reform. *Policy & Politics, 28*(1), pp. 5–18.

della Porta, Donnatella. (2010). Left-Wing Terrorism in Italy. In Martha Crenshaw (Ed.), *Terrorism in Context* (pp. 106–160). University Park, PA: Penn State Press.

BIBLIOGRAPHY

Deng, Chao, Simmons, Ann M., Gershkovich, Evan, & Mauldin, William. (2022, 4 February). Putin, Xi Aim Russia-China Partnership Against U.S. Retrieved 20 June 2022, from https://www.wsj.com/articles/russias-vladimir-putin-meets-with-chinese-leader-xi-jinping-in-beijing-11643966743

Denmark, Abraham. (2018, 19 December). 40 years ago, Deng Xiaoping changed China — and the world. Retrieved 6 April 2022, from https://www.washingtonpost.com/news/monkey-cage/wp/2018/12/19/40-years-ago-deng-xiaoping-changed-china-and-the-world/

Department of Justice. (2022, 28 June). Ghislaine Maxwell Sentenced To 20 Years In Prison For Conspiring With Jeffrey Epstein To Sexually Abuse Minors. Retrieved 27 July 2022, from https://www.justice.gov/usao-sdny/pr/ghislaine-maxwell-sentenced-20-years-prison-conspiring-jeffrey-epstein-sexually-abuse

Department of Legal Cooperation. (2011). Text of the Draft Model Law on the Declaration of Interests, Income, Assets and Liabilities of Persons performing Public Functions (p. 10): Organization of American States.

Diamond, Yonah. (2021). The Uyghur Genocide: An Examination of China's Breaches of the 1948 Genocide Convention (p. 55): Newlines Institute for Strategy and Policy.

Dickinson, Peter. (2020, 22 November). How Ukraine's Orange Revolution shaped twenty-first century geopolitics. Retrieved 14 April 2022, from https://www.atlanticcouncil.org/blogs/ukrainealert/how-ukraines-orange-revolution-shaped-twenty-first-century-geopolitics/

Dorling, D. (2015). *Injustice*. Bristol: Policy Press.

Douglas, Karen M, Uscinski, Joseph E, Sutton, Robbie M, Cichocka, Aleksandra, Nefes, Turkay, Ang, Chee Siang, & Deravi, Farzin. (2019). Understanding conspiracy theories. *Political Psychology, 40*, 3–35.

Douglas, Karen M., Sutton, Robbie M., & Cichocka, Aleksandra. (2017). The Psychology of Conspiracy Theories. *Current Directions in Psychological Science, 26*(6), pp. 538–542.

Draper, Robert. (2020). *To Start a War: How the Bush Administration Took America Into Iraq*. New York: Penguin.

BIBLIOGRAPHY

El-Geressi, Yasmine. (2020, 8 September). Climate change, water woes, and conflict concerns in the Middle East: A toxic mix. Retrieved 1 June 2021, from https://www.earthday.org/climate-change-water-woes-and-conflict-concerns-in-the-middle-east-a-toxic-mix/

Elson, Anthony. (2019). Trade Globalization and the US Economy. In Anthony Elson (Ed.), *The United States in the World Economy*. (pp. 43–74). Cham: Palgrave Macmillan.

Engel, Pamela. (2016, 28 August). Obama's biggest achievement in Syria fell short — and Assad is rubbing it in his face. Retrieved 31 August 2016, from http://linkis.com/8XzI6

European Parliament. (2015). Consumer Protection in the EU (pp. 24). Brussels: European Parliament.

EUROPOL. (2016). Migrant Smuggling in the EU (p. 15). Brussels: Europol.

Falkenstein, Eric. (2009, 10 August). We Need Less Regulation, Not More. Retrieved 23 November 2021, from https://www.cbsnews.com/news/we-need-less-regulation-not-more/

Fawcett, Edmund. (2020). *Conservatism: The Fight for a Tradition*. Princeton, NJ: Princeton University Press.

Federal Reserve System. (2021, 13 May). Financial Stability Report. Retrieved 4 December 2021, from https://www.federalreserve.gov/publications/may-2021-asset-valuations.htm

Fediy, Olga, Protsai, Liudmyla, & Gibalova, Nataliia. (2021). Pedagogical Conditions for Digital Citizenship Formation among Primary School Pupils. *Revista Romaneasca pentru Educatie Multidimensionala, 13*(3), pp. 95–115.

Felice, Emanuele, & Vecchi, Giovanni. (2015). Italy's modern economic growth, 1861–2011. *Enterprise & Society, 16*(02), pp. 225–248.

Feng, Wenmeng. (2018). The Silver and White Economy: The Chinese Demographic Challenge (pp. 36): OECD.

Ferguson, Charles D. (2010). The Long Road to Zero: Overcoming the Obstacles to a Nuclear-Free World. *Foreign Affairs, 89*(1), pp. 86–94.

Finlayson, Alan. (2004). Imagined Communities. In Kate Nash & Alan Scott (Eds.), *The Blackwell Companion to Political Sociology* (pp. 281–290). Oxford: Blackwell.

BIBLIOGRAPHY

Fister, Barbara. (2021, February 18). The Librarian War Against QAnon Retrieved 29 January 2022, from https://www.theatlantic.com/education/archive/2021/02/how-librarians-can-fight-qanon/618047/

Foreign Affairs Committee. (2019). Responding to irregular migration: A diplomatic route (p. 30). London: House of Commons.

Foy, Henry. (2021, 18 June). Vladislav Surkov: 'An overdose of freedom is lethal to a state'. Retrieved 20 June 2021, from https://www.ft.com/content/1324acbb-f475-47ab-a914-4a96a9d14bac

Freitas, Any. (2013). Water as a stress factor in sub-Saharan Africa (pp. 4). Brussels: European Union Institute for Security Studies.

Friedman, Milton. (2007). The Social Responsibility of Business Is to Increase Its Profits. In Walther Ch Zimmerli, Markus Holzinger & Klaus Richter (Eds.), *Corporate Ethics and Corporate Governance* (pp. 173–178). Berlin: Springer Berlin Heidelberg.

Friedman, Thomas L. (1999). *The Lexus and the Olive Tree*. New York: Farrar, Straus and Giroux.

Frost, Rosie. (2022, 5 April). UK government 'exploiting' Ukraine war to continue fossil fuel investment, oil protesters say. Retrieved 21 June 2022, from https://www.euronews.com/green/2022/04/05/protesters-block-10-oil-terminals-as-uk-government-doubles-down-on-fossil-fuel-expansion

Fukuyama, Francis. (1992). *The End of History and the Last Man*. New York: Free Press.

Fuller, Nicholas. (2016). Xinjiang: The History and Context of Modern Issues. *IUSB Undergraduate Research Journal of History, 6*, pp. 11–20.

Ganser, Daniele. (2005). *NATO's Secret Armies: Operation Gladio and Terrorism in Western Europe*. London: Frank Cass.

Gat, Azar. (2001). *A History of Military Thought*. Oxford: Oxford University Press.

Gat, Azar. (2007). The Return of Authoritarian Great Powers. *Foreign Affairs, 86*(4), pp. 59–69.

Gebhardt, Christiane. (2013). Upgrading the Chinese Economy by Overhauling Special Economic Zones: Innovation Model Shopping or the Emergence of a Chinese Innovation Model? *Industry and Higher Education, 27*(4), pp. 297–312.

BIBLIOGRAPHY

Geoghegan, Peter, & Corderoy, Jenna. (.2018, 4 May). Revealed: Legatum's 'extraordinary' secretive monthly meetings with Brexit minister Retrieved 12 December 2019, from https://www.opendemocracy.net/en/opendemocracyuk/revealed-legatum-s-extraordinary-secretive-monthly-meetings-with-brexit/?utm_source=tw

Gibney, Matthew J. (2008). Asylum and the Expansion of Deportation in the United Kingdom. *Government and Opposition, 43*(2), pp. 146–167.

Ginsborg, Paul. (1990). *A History of Contemporary Italy: 1943–1980.* London: Penguin.

Ginsborg, Paul. (2001). *Italy and Its Discontents: 1980–2001.* London: Penguin.

Glenny, Misha. (2008). *McMafia: Crime Without Frontiers.* London: Bodley Head.

Goertz, Gary. (2006). *Social Science Concepts: A User's Guide.* Princeton, NJ: Princeton University Press.

Gould, Elise. (2020, 20 February). State of Working America Wages 2019. Retrieved 22 November 2021, from https://www.epi.org/publication/swa-wages-2019/

Gower, Melanie. (2011). Immigration and asylum policy: the Government's plans (p. 9): House of Commons Library.

Gracie, Carrie. (2015, 19 October). China and 'the Osborne Doctrine'. Retrieved 1 March 2019, from https://www.bbc.co.uk/news/world-asia-china-34539507

Graham, Loren R. (1984). Science and Computers in Soviet Society. *Proceedings of the Academy of Political Science, 35*(3), pp. 124–134.

Grubel, Herbert. (2002, 3 October). Why We Need Less Regulation of Capital Markets. Retrieved 23 November 2021, from https://www.fraserinstitute.org/article/why-we-need-less-regulation-capital-markets

Haidt, Jonathan. (2012). *The Righteous Mind.* London: Penguin.

Hanna, Rema, Bishop, Sarah, Nadel, Sara, Scheffler, Gabe, & Durlacher, Katherine. (2011). The effectiveness of anti-corruption policy What has worked, what hasn't, and what we don't know. In Social Science Research Unit EPPI-Centre (Ed.), (p. 127). London: Institute of Education.

BIBLIOGRAPHY

Hastings, Justin V. (2011). Charting the Course of Uyghur Unrest. *The China Quarterly, 208*, pp. 893–912.

Hayek, FA. (1944). *The Road to Serfdom*. London: University of Chicago Press.

Hayes, Chris. (2021, 8 February). The Republican Party Is Radicalizing Against Democracy. Retrieved 5 June 2022, from https://www.theatlantic.com/ideas/archive/2021/02/republican-party-radicalizing-against-democracy/617959/

Heathershaw, John, Cooley, Professor Alexander, & Mayne, Thomas. (2021). The UK's kleptocracy problem: How servicing post-Soviet elites weakens the rule of law London: Chatham House.

Heller, Richard. (2017, 9 October). Digging into Corbyn's silence on Putin. Retrieved 5 June 2019, from https://www.politics.co.uk/comment-analysis/2017/10/09/digging-into-corbyn-s-silence-on-putin

Hennessy, Peter. (1992). *Never Again: Britain 1945–1951*. London: Penguin.

Herman, Lise Esther. (2014, 16 June). Book Review: Revolt on the Right: Explaining Support for the Radical Right in Britain by Robert Ford and Matthew J. Goodwin. Retrieved 12 September 2016, from http://blogs.lse.ac.uk/lsereviewofbooks/2014/06/16/book-review-revolt-on-the-right-explaining-support-for-the-radical-right-in-britain-by-robert-ford-and-matthew-j-goodwin/

Hidalgo, F. Daniel, & Nichter, Simeon. (2015). Voter Buying: Shaping the Electorate through Clientelism. *American Journal of Political Science*, n/a-n/a.

Hirschmann, Albert O. (1970). *Exit, Voice and Loyalty: Responses to Decline in Firms, Organizations and States*. New York: Harvard University Press.

Hobsbawm, Eric. (1987). *The Age of Empire 1875–1914*. London: Sphere Books.

Hobsbawm, Eric. (1992). *Nations and Nationalism Since 1780: Programme, Myth, Reality*. Cambridge: Cambridge University Press.

Hochschild, Arlie Russell. (2018). *Strangers in their Own Land* (2nd ed.). New York: New Press.

Horgan, John. (2008). From Profiles to Pathways and Roots to Routes: Perspectives from Psychology on Radicalization into Terrorism. *The*

BIBLIOGRAPHY

Annals of the American Academy of Political and Social Science, 618(1), pp. 80–94.

House of Commons. (2022a). Countering Russian influence in the UK (p. 32). London: UK Parliament.

House of Commons. (2022b, 22 March). The EU response to the Russian invasion of Ukraine. Retrieved 10 June 2022, from https://commonslibrary.parliament.uk/research-briefings/cbp-9503/

Ibrahim, Azeem. (2014). The Resurgence of Al-Qaeda in Syria and Iraq (p. 80). Washington, DC: SSI.

Ibrahim, Azeem. (2016). *The Rohingyas: Inside Myanmar's Hidden Genocide*. Oxford: Oxford University Press.

Ibrahim, Azeem. (2017). *Radical Origins: Why We Are Losing the Battle Against Islamic Extremism?* New York: Pegasus Books.

Ibrahim, Azeem. (2019). The Prospective Foreign Policy of a Corbyn Government and its U.S. National Security Implications (p. 39). Washington, DC: Hudson Institute.

Ingrao, Charles W. (2019). *The Habsburg Monarchy 1618–1815* (3rd ed.). Cambridge: Cambridge University Press.

International Consortium of Investigative Journalists. (2019). The Panama Papers: Exposing the Rogue Offshore Finance Industry. Retrieved 24 November 2019, from https://www.icij.org/investigations/panama-papers/

International Court of Justice. (2015). Case Concerning Application of the Convention on the Prevention and Punishment of the Crime of Genocide (Croatia v Serbia) (p. 153). The Hague: International Court of Justice.

Ioffe, Julia. (2010, 1 October). What Is Russia Today? Retrieved 1 May 2017, from https://archives.cjr.org/feature/what_is_russia_today.php

Jacques, Martin. (2009). *When China Rules the World: The Rise of the Middle Kingdom and the End of the Western World*. London: Allen Lane.

James, C.L.R. (1980). *The Black Jacobins: Toussaint L'Ouverture and the San Domingo Revolution* (3rd ed.). London: Alison and Busby.

Jensen, Eric Allen, Pfleger, Axel, Herbig, Lisa, Wagoner, Brady, Lorenz, Lars, & Watzlawik, Meike. (2021). What Drives Belief in Vaccination

Conspiracy Theories in Germany? [Brief Research Report]. *Frontiers in Communication, 6.*

Jie, Yu, & Wallace, Jon. (2021). What is China's Belt and Road Initiative (BRI)? (p. 5): Chatham House.

Johnson, Simon. (2011). Did the Poor Cause the Crisis? *Project Syndicate* (Vol. 2012). Washington.

Jones, Lee, & Hameiri, Shahar. (2020). Debunking the Myth of 'Debt-trap Diplomacy' (pp. 20): Chatham House.

Jones, Seth G., & Doxsee, Catrina. (2020, 17 June). The Escalating Terrorism Problem in the United States. Retrieved 1 May 2022, from https://www.csis.org/analysis/escalating-terrorism-problem-united-states

Karns, Margaret P., & Mingst, Karen A. (2004). *International Organizations: The Politics and Processes of Global Governance.* Boulder, CO: Lynne Rienner.

Kempe, Frederick. (2022, 6 February). The world's top two authoritarians have teamed up. The US should be on alert. Retrieved 15 June 2022, from https://www.atlanticcouncil.org/content-series/inflection-points/the-worlds-top-two-authoritarians-have-teamed-up-the-us-should-be-on-alert/

Kint, Jason. (2022, 10 February). Facebook Accountability. Retrieved 11 February 2022, from https://threadreaderapp.com/thread/1491933693346299913.html

Kirchick, James. (2017, 17 March). Russia's plot against the West. Retrieved 11 June 2019, from https://www.politico.eu/article/russia-plot-against-the-west-vladimir-putin-donald-trump-europe/

Knox, MacGregor. (1982). *Mussolini Unleashed 1939–1941.* Cambridge: Cambridge University Press.

Kotkin, Stephen. (2001). *Armageddon Averted: The Soviet Collapse 1970–2000.* Cambridge: Cambridge University Press.

Kramarenko, Alexander. (2022). The Great Patriotic War 2.0 (p. 2).

Krange, Olve, Kaltenborn, Bjørn P., & Hultman, Martin. (2021). 'Don't confuse me with facts'—how right wing populism affects trust in agencies advocating anthropogenic climate change as a reality. *Humanities and Social Sciences Communications, 8*(1), p. 255.

Kroenig, Matthew. (2009). Exporting the Bomb: Why States Provide Sensitive Nuclear Assistance. *The American Political Science Review, 103*(1), pp. 113–133.

Kruk, Katya. (2019, 7 May). The Crimean Factor: How the European Union Reacted to Russia's Annexation of Crimea. Retrieved 10 June 2022, from https://warsawinstitute.org/crimean-factor-european-union-reacted-russias-annexation-crimea/

Kuo, Mercy A. (2022, 8 March). Lithuania as a Litmus Test of EU-China Relations. Retrieved 20 June 2022, from https://thediplomat.com/2022/03/lithuania-as-a-litmus-test-of-eu-china-relations/

Kwarteng, Kwasi, Patel, Priti, Raab, Dominic, Skidmore, Chris, & Truss, Elizabeth (Eds.). (2012). *Britannia Unchained: Global Lessons for Growth and Prosperity*. London: Palgrave MacMillan.

Lane, David. (2004). *Berlusconi's Shadow*. London: Penguin.

Langmuir, Gavin I. (1993). *History, Religion, and Antisemitism*. Berkeley, CA: University of California Press.

Leigh, Andrew. (2021, 5 November). How Populism Imperils the Planet. Retrieved 25 June 2022, from https://thereader.mitpress.mit.edu/how-populism-imperils-the-planet/

Levitt, Matthew A. (2002). The Political Economy of Middle East Terrorism. *Middle East Review of International Affairs, 6*(4), pp. 49–65.

Levy, Carl. (2005). The European Union after 9/11: The Demise of a Liberal Democratic Asylum Regime? *Government and Opposition, 40*(1), pp. 26–59.

Levy, Steven. (2011). *In the Plex: How Google Thinks, Works, and Shapes Our Lives*. New York: Simon and Schuster.

Liang, Christina Schori, & Cross, Matthew John. (2020). White Crusade: How to Prevent Right-Wing Extremists from Exploiting the Internet (p. 27). Geneva: Geneva Centre for Security Policy.

Lichbach, Mark Irving. (1998). *The Rebel's Dilemna*. Michigan: University of Michagan Press.

Lissner, Rebecca, & Rapp-Hooper, Mira. (2020). *An Open World*. New Haven, CT: Yale University Press.

Lucas, Scott. (2016, 7 October). Who are Syria's White Helmets, and why are they so controversial? Retrieved 23 May 2019, from http://

theconversation.com/who-are-syrias-white-helmets-and-why-are-they-so-controversial-66580

Lundberg, Erik. (1985). The Rise and Fall of the Swedish Model. *Journal of Economic Literature, 23*(1), pp. 1–36.

Mac, Ryan, Silverman, Craig, & Lytvynenko, Jane. (2021, 26 April). Facebook Stopped Employees From Reading An Internal Report About Its Role In The Insurrection. You Can Read It Here. Retrieved 5 June 2022, from https://www.buzzfeednews.com/article/ryanmac/full-facebook-stop-the-steal-internal-report

Mackay, Neil. (2021, 26 September). SNP MP's warning over Russian disinformation ops targeting Indyref2. Retrieved 29 July 2022, from https://www.heraldscotland.com/politics/19605624.neil-mackays-big-read-snp-mps-warning-russian-disinformation-ops-targeting-indyref2/

Mackintosh, Eliza. (2021, 25 October). Facebook knew it was being used to incite violence in Ethiopia. It did little to stop the spread, documents show. Retrieved 15 February 2022, from https://edition.cnn.com/2021/10/25/business/ethiopia-violence-facebook-papers-cmd-intl/index.html

Maclean, Fitzroy. (1949). *Eastern Approaches*. London: The Reprint Society.

MacMillan, Margaret. (2002). *Peacemakers: Six Months that Changed the World*. London: John Murray.

Mansfield, Edward D., & Pevehouse, Jon C. (2000). Trade Blocs, Trade Flows, and International Conflict. *International Organization, 54*(4), pp. 775–808.

Marineau, Sophie. (2020, 29 September). Fact check US: What is the impact of Russian interference in the US presidential election? Retrieved 5 June 2022, from https://theconversation.com/fact-check-us-what-is-the-impact-of-russian-interference-in-the-us-presidential-election-146711

Mazzucato, Mariana. (2018). *The Value of Everything: Making and Taking in the Global Economy*. London: Allen Lane.

McBride, James, & Siripurapu, Anshu. (2022, 10 June). What's Next for the WTO? Retrieved 20 June 2022, from https://www.cfr.org/backgrounder/whats-next-wto

BIBLIOGRAPHY

McDonald, Steward. (2022, 29 April). A Scottish National Security Strategy. Retrieved 2 May 2022, from https://reformscotland. com/2022/04/a-scottish-national-security-strategy-stewart-mcdonald-mp/

McGreevy, Nora. (2020, 12 March). Pigasus, the Naked Cowboy, and Other Presidential Candidates Who Never Had a Shot. Retrieved 20 March 2022, from https://www.washingtonian.com/2020/03/12/pigasus-the-naked-cowboy-presidential-fringe-candidates-mark-stein/

McHugh, Lucy Holmes, Lemos, Maria Carmen, & Morrison, Tiffany Hope. (2021). Risk? Crisis? Emergency? Implications of the new climate emergency framing for governance and policy. *WIREs Climate Change, 12*(6), e736.

McIlvenna-Davis, Dylan. (2019, 16 December). Gangs and Gulags: How Vladimir Putin Utilizes Organized Crime to Power his Mafia State. *Berkeley Political Review*. Retrieved 4 June 2021, from https://bpr. berkeley.edu/2019/12/16/gangs-and-gulags-how-vladimir-putin-utilizes-organized-crime-to-power-his-mafia-state/

Mearsheimer, John J. (1993). The Case for a Ukrainian Nuclear Deterrent. *Foreign Affairs, 72*(3), pp. 50–66.

Megerisi, Tarek. (2020, 24 March). Why the 'ignored war' in Libya will come to haunt a blinkered west. Retrieved 24 March 2020, from https://www. theguardian.com/global-development/commentisfree/2020/mar/24/why-the-ignored-war-in-libya-will-come-to-haunt-a-blinkered-west

Meijer, Roel (Ed.). (2009). *Global Salafism: Islam's New Religious Movement.* Oxford: Oxford University Press.

Meyer, Robinson. (2018, 8 March). The Grim Conclusions of the Largest-Ever Study of Fake News. Retrieved 5 June 2022, from https://www. theatlantic.com/technology/archive/2018/03/largest-study-ever-fake-news-mit-twitter/555104/

Migration Data. (2019, 15 October). Human Trafficking. Retrieved 12 November 2019, from https://migrationdataportal.org/themes/human-trafficking

Migration Policy Centre. (2019). The Syrian refugee crisis and its repercussions for the EU. Retrieved 20 June 2019, from http:// syrianrefugees.eu/

BIBLIOGRAPHY

Milne, Seamus. (2008, 14 August). This is a tale of US expansion not Russian aggression. Retrieved 21 April, 2019, from https://www.theguardian.com/commentisfree/2008/aug/14/russia.georgia

Milne, Seamus. (2015, 4 March). The demonisation of Russia risks paving the way for war Retrieved 22 April 2019, from https://www.theguardian.com/commentisfree/2015/mar/04/demonisation-russia-risks-paving-way-for-war

Moak, Ken. (2017). *Developed Nations and the Economic Impact of Globalization*. New York: Palgrave Macmillan.

Mohammed, Ruzwan. (2016). *Caliphate Reloaded: Past, present and future Muslim discourse on Power*.

Morris, Anne. (2013, 7 June). UK chancellor defends Huawei after security report spooks MPs. Retrieved 3 March 2019, from https://www.fiercewireless.com/europe/uk-chancellor-defends-huawei-after-security-report-spooks-mps

Moynihan, Harriet, & Patel, Champa. (2021). Restrictions on online freedom of expression in China. London: Chatham House.

Muelle, Robert S. (2019). Report On The Investigation Into Russian Interference In The 2016 Presidential Election (p. 448). Washington, DC: US Department of Justice.

Mueller, Axel. (2019). The meaning of 'populism'. *Philosophy & Social Criticism, 45*(9-10), pp. 1025–1057.

Mueller, John. (1988). The Essential Irrelevance of Nuclear Weapons: Stability in the Postwar World. *International Security, 13*(2), pp. 55–79.

Müller, Jan-Werner. (2016). *What Is Populism?* Philadelphia, PN: University of Pennsylvania Press.

Munck, Gerardo L. (2009). *Measuring Democracy*. Baltimore, MD: Johns Hopkins University Press.

Murphy, J. T. (1941). *Russia on the March: A study of Soviet Foreign Policy*. Hertford: Stephen Austin and Sons, Ltd.

OECD. (2018). China's Belt and Road Initiative in the global trade,investment and finance landscape *OECD Business and Finance Outlook* (p. 46): OECD.

OECD. (2021a). General government debt. Retrieved 4 December 2021, from https://data.oecd.org/gga/general-government-debt.htm

OECD. (2021b). Household Debt. Retrieved 22 November 2021, from https://data.oecd.org/hha/household-debt.htm

Ongaro, Edoardo, Di Mascio, Fabrizio, & Natalini, Alessandro. (2022). How the European Union responded to populism and its implications for public sector reforms. *Global Public Policy and Governance, 2*(1), pp. 89–109.

Page, Mercedes. (2022, 6 April). The mysterious missing UN report on human rights abuses in Xinjiang. Retrieved 21 June 2022, from https://www.lowyinstitute.org/the-interpreter/mysterious-missing-un-report-human-rights-abuses-xinjiang

Page, Robert M. (2007). Without a Song in their Heart: New Labour, the Welfare State and the Retreat from Democratic Socialism. *Journal of Social Policy, 36*, pp. 19–37.

Palese, Michela. (2018, 29 May). The Irish abortion referendum: How a Citizens' Assembly helped to break years of political deadlock. Retrieved 22 June 2022, from https://www.electoral-reform.org.uk/the-irish-abortion-referendum-how-a-citizens-assembly-helped-to-break-years-of-political-deadlock/

Parker, Geoffrey. (1985). *The Dutch Revolt* (2nd ed.). London: Penguin.

Passmore, Kevin. (2010). The Ideological Origins of Fascism before 1914. In R. J. B. Bosworth (Ed.), *The Oxford Handbook of Fascism*. Oxford: Oxford University Press.

Pavel, Barry. (2022). The next National Defense Strategy is coming. These seven points are key to understanding it. Retrieved 15 June 2022, from https://www.atlanticcouncil.org/blogs/new-atlanticist/the-next-national-defense-strategy-is-coming-these-seven-points-are-key-to-understanding-it/

Pennings, Paul. (2017). When and where did the great recession erode the support of democracy? *Zeitschrift für Vergleichende Politikwissenschaft, 11*(1), pp. 81–103.

Peterson, Dahlia. (2020). Foreign technology and the surveillance state *China's Quest for Foreign Technology: Beyond Espionage* (pp. 241–257). London: Routledge.

Petri, Peter A., & Banga, Meenal. (2020). The Economic Consequences of Globalisation in the United States (p. 28). Waltham, MA: Brandeis University.

BIBLIOGRAPHY

Philo, G., & Beattie, L. (1999). Race, Migration and the Media. In G. Philo (Ed.), *Message Received* (pp. 171–196). London: Routledge.

Piven, Frances Fox, & Cloward, Richard, A. (1979). *Poor People's Movements: Why They Succeed, How They Fail.* New York: Pantheon Books.

Plant, Raymond. (2008). Blair's Liberal Interventionism (pp. 151–169).

Podnar, Rachel. (2017, 6 March). Blog Log: Google Home shares conspiracy theory; people are putting pizza in milk. Retrieved 24 May 2022, from https://www.washingtonpost.com/express/wp/2017/03/06/blog-log-google-home-shares-conspiracy-theory-people-are-putting-pizza-in-milk/

Pop, Valentina. (2009, 21 March). EU expanding its 'sphere of influence,' Russia says. Retrieved 11 June 2019, from https://euobserver.com/foreign/27827

Posen, Adam S. (2021, 28 September). The Interconnected Economy: The Effects of Globalization on US Economic Disparity. Retrieved 23 November 2021, from https://www.piie.com/commentary/testimonies/interconnected-economy-effects-globalization-us-economic-disparity

Posen, Barry R., & Ross, Andrew L. (1996). Competing Visions for U.S. Grand Strategy. *International Security, 21*(3), pp. 5–53.

Press Association. (2016, 1 August). Osborne rejected safeguards over Chinese role in Hinkley Point, says ex-minister. Retrieved 1 March 2019, from https://www.theguardian.com/uk-news/2016/aug/01/osborne-rejected-safeguards-over-chinese-role-in-hinkley-point-says-ex-energy-minister

Price, Richard M, & Zacher, Mark W. (2004). *The United Nations and Global Security.* New York: Palgrave Macmillan.

Qvortrup, Matt. (2018). *Referendums around the world. Basingstoke*: Palgrave Macmillan.

Rajan, Raghuram G. (2010). *Fault Lines: How Hidden Fractures Still Threaten the World Economy.* Princeton, NJ: Princeton University Press.

Ramzy, Austin, & Buckley, Chris. (2019, 16 November). Absolutely No Mercy': Leaked Files Expose How China Organized Mass Detentions of Muslims. Retrieved 16 February 2021, from www.nytimes.com/interactive/2019/11/16/world/asia/china-xinjiang-documents.html

Rees, Ray, Kessner, Ekkehard, Klemperer, Paul, & Matutes, Carmen. (1999). Regulation and Efficiency in European Insurance Markets. *Economic Policy, 14*(29), pp. 365–397.

Ritchie, Hannah, Hasell, Joe, Appel, Cameron, & Roser, Max. (2019, November). Terrorism. Retrieved 12 May 2022, from https://ourworldindata.org/terrorism

Rodrik, Dani. (2006). Goodbye Washington Consensus, Hello Washington Confusion? A Review of the World Bank's 'Economic Growth in the 1990s: Learning from a Decade of Reform'. *Journal of Economic Literature, 44*(4), pp. 973–987.

Rodrik, Dani. (2015). *Economics Rules*. Oxford: Oxford University Press.

Rostow, W. W. (1959). The Stages of Economic Growth. *The Economic History Review, New Series, 12*(1), pp. 1–16.

Rudd, Kevin. (2021). Reflections on China and U.S.-China Relations in 2021 (p. 94): Asia Society Policy Institute.

Russonello, Giovanni. (2021). QAnon Now as Popular in U.S. as Some Major Religions, Poll Suggests. Retrieved 29 January 2022, from https://www.nytimes.com/2021/05/27/us/politics/qanon-republicans-trump.html

Rutenberg, Jim, Corasaniti, Nick, & Feuer, Alan. (2020, 26 December). Trump's Fraud Claims Died in Court, but the Myth of Stolen Elections Lives On. Retrieved 15 May 2021, from https://www.nytimes.com/2020/12/26/us/politics/republicans-voter-fraud.html

Sagan, Scott D., & Waltz, Kenneth N. (2002). Indian and Pakistani Nuclear Weapons: For Better or Worse. In Scott D. Sagan & Kenneth N. Waltz (Eds.), *The Spread of Nuclear Weapons: A Debate Renewed* (pp. 88–124). New York: WW Norton.

Samuel, Henry. (2008, 8 February). Le Pen found guilty of Holocaust denial. Retrieved 11 January 2016, from http://www.telegraph.co.uk/news/worldnews/1578053/Le-Pen-found-guilty-of-Holocaust-denial.html

Sassoon, Donald. (1997). *One Hundred Years of Socialism: The West European Left in the Twentieth Century*. London: Fontana.

Scurr, Ruth. (2006). *Fatal Purity: Robespierre and the French Revolution*. London: Vintage Books.

Seifert, J. W., & Chung, J. (2005). *Comparing E-Government in the United States and China: Mobilizing Democracy or Empowering Government?* Paper presented at the American Political Science Association, Marriott Wardman Park, Omni Shoreham, Washington Hilton, Washington, DC.

Serdült, Uwe. (2014). Referendums in Switzerland *Referendums around the World* (pp. 65–121). Basingstoke: Palgrave Macmillan.

Shafir, Eldar, & LeBoeuf, Robyn A. (2008). Context and Conflict in Multiattribute Choice *Blackwell Handbook of Judgment and Decision Making* (pp. 339–359): Blackwell Publishing Ltd.

Shipman, Tim. (2016). *All Out War: The Full Story of Brexit*. London: William Collins.

Shipman, Tim. (2017). *Fall Out*. London: William Collins.

Silberman, Laurence, & Robb, Charles. (2005). The Commission on the Intelligence Capabilities of the United States Regarding Weapons of Mass Destruction (p. 618). Washington.

Simms, Brendan. (2001). *Unfinest Hour: Britain and the Destruction of Bosnia*. London: Penguin.

Slaughter, Anne-Marie. (2004). *A New World Order*. Princeton, NJ: Princeton University Press.

Sputnik. (2015, 30 September). Homs Airstrike: White Helmets Caught Faking Syria Casualties Report. Retrieved 23 May 2019, from https://sputniknews.com/middleeast/201509301027807644-ngo-caught-faking-syria-casualties-report/

Srnicek, Nick. (2017). *Platform Capitalism*. Cambridge: Polity Press.

Stanley, Jason. (2018). *How Fascism Works: The Politics of Us and Them*. New York: Random House.

Statista. (2022, 18 February). Meta's (formerly Facebook Inc.) advertising revenue worldwide from 2009 to 2021. Retrieved 4 March 2022, from https://www.statista.com/statistics/271258/facebooks-advertising-revenue-worldwide/

Steck, Em, & Kaczynski, Andrew. (2021, 5 February). Marjorie Taylor Greene's history of dangerous conspiracy theories and comments.

Retrieved 3 February 2022, from https://edition.cnn.com/2021/02/04/politics/kfile-marjorie-taylor-greene-history-of-conspiracies/index.html

Steele, Jonathan. (1994). *Eternal Russia*. London: Faber and Faber.

Stets, Jan E., & Burke, Peter J. (2000). Identity Theory and Social Identity Theory. *Social Psychology Quarterly, 63*(3), pp. 224–237.

Stevenson, Alexandra. (2018, 6 November). Facebook Admits It Was Used to Incite Violence in Myanma. Retrieved 1 March 2020, from https://www.nytimes.com/2018/11/06/technology/myanmar-facebook.html

Stillito, David. (2021, 13 September). Andrew Neil resigns from GB News three months after channel's launch. Retrieved 19 April 2022, from https://www.bbc.co.uk/news/entertainment-arts-58464664

Stourzh, Gerald. (1992). The Multinational Empire Revisited: Reflections on Late Imperial Austria. *Austrian History Yearbook, 23*, 1-22.

Sweeney, John. (2022, 23 February). Has the Prime Minister Been Compromised by Russia? Retrieved 1 March 2022, from https://bylinetimes.com/2022/02/23/has-prime-minister-boris-johnson-been-compromised-by-russia/

Sweet, Pat. (2020, 8 April). Google revenue hits £1.6bn, pays only £44m in corporation tax. Retrieved 4 March 2022, from https://www.accountancydaily.co/google-revenue-hits-ps16bn-pays-only-ps44m-corporation-tax

Tajfel, Henri, & Turner, J. C. (1986). The Social Identity Theory Of Inter-Group Behavior. In S. Worchel & L. W. Austin (Eds.), *Psychology of Intergroup Relations*. Chicago: Nelson-Hall.

Tarabay, Jamie. (2021, 30 August). How Hackers Hammered Australia After China Ties Turned Sour. Retrieved 25 July 2022, from https://www.bloomberg.com/news/features/2021-08-30/covid-origin-probe-calls-australian-government-businesses-universities-hacked

Tarrow, Sidney. (1998). *Power In Movement: Social Movements and Contentious Politics* (2nd ed.). Cambridge: Cambridge University Press.

Taylor, Alan. (2012, 13 April). 20 Years Since The Bosnian War. Retrieved 5 January 2017, from http://www.theatlantic.com/photo/2012/04/20-years-since-the-bosnian-war/100278/

BIBLIOGRAPHY

The Economist. (2021, 30 January). The world is facing an upsurge of nuclear proliferation. Retrieved 25 June 2022, from https://www.economist.com/leaders/2021/01/30/the-world-is-facing-an-upsurge-of-nuclear-proliferation

The Joint Staff. (2018). National Military Strategy (p. 8).

Theuns, Tom. (2020). Containing Populism at the Cost of Democracy? Political vs. Economic Responses to Democratic Backsliding in the EU. *Global Justice: Theory, Practice, Rhetoric, 12*(2), pp. 141–161.

Thompson, Stuart A. (2022, 15 April). How Russian Media Uses Fox News to Make Its Case. Retrieved 19 April 2022, from https://www.nytimes.com/2022/04/15/technology/russia-media-fox-news.html

Tilly, Charles. (2003). *Contention and Democracy in Europe, 1650–2000.* Cambridge: Cambridge University Press.

Treck, Till von. (2012). Did inequality cause the U.S. financial crisis? (p. 42). Düsseldorf: Macroeconomic Policy Institute (IMK).

Tusalem, Rollin F. (2007). A Boon or a Bane? The Role of Civil Society in Third- and Fourth-Wave Democracies. *International Political Science Review, 28*(3), pp. 361–386.

Ullah, I., Khan, K. S., Tahir, M. J., Ahmed, A., & Harapan, H. (2021). Myths and conspiracy theories on vaccines and COVID-19: Potential effect on global vaccine refusals. *Vacunas (English Edition), 22*(2), pp. 93–97.

UNEP. (2022). Facts about the climate emergency. Retrieved 25 June 2022, from https://www.unep.org/explore-topics/climate-action/facts-about-climate-emergency

UNHCR. (2011). The 1951 Convention relating to the Status of Refugees and its 1967 Protocol (p. 16). Geneva: UNHCR.

UNHCR. (2021, 22 April). Data reveals impacts of climate emergency on displacement. Retrieved 23 June 2022, from https://www.unhcr.org/uk/news/stories/2021/4/60806d124/data-reveals-impacts-climate-emergency-displacement.html

United Nations. (1947). The Prevention Of Corruption Act, 1947. Retrieved 24 June 2012, from http://unpan1.un.org/intradoc/groups/public/documents/apcity/unpan047878.pdf

BIBLIOGRAPHY

United Nations. (1948). Universal Declaration of Human Rights, (p. 8). New York: UN General Assembly.

United Nations. (1951). Convention on the Prevention and Punishment of the Crime of Genocide (p. 25). Geneva: United Nations.

United States District Court. (2022, 10 February). In re: Facebook, Inc. Consumer Privacy User Profile Litigation. Retrieved 11 February 2022, from https://www.cand.uscourts.gov/judges/chhabria-vince-vc/in-re-facebook-inc-consumer-privacy-user-profile-litigation/

United States Senate. (2018). Putin's Asymmetric Assault on Democracy in Russia and Europe: Implications for U.S. National Security (p. 206). Washington: Congress.

Urban, Joan Barth. (1986). *Moscow and the Italian Communist Party: From Togliatti to Berlinguer*. Ithaca, NY: Cornell University Press.

Vaughn, Karen I. (1998). *Austrian Economics in America: The Migration of a Tradition*. Cambridge: Cambridge University Press.

von Brömssen, Kerstin. (2013). '2083 – A European Declaration of Independence' – An Analysis of Discourses from the Extreme. *Nordidactica – Journal of Humanities and Social Science Education, 2013*, pp. 12–33.

Walter, Barbara F. (2022). *How Civil Wars Start: And How to Stop Them*. London: Penguin Books.

Wang, Jue, & Simpson, Michael. (2021). China's approach to global economic governance (p. 15). London: Chatham House.

Wang, Xue, Zuo, Shi-Jiang, Chan, Hoi-Wing, Chiu, Connie Pui-Yee, & Hong, Ying-yi. (2021). COVID-19-related conspiracy theories in China:The role of secure versus defensive in-group positivity and responsibility attributions. *Journal of Pacific Rim Psychology, 15*, 18344909211034928.

Watson, Dale. (2002, 6 February). The Terrorist Threat Confronting the United States. Retrieved 7 February 2017, from https://archives.fbi.gov/archives/news/testimony/the-terrorist-threat-confronting-the-united-states

Weiss, DJ, & Shanteau, J. (2004). The Vice of Consensus and the Virtue of Consistency. In K. Smith, J. Shanteau & P. Johnson (Eds.), *Psychological Investigations of Competence in Decision Making* (pp. 226–240). Cambridge: Cambridge University Press.

BIBLIOGRAPHY

Wesslau, Fredrik. (2016, 19 October). Putin's friends in Europe. Retrieved 1 May 2019, from https://ecfr.eu/article/commentary_putins_friends_in_europe7153/

Willan, Philip. (2002). *Puppet Masters: The Political Use of Terrorism in Italy* (2nd ed.). New York: Authors Choice Press.

Williamson, John. (2005). The Washington consensus as policy prescription for development. In Timothy Besley & Roberto Zagha (Eds.), *Development challenges in the 1990s: leading policymakers speak from expertise* (pp. 33–53): World Bank Publications.

Williamson, Peter J., Hoenderop, Simon, & Hoenderop, Jochem. (2018). An alternative benchmark for the validity of China's GDP growth statistics. *Journal of Chinese Economic and Business Studies, 16*(2), pp. 171–191.

Winder, R. (2005). *Bloody Foreigners: The Story of Immigration to Britain.* London: Abacus.

Winter, Charlie. (2015). Libya: The Strategic Gateway for the Islamic State (p. 15). London: Quilliam Foundation.

Wohlforth, William C. (1999). The Stability of a Unipolar World. *International Security, 24*(1), pp. 5–41.

Wolford, Ben. (2016). Everything you need to know about the 'Right to be forgotten'. Retrieved 1 March 2022, from https://gdpr.eu/right-to-be-forgotten/

World Trade Organization. (2007). Understanding the WTO (p. 111).

Yang, Z., Luo, X., & Jia, H. (2021). Is It All a Conspiracy? Conspiracy Theories and People's Attitude to COVID-19 Vaccination. *Vaccines (Basel), 9*(10).

Yu, Lili. (2014). *The reliability of Chinese economic statistics.* Denver, CO: University of Denver.

Zerilli, John, Danaher, John, Maclaurin, James, Gavaghan, Colin, Knott, Alistair, Liddicoat, Joy, & Noorman, Merel. (2021). *A Citizen's Guide to Artificial Intelligence.* Cambridge, MA: MIT Press.

Zingales, Luigi. (2008). Causes and effects of the Lehman Brothers bankruptcy *Committee on Oversight and Government Reform US House of Representatives* (pp. 23–25).

Zuboff, Shoshana. (2019). *The Age of Surveillance Capitalism.* London: Profile Books.

INDEX

Note: Page numbers followed by "*n*" refer to notes, "*f*" refer to figures.

INDEX

INDEX

INDEX

INDEX

INDEX

INDEX

INDEX